CHAUCER, GOWER,

AND THE

VERNACULAR RISING

CHAUCER, GOWER,

AND THE

VERNACULAR RISING

POETRY AND THE

PROBLEM

OF THE POPULACE

AFTER 1381

LYNN ARNER

THE PENNSYLVANIA STATE UNIVERSITY PRESS
UNIVERSITY PARK, PENNSYLVANIA

An earlier version of the first half of chapter 3 appeared as
"History Lessons from the End of Time: Gower and
the English Rising of 1381," *Clio: A Journal of Literature,
History, and the Philosophy of History* 31 (2002): 237–55,
reprinted by permission of *Clio: A Journal of Literature,
History, and the Philosophy of History.*

Library of Congress Cataloging-in-Publication Data

Arner, Lynn.
Chaucer, Gower, and the vernacular rising : poetry and the
problem of the populace after 1381 / Lynn Arner.
    p.   cm.
Summary: "Examines the transmission of Greco-Roman
and European literature into English in the late fourteenth
and early fifteenth centuries, when literacy was burgeoning
among men and women from the nonruling classes in
England"—Provided by publisher.
Includes bibliographical references and index.
ISBN 978-0-271-05893-1 (cloth : alk. paper)
ISBN 978-0-271-05894-8 (pbk. : alk. paper)
1. English poetry—Middle English, 1100–1500—History
and criticism.
2. Literature and society—England—History—To 1500.
3. Gower, John, 1325?–1408. Confessio amantis.
4. Gower, John, 1325?–1408—Criticism and interpretation.
5. Chaucer, Geoffrey, d. 1400. Legend of good women.
6. Chaucer, Geoffrey, d. 1400—Criticism and
interpretation.
7. Social classes—England—History—To 1500.
8. England—Social conditions—1066–1485.
9. Literacy—England—History—To 1500.
10. Tyler's Insurrection, 1381.
I. Title.
PR311.A76   2013
821'.109—dc23
2012034456

The Pennsylvania State University Press is a member of the
Association of American University Presses.

It is the policy of The Pennsylvania State University Press
to use acid-free paper. Publications on uncoated stock
satisfy the minimum requirements of American National
Standard for Information Sciences—Permanence of Paper
for Printed Library Material, ANSI Z39.48-1992.

FOR MARK

CONTENTS

ACKNOWLEDGMENTS

First and foremost, I thank The Gower Project, most notably Georgiana Donavin and Eve Salisbury, for helping to make another version of Gower studies possible. I am grateful to fellow members of the Society for Medieval Feminist Scholarship over the past two decades, for their comradery and for their work to make medieval studies a more compelling field. In the Department of English at Brock University, I have the good fortune of teaching among a very collegial group of faculty members, and I thank them all for their support, especially Elizabeth M. Sauer. Thanks also go to Brock historian Tami J. Friedman for her support. Regarding *Chaucer, Gower, and the Vernacular Rising*, I thank Sheila Delany for reading an early draft of chapter 4 and Andrew Prescott for reading the first half of chapter 3. I am grateful to the two anonymous reviewers at Pennsylvania State University Press for their helpful feedback and suggestions, which made the manuscript stronger. I thank Kendra Boileau, the editor in chief at Pennsylvania State University Press, and Stephanie Lang, editorial assistant, for their immediate enthusiasm for the project and for their kindness and generosity. I appreciate Brock University's Council for Research in the Social Sciences, for providing funds for the final stages of manuscript preparation. My most profound thanks go to Mark Lynn Anderson, for his boundless love and support, for his tireless enthusiasm for this book, and for two decades of wonderful conversations about historiography, institutional power, political economy, classism, knowledge and power, and the politics of culture.

he spring and summer of 1381 witnessed the most geographically widespread series of rebellions, featuring the largest
number of insurgents, in medieval English history. In the
immediate aftermath, John Gower composed book 1 of the
Vox Clamantis, describing the event in vitriolic terms and portraying rebels
as beasts ontologically incapable of intelligible speech. Preaching to the
demographics who overwhelmingly opposed the English Rising of 1381, the
Vox staged a dramatic refusal to engage with subordinate classes, as the
poem's educational prerequisites attest.[1] Around 1386 Gower began the
Confessio Amantis,[2] in which the memory of the rising persists,[3] although
the two poems offer dramatically divergent strategies for grappling with the
event. Requiring neither fluency in Latin nor conversance with Greco-
Roman antecedents, the *Confessio* acknowledged that the eagerness of the
ruling classes alone was insufficient to reproduce social relations and that
recruitment is easier when the ruling and subordinate classes speak a shared
language. Spending far less time than the *Vox* on explicitly politicized
speech, the *Confessio* relocated the debate to an expressly literary register,
promoting culture as a powerful site at which to engage in political struggle.
No longer the preserve of the ruling classes, learned poetry structured by a
Greco-Roman and erudite European literary tradition addressed members
of the populace directly in late fourteenth- and early fifteenth-century
England, and, as the *Confessio* testifies, offered a viable locus for intersecting
with the consciousness of the subordinate classes. Ultimately, this study is
less concerned with the English Rising of 1381 than with the larger "crisis
of authority" that the rebellion signaled and with responses to this crisis.[4]
This crisis of authority was an incitement to discourse, and one response

was the flourishing of an erudite, highly literary Greco-Roman English poetry, a key site of political struggle in late medieval England.

Chaucer, Gower, and the Vernacular Rising: Poetry and the Problem of the Populace After 1381 examines the transmission of Greco-Roman and European literature into English while the ability to read was burgeoning among significant numbers of men and women from the nonruling classes in late fourteenth- and early fifteenth-century England.[5] This transmission required a dissemination of cultural authority and offered a radically democratizing potential for accessing, interpreting, and deploying learned texts. The late medieval vernacular turn meant that large portions of the nonruling classes no longer needed the more highly educated to dispense this knowledge or to interpret it for them. *The Vernacular Rising* argues that while Geoffrey Chaucer's and John Gower's writings were key conduits of these cultural riches into the language of the populace, these writings simultaneously engaged in elaborate processes of constructing cultural expertise and defining gradations of cultural authority. At the founding of a highly literate English tradition, this poetry attempted to circumscribe the democratizing potential of this new knowledge and worked to grant certain socioeconomic groups leverage in public affairs, all the while promoting relations of dependency for others. As part of its analysis, *The Vernacular Rising* scrutinizes multiple addresses to different sectors of the early readership for Chaucer's and Gower's English poetry, with particular attention to the *Confessio*'s complex, often contradictory address to sizeable portions of nonruling groups upon their entrée, as a significant readership, into an erudite literary legacy. Classificatory systems in Chaucer's and Gower's texts encouraged all sectors of their early readership to make social distinctions: first, among varied groups of readers; and, second, between these groups and those not among them. By doing so, these writings participated in determining, at the sites of vernacular poetry and poetics, who could legitimately contribute to the production of knowledge in late medieval England.

Furthermore, *The Vernacular Rising* argues that at formative moments in the English literary tradition (as it is now conventionally celebrated), the poetry of Chaucer and Gower circumscribed the field of debate regarding appropriate responses to poetry and acceptable categories of analysis for understanding and for adjudicating texts, helping to establish which conversations about literature were possible. Chaucer's and Gower's writings jointly participated in forging a highly effective set of discourses about English poetry, some premises of which subtend current praxes surrounding

English literature. While their writings were typically consonant regarding constructions of cultural expertise, gradations of cultural authority, and the circumscription of the democratizing potential of English literature, regarding other terms, Chaucer's and Gower's poetics frequently clashed. Gower's version of poetics envisions poetry as an explicit, direct participant in political debates, especially in socioeconomic struggles in late fourteenth-century England, although Gower's expressed stances and the ways in which his writings attempted to intervene in the sociopolitical terrain were not always congruous. By contrast, Chaucer's version of poetics not only disavows that poetry intervenes in political debates but denies that the poet or his art *can* do so. While forwarding this stance, Chaucer's *Legend of Good Women* offers a sustained attempt to disarticulate both Gower's vision of poetics and the recognition that poetry is a powerful arena for sociopolitical struggles. This study examines negotiations, enacted in the texts of these two key figures, over the roles vernacular poetry should play in the late medieval English social formation and considers how their writings positioned poetry to be a powerful participant in processes of social control.

The Vernacular Rising is keenly interested in engagements of erudite English poetry with readers from the nonruling classes. Although after Steven Justice's *Writing and Rebellion: England in 1381* it became difficult to discount the possibility of at least some members of the nonruling classes being among the audiences for vernacular writings,[6] there has not yet been much consideration of subordinate classes specifically as readers of highly literary English poetry derived from Greco-Roman and European texts in the late fourteenth and early fifteenth centuries. Discussions of lay readers of vernacular literature from 1380 to 1425 have been heavily influenced by Anne Middleton, Paul Strohm, Kathryn Kerby-Fulton, and Steven Justice. Middleton suggests that early readers for poetry such as Chaucer's included "New Men," resembling his fictive Man of Law, Franklin, Monk, Clerk, and Squire, and Strohm argues that Chaucer's primary reading circle for his poetry during his lifetime consisted of fellow knights and esquires in Richard II's household and civil servants and lawyers in the London-Westminster area, while additional readers may have included educated women at the court and, in the early fifteenth century, wealthy merchants.[7] As chapter 1 explains, Middleton and especially Strohm focus primarily on the protobourgeoisie and aristocracy (including the gentry), the classes from which Chaucer and Gower emerged. Middle English scholars frequently reiterate Strohm's problematic identification of these readers as being from the "middle strata" or "middle class," thereby mistaking members of the ruling classes for less privileged ranks.[8] These scholars also often echo Middleton's formulation "public poetry"[9] and maintain that English-language texts were potentially available to a reading public. Typically in these commonplace invocations of the "middle strata" and "reading public," the demographics of readers are unstable.[10] After delineating the relationships among various socioeconomic groups in Chaucer's and Gower's lay readership in late fourteenth- and early fifteenth-century England, chapter 1 examines which men and women from the nonruling classes in cities and towns typically possessed the ability to read English and were among the readership for Chaucer's and Gower's vernacular poetry prior to 1425. Mapping out this territory enables more complicated analyses of social class in relation to negotiations over the terms of an emergent highly literary English poetry in late fourteenth- and early fifteenth-century England.

Kerby-Fulton and Justice argue that bureaucrats, sergeants and justices of law, civil servants, and scribes in London, Westminster, and Dublin formed a central readership for William Langland, Chaucer, and Gower from 1380 to 1427.[11] Although Kerby-Fulton and Justice do not pursue this line of inquiry, the higher-ranking members of these London, Westminster, and Dublin reading circles emerged from the ranks of the gentry and merchant class. However, of greater interest to me are those men whom Kerby-Fulton and Justice identify at the lower levels of the London-Westminster reading circles, including anonymous legal scribes who intermittently helped produce literary manuscripts, such as the poetry of Chaucer and Gower. I argue that these legal scribes need to be placed alongside London's large cadre of booktrade artisans and, in turn, located among craftspeople as readers of Chaucer's and Gower's poetry in the late fourteenth and early fifteenth centuries. To investigate the ways in which this new, highly literary poetry spoke to subordinate classes in the aftermath of the insurrection, I offer, as a concrete example, what I dub the "upper strata of nonruling urban classes," roughly, lesser merchants and prosperous artisans, strata that had generated substantial numbers of rebels in 1381, demographics described more fully in chapter 1. Despite records of book ownership and despite extensive documentation of these ranks' abilities to read English prior to 1425, literary scholars have generally overlooked these men and women as readers in late fourteenth- and early fifteenth-century England. It is important to reframe discussions of medieval readers to make these ranks visible, since members of these strata typically possessed the ability to read English, often owned texts, and intermittently consumed literature. *The Vernacular Rising* demonstrates that the upper strata of nonruling classes must be seriously considered part of Chaucer's and Gower's readership prior to 1425, opening up new possibilities for critical engagements with the writings of these two poets.

Emphasizing this readership, but also keeping in mind the broader spectrum of late fourteenth- and early fifteenth-century readers, one central concern of *The Vernacular Rising* is the flourishing of a highly literary English poetry vis-à-vis a nexus of issues surrounding entitlement, exclusivity, cultural prestige, and suitability for social mobility. Although scholars have discussed sundry ways in which Middle English poets legitimated their use of the language of the populace,[12] explorations of the simultaneous multiple addresses of a text, especially according to socioeconomic position, have been rare in medieval English literary studies. *The Vernacular Rising* scrutinizes the emergence of (what is now celebrated as) the English literary tradition while this poetry addressed different groups of readers according to varied degrees of alleged election, deservedness, and preparedness, thereby assigning these readers differing qualities for claiming and exercising cultural authority. Chaucer's and Gower's writings engaged in processes of classifying readers, in part, through readers' different connections to the Greco-Roman and European literary traditions that Chaucer's and Gower's texts conferred. These classificatory systems were simultaneously intertwined with a seemingly contradictory project of forging unity among readers. I am not arguing that Chaucer's and Gower's writings had specific effects on early readers, only that the discourses speaking through these writings attempted to reshape readers' consciousness. I understand the social terrain of cultural production in ways indebted to theorists who have pursued questions about culture's participation in the recruitment of populations from a range of socioeconomic positions, especially Pierre Bourdieu, Antonio Gramsci, Stuart Hall, and Raymond Williams. Gramsci and Hall have argued that politics must be understood as a production and that effective recruitment involves an acknowledgment of a variety of social antagonisms, aligning different interests within a common project. The production of such alignments entails altering how subordinate subjects view themselves and their relationships with others; severing former alliances and forming new ones among groups who might appear to have very diverse interests; speaking to different identities, projects, and aspirations;

and constructing unity from difference by seeming to represent some of the interests of everyone.[13]

In social projects forging unity, as Williams points outs, tradition often plays a central role. Williams argues that tradition is an actively shaping force, a powerful practical means of incorporation, powerful in the processes of social and cultural definition and identification. Most versions of tradition are radically selective: from an expansive arena of past and present events in a given society, certain meanings and practices are emphasized, while others are excluded, although this selection is usually passed off as "the tradition" or "the significant past." Tradition, Williams writes, "is a version of the past which is intended to connect with and ratify the present. . . . The hegemonic sense of tradition is always the most active: a deliberately selective and connecting process which offers a historical and cultural ratification of a contemporary order." It is at the vital points of connection, where a rendition of the past is employed to ratify the present, that a selective tradition is most effective, because it is tied to many practical continuities—such as places, institutions, a language—that are directly experienced. When Williams explains that tradition is a version of the past "used to ratify the present and to indicate directions for the future," he implies that a construction of history and tradition makes certain possibilities in that present moment, and potentially in the future, more probable, while simultaneously decreasing the likelihood of alternatives.[14] *The Vernacular Rising* examines the mustering of tradition in Chaucer's and Gower's poetry, the excerpting and molding of earlier cultural artifacts for use in political debates in late medieval England, often working to consolidate power relations in the aftermath of the English Rising of 1381 and to circumscribe political possibilities at the time and impede their likelihood thereafter. The very terms in which the writings of Chaucer and Gower shaped a previously largely exclusive cultural history produced a new readership and a new set of possibilities for governance.

The Vernacular Rising foregrounds the incoherence and fragmentation of the consciousness of the late medieval English nonruling classes. Regarding rebels' consciousness, Justice's seminal *Writing and Rebellion*, which continues to influence most literary scholars' perceptions of the insurrection, seeks to reconstruct rebels' consciousness by drawing together scant, often contradictory extant evidence surrounding the rising.[15] Concentrating on priests and peasants, Justice strives to uncover rebels' intentions, experiences, and consciousness in some illusory fullness, answering the Freudianesque question "What did rebels want?" While the chronicles and other writings by members of the ruling classes betray a great deal about their own projections, interests, and ideologies, they reveal little about the thoughts of men and women who rebelled. Although Strohm also voices this sentiment, he nonetheless strives, albeit much more cautiously and reservedly, to restore rebels' ideologies, intentions, and speech.[16] In part because the consciousness of subaltern groups is by definition fragmentary, studies offering to reconstruct, especially in any authentic way, the consciousness of nonruling classes from medieval England are highly fraught.[17] Hence, rather than pursuing consciousness as a lost object waiting to be found in the archive, I trace the ways in which rebels and members of subordinate classes more generally were addressed and instructed through a set of key texts in late fourteenth- and early fifteenth-century England.

In addition to its inherent fragmentation, the consciousness of these strata is further lost to us because of the distance of more than six hundred years and because these are not the ranks whose worldviews are expressed in extant cultural artifacts from the period. The emergence of English literature can be read elegiacally, as a memorial to those whom Gower and Chaucer were writing over and against, intentionally or not. Responding to insurgents' comprehensions of themselves, of their actions, and of their larger society, the poetry of Chaucer and Gower worked, albeit often differently, to guarantee the incoherency of these subjectivities. Ultimately, the project of disarticulation in which the *Vox, Confessio, Nun's Priest's Tale*, and various late medieval chronicles participated succeeded: what must have been the varied, complicated web of rebels' perceptions of their actions, and their larger worldviews, remains largely inaccessible or unintelligible to us now. *The Vernacular Rising* investigates this process of disarticulation and the cultural project of thwarting the uprising from living compellingly in the minds of readers. More broadly, this study connects attempts to ensure the fragmentation of subaltern consciousness in late medieval England to a metaliterary formation in which Chaucer's and Gower's poetry rendered incoherent alternate ways of understanding and being in the world. Simultaneously, at the sites of poetry and poetics, Chaucer's and Gower's writings promoted certain new social identities and cultural relations in late medieval England.

The long-enduring hegemonic stance in Gower studies of sympathizing with Gower and the ruling classes against rebels and the poor is the legacy of this disarticulation.[18] With respect to Gowerian poetry and class relations more generally, Gower studies has been structured by a simultaneous acknowledgement and disavowal of social class in Gower's writings. On the one hand, as the need for scholarship such as David Aers's work on Gower's politics reveals,[19] there has been a strong defense of a beloved poet by the humanist gesture of locating Gower outside the sociopolitical fray, aiming his arrow equally at the three estates.[20] On the other hand, because Gower ferociously pronounces the social order to be decreed by God and nature alike, there are commonplace assumptions that the class politics of his texts are self-evident and hence that we need not analyze them. Both stances have resulted in a dearth of class-based analyses of Gower's writings.[21] Negotiations surrounding class in Gower's texts, particularly in the *Confessio*, are much more complex and fascinating than they initially appear and hence merit further investigation, even as the texts themselves and the legacy of their critical reception thwart such an endeavor.

Although this study locates Chaucer and Gower at the beginnings of English literature, their writings do not represent the founding of English literature in any absolute sense, as extant Anglo-Saxon poetry and as *Piers Plowman*, with its earliest complete version of the B-text dating from 1378 to 1381,[22] attest. Exemplifying Williams's formulations surrounding tradition, the beginnings of English literature are, of course, heavily constructed and contested. John M. Bowers's rendition of the origins of English literature, for example, privileges William Langland, pronouncing Langland's writing indigenous to England and insular in style and content, noting that *Piers Plowman* features many Latinate references to bureaucratic culture rather than offering the literary allusiveness of Chaucerian poetry.[23] Keenly aware that there are numerous potential loci at which to posit the foundations of English letters and that sundry aesthetic and ideological criteria determine these loci, *The Vernacular Rising* positions Chaucer and Gower at the nascence of a *particular type* of English literature, a type frequently valorized in conventional histories of English literature: a legacy structured by Greco-Roman texts and in dialogue with French and Italian poetry; a corpus with identifiable, individuated authors; an English-language heritage without the embarrassing interlude of a Norman conquest; and a corpus with a subsequent history of allusions to Gower's and especially Chaucer's poetry. Multiple artistic and political possibilities existed in the embryonic moments of the versions of English letters propelled by Chaucer and Gower, and this book is, in some ways, a memorial to what the English literary canon did not become, including a memorial to some, curiously, politically progressive options that Gower's writings proposed for English literature but that have failed to become dominant. In its analysis of these lost possibilities, this study eschews the romantic paradigm of the struggling poet structuring Bowers's book, investigating instead the participation of Chaucer's and Gower's poetry in emergent discourses about erudite poetry and poetics.

Gower scholars have not infrequently paired Gower with Chaucer,[24] as two scholarly monographs, both recent, attest: J. Allan Mitchell's *Ethics and Exemplary Narrative in Chaucer and Gower* and Malte Urban's *Fragments: Past and Present in Chaucer and Gower*. Mitchell examines ethics in Gower's and Chaucer's writings, but since ethics is one of the most traversed territories in Gower scholarship, it is not a topic I pursue.[25] In the preface to *Amoral Gower: Language, Sex, and Politics*, a study of Gower's ethics and politics in relation to gender and sexuality, Diane Watt cursorily compares Chaucer and Gower, noting that Gower intervenes in politics in a way Chaucer did not. Similarly, Elizabeth Allen interprets the *Confessio*'s explicit reference to Chaucer as a "specific challenge to Chaucer's notorious political reticence," where Gower "charges his fellow-poet to take a personal stand." Speaking more generally, in *John Gower: Moral Philosopher and Friend of Chaucer*, John H. Fisher writes, "Gower was Chaucer's senior and mentor; their allusions to one another and the evolving pattern of the parallels in their works suggest that Gower was a sort of conscience to his brilliant but volatile friend, encouraging him by both precept and example to turn from visions of courtly love to social criticism."[26] *The Vernacular Rising* explores the striking political disparity between Chaucer's and Gower's stances on the role of poetry, an incongruence not infrequently remarked on but less commonly pursued. Urban's book might be a possible exception here, although, deploying deconstruction, queer theory, and postmodern theory, the methodology and politics of Urban's study differ greatly from mine and, predictably, class is not of much concern in his book, nor is literacy. Urban does, however, foreground the instability of meaning in Chaucerian texts.[27] Chaucer's political elusiveness, whether volitional or discursive, is no secret. Several Chaucerians, including Lee Patterson, Sheila Delany, and Strohm, have commented on Chaucer's avoidance of explicit political stances.[28] An innovation I bring to the conversation is to argue that the *Legend of Good Women* directly grapples with a Gowerian version of poetics and seeks to render uncompelling and incoherent Gower's explicit stance that poetry actively participates in the production of the social formation.

The Vernacular Rising, in part, investigates a debate between two of the most prolific, important authors in late medieval England over the function of poetry, while these men were vernacularizing a rich Greco-Roman and European cultural legacy. Gower understands Art to be inherently political and maintains that authors have an obligation to intervene explicitly in sociopolitical affairs. Gower offers heightened emphases on socioeconomic conflicts, and his poetry generally privileges history and political struggles. By contrast, Chaucer privileges art and aesthetics. The *Legend of Good Women* can be viewed as a protracted response to the version of poetics for which Gower stands. I argue that the *Legend* is an *ars poetica* intently concerned with the question of Art and social responsibility and that the *Legend* launches this inquiry specifically at the site of gender. The *Legend* undertakes a sustained investigation of the accountability a poet bears for his art and insists that neither the poet nor his creations are subject to any imperative to correct social maladies or to uplift society. The *Legend* seeks not only to undermine Gower's stance that poetic production entails such obligations but also to fragment social responsibility as a possible category through which to assess—and, more foundationally, through which to comprehend—poetry. By means of its investigation, the *Legend* seeks to establish the parameters of debate for suitable responses to poetry.

Although considering other poems by both Gower (most notably the *Vox*) and Chaucer (including *Troilus and Criseyde* and the *Canterbury Tales*), *The Vernacular Rising* focuses the most intently on the *Confessio* and the *Legend*. As Gower's only major composition in English, the *Confessio* is a self-evident selection on which to center an interrogation of his vernacular poetics, and the *Confessio* is coupled with the *Legend* because the latter constitutes an important Chaucerian treatise on poetics and because the *Legend* is arguably the most pronounced articulation of the debate between Chaucer's and Gower's poetics. More minor considerations also make the *Confessio* and the *Legend* an obvious pair. Both texts were composed around London at roughly the same time: Gower is conventionally believed to have begun the *Confessio* after penning the *Visio Anglie* (ca. 1381) and to have finished the *Confessio* around 1390, while the *Legend* is conventionally dated around 1386, with the Prologue possibly being revised as late as eight to ten years thereafter.[29] Even apart from the simultaneous composition of the *Confessio* and the *Legend*, the junior poet had seen earlier demonstrations of

Gowerian poetics in the *Vox* and the *Mirour de l'Omme*. As chapter 3 explains, Chaucer's dedication to Gower in *Troilus and Criseyde* connects Gower to the *Legend*, especially to the *Legend*'s investigation of Art and accountability. Regarding verbal exchanges and mutual textual references, Joyce Coleman has detailed the sustained, ubiquitous verbal echoes and literary parallels between the *Legend* and the end of book 8 of the *Confessio* (i.e., Amans's conversion scene),[30] two sections of Chaucer's and Gower's writings this study scrutinizes at length.

Apart from its dialogue with Gowerian poetics, the *Legend* is a response in its own right to socioeconomic conflicts in late fourteenth-century England. Although saying little about the *Legend* specifically, in *Chaucer's Jobs* David R. Carlson argues that Chaucer's literary devotion to amorous affairs is a response to the crisis of order in late medieval England. Despite well-documented flaws in his study,[31] Carlson's stance deserves serious consideration. Carlson believes that Chaucer's amatory complaints supported the interests of the dominant class through several maneuvers: by retreating into individualism; by distracting, namely, by pretending that there was no crisis and by shifting attention to other concerns; by promoting an ideal of the noble good life, a leisurely life to which to aspire, an existence untroubled by social conflict; and by cultivating a capacity for elegantly saying little or nothing, to establish that nothing need be said.[32] Although I interpret Chaucer's love visions as more contradictory texts than Carlson seems to, Carlson is right to insist that Chaucer's interest in *l'amour* should be understood at least, in part, as a response to socioeconomic conflicts, including the English Rising of 1381. Discarding Carlson's models of authorial intention (including servility) and false consciousness in favor of complex models of the production of consciousness and subjectivity formulated in poststructuralist theory and British cultural studies, I offer more mediated understandings of the relation between Chaucer's amatory writings and socioeconomic struggles and argue that Chaucer is engaged with the socioeconomic in much more expansive ways than Carlson investigates.

I also bring gender into the conversation. While chapters 2 and 3 (primarily discussions of Gower) privilege class as the primary category of analysis, in chapters 4 and 5 (primarily discussions of Chaucer), class recedes while gender predominates. The *Legend*'s considerations of gender, however, are ultimately tied to class and to the socioeconomic conflicts with which the *Confessio* grapples. Through a complicated nexus of issues surrounding gender, the *Legend* seeks to fracture discourses of inequality, both in the domain of literature and in late medieval England. The *Legend* works to make discourses of inequality ineffectual and incoherent as possibilities for understanding one's place in the world. The poem's attempts to dislodge discourses of inequality have profound implications for understandings of class and can be viewed, in part, as an engagement with the insurrection and with rebels' dramatic challenges to inequitable distributions of wealth and power. Likewise, the *Legend* adopts a strong anti-identity stance. Rendered ridiculous, it is easy to dismiss identity-based claims within the universe of the poem, and readers are encouraged to dismiss identity politics more generally, whether rooted in gender or class. Moreover, the *Legend* dramatizes what happens when special interests are given audience: the imperilment of Art, tradition, and even civilization itself. People who argue from identity, the *Legend* maintains, muster no rational intellectual arguments, and the *Legend* instructs readers how to recognize and comprehend identity-based logic, discounting such concerns as unartful, ignorant, and ultimately dismissible. Furthermore, the *Legend* teaches readers to perceive protestations as mere products of a culture of complaint, voiced by malcontents, not as sincere concerns by those with legitimate grievances. By maintaining that poetry does not help shape consciousness or affect lives and that an author bears no social responsibility for his creations, the *Legend* works to frustrate Art's potential to be a forum for interrogations of societal strife, including gendered and class-based inequities in late medieval England, and to be an explicit vehicle for social transformation. While forwarding its elaborate argument about the unsuitability of serious considerations of gendered and class-based inequities in assessments of poetry, the *Legend* simultaneously engaged in the reproduction of gendered and class-based relations in late medieval England by advancing this very argument. Disavowing poetry's participation in the generation of the sociopolitical terrain, the *Legend* was thereby better poised than Gower's frequently didactic writings to intervene effectively in this terrain.

Their approaches to poetics often at odds, Chaucer's writings do not consistently permit the same types of analyses as Gower's. More specifically, the frequent incommensurability of their respective poetry's responses to socioeconomic conflicts renders it impossible to entertain questions of class in the *Legend* in several of the ways in which they are entertained in the *Confessio*. *The Vernacular Rising* explores the *Confessio* first, a text that bears witness to intense political upheavals, that provides significant insights into England's socioeconomic contestations in the 1380s and 1390s, and that, through contrast, demonstrates what the *Legend* expressly writes out. Among the multiple addresses inscribed therein, the *Confessio* documents the presence of readers from the upper strata of nonruling urban classes in the late fourteenth- and early fifteenth-century England, an address scrutinized at length in this study. However, the conflicts the *Confessio* marks at the level of address are eclipsed in the *Legend*. Regarding readers from the upper strata of nonruling urban classes, the *Legend* thwarts this level of decipherability in its address: just as the poem works to frustrate understandings of socioeconomic conflict and, especially, to frustrate understandings of poetry's relation to such conflict, the *Legend* makes specifying address much more difficult and erases traces of these strata, largely eliding competing ranks. Hence, while chapters 2 and 3 focus on the *Confessio*'s attempts to speak to these strata, chapters 4 and 5 instead examine the ways in which the *Legend* renders socioeconomic struggles in late fourteenth-century England as a possible concern of poetry incomprehensible. Consequently, this book's heightened emphasis on class in discussions of Gower and diminished attention to class in discussions of Chaucer reflect two competing discourses about poetry's relation to the social and to history. *The Vernacular Rising*'s shift regarding address mimics the *Legend*'s containment of an address to these readers. While Chaucer insists on the autonomous work of art and on the separation of poetic from political discourses, Gower conceptualizes literature as a vehicle for conferring social and political identities—and for constructing groups' interests—not merely as reflective of such identities. Gower views culture as a tool of social management or transformation. Although Chaucer maintains a divergent point of view, nonetheless, his poetry participates in social control, irrespective of his agency. Hence, not only do Chaucer and Gower volitionally voice disparate visions of poetry, but discursively their writings forwarded frequently competing models for what the rising vernacular literature could become.

The first chapter, "Chaucer's and Gower's Early Readership Expanded," widens the demographics of the lay readership whom literary scholars have envisioned for English poetry in the late fourteenth and early fifteenth centuries. This chapter defines the "upper strata of nonruling urban classes," explains their importance, and, drawing on scholarship of historians, briefly outlines political and economic alliances between these strata and different ranks in English cities and towns. Piecing together evidence from wills, court records, documents surrounding formal and informal educations, and various other historical records, chapter 1 demonstrates that substantial portions of the upper strata of nonruling urban classes possessed the ability to read the vernacular in late fourteenth- and early fifteenth-century England. Presenting a constellation of evidence grounded in social practices surrounding the consumption of vernacular texts at the time, this chapter argues that men and women from the upper strata of nonruling urban classes were among the readership for Chaucer's and Gower's writings prior to 1425, indicating that erudite Middle English poetry had a sizeable readership among the nonruling classes at its emergence, with many of these readers occupying demographics that had that produced large numbers of rebels in the English Rising of 1381.

After considering what Chaucer's Man of Law betrays about the *Confessio*'s cultural logic, chapter 2, "Against the Greyness of the Multitude: Poetry, Prestige, and the *Confessio Amantis*," argues that the *Confessio* attached prestige to an erudite English vernacular tradition, while engaged in founding this tradition, and granted this nascent heritage, and conversance with it, cachet, not unlike what Bourdieu identifies as "cultural capital."[33] The *Confessio*'s portrayal of the acquisition of this cultural knowledge is heavily mystified, an enchanted tale participating in something akin to what Bourdieu and Jean-Claude Passeron dub an "ideology of 'gifts.'"[34] The poem offered readers a similar gift and coded conversance with its textual legacy as a signifier of transformation, proof of intellectual, moral, and spiritual superiority over the populace. Familiarity with this heritage was the mark of distinction by which readers and other inheritors of these cultural treasures could recognize one another against the greyness of the multitude. Using this standard of measurement, the *Confessio* attempted to police debates about England's welfare, determining who was equipped to participate in such dialogues. Although inviting all readers to be inheritors of this legacy, the *Confessio* deemed some readers worthier than others, pronouncing certain readers members full inheritors of the bequest, while positioning less experienced readers as only partial beneficiaries. The poem instructed readers alienated by the text to differentiate between their deficient selves and the more deserving scions and to defer to the latter as the only legitimate producers of knowledge. This chapter examines how the terms of the poem's conferral of this new heritage worked to reorganize political alliances among various socioeconomic groups in the aftermath of the English Rising of 1381.

Chapter 3, "Time After Time: Historiography and Nebuchadnezzar's Dream," focuses primarily on the competing models of history embedded in the rendition of Nebuchadnezzar's dream recounted in the *Confessio*'s Prologue. This regal vision represents history both as a homogeneous, static mass and as a teleological progression into ruin. This chapter investigates how, through these contradictory models of history, the poem proposed to alter the terms in which readers from the upper strata of nonruling urban classes understood how history happens and perceived their relation to the past and future. Through these competing versions of history, the text offered to change the ways in which readers understood their interests, conceptualized their agency, chose their allies, comprehended their connections to the English Rising of 1381, and perceived insurrection more generally.

The final section of this chapter considers two other competing understandings of time in the *Confessio*: historical time versus the seemingly eternal realm of *l'amour*. These incongruent versions of time both mark a shift in Gower's oeuvre and reflect a strong divergence between Gowerian and Chaucerian poetics. Tying these versions of time to Chaucer's and Gower's explicit mutual references, this section argues that each author's comments about the other foreground their disparate understandings of the nature and function of Art. Gower's message to his colleague betrays a recruitment fantasy of Chaucer and of Chaucerian readers to a poetics centered on intense engagements with social issues, while Chaucer warns "moral Gower" about the perils of zealousness, advice dispensed at the end of *Troilus and Criseyde* and writ large in the *Legend*, as the subsequent two chapters demonstrate.

Chapter 4, "In Defense of Cupid: Poetics, Gender, and the *Legend of Good Women*," argues that a central concern of Chaucer's *Legend of Good Women* is the issue of art and social responsibility, a discussion instigated narratively by Cupid's complaint about construals of gender in *Troilus and Criseyde*, since cultural artifacts shape readers' consciousness and affect lives. This chapter maintains that the *Legend* launches a full-blown investigation into the problem of poetry and accountability, conducting this investigation at the site of gender. The poem examines the conundrum of where culpability for suspicious gendered practices in and surrounding the field of cultural production lies. Through its investigation, the *Legend* attempted to delimit the parameters of debate regarding acceptable responses to poetry and to establish which conversations about literature were proper to its domain. The poem worked to thwart readers' recognition of gender, and of social inequities in general, as an appropriate, or even possible, category of analysis through which to evaluate literature. The poem simultaneously attempted to block understandings that cultural artifacts shape consciousness and hence affect lives, while proceeding as if poetry does exactly that.

The fifth chapter, "Chaucer on the Effects of Poetry," demonstrates the *Legend*'s second pronounced strategy for dealing with concerns about the stakes of poetry: the *Legend* conducts an extensive theoretical inquiry into how to measure and adjudicate the effects of a text. In part, through repeated, dramatic stagings of endeavors by the narrator and by fictive authors to elicit defined responses from their respective readers, the poem investigates methodological complications involved in claims that a text induces a specific action or affect. The *Legend* scrutinizes difficulties surrounding how to delineate and how to gauge the influence of a piece of writing, and the poem explores the mediation of a constellation of factors in the production of the meaning of a cultural artifact or literary practice. This chapter then analyzes the political implications of the *Legend*'s assessments of difficulties surrounding the adjudication of a text's effects.

Building on preceding chapters, and placing the *Legend* alongside the *Canterbury Tales*, the conclusion compares the political possibilities for English poetry forwarded by Chaucer's and Gower's writings. The conclusion examines the specific terms their respective poetry legitimated, discredited, or disarticulated for comprehending and for assessing this new cultural form. This discussion considers, for example, the ways in which their texts participate in discourses regarding identity politics, as well as valuations of identity as a legitimate category of knowledge about the world and for engagements with literature. While forwarding sometimes coincident, sometimes divergent, and frequently contradictory understandings of the roles the poet and poetry should play in the social formation, Chaucer's and Gower's poetry jointly helped set up vernacular literature to be a compelling force in processes of recruitment, cultural identification, and social identification in late medieval England. The conclusion also investigates recurrent alignments of Gower with morbidity and nihilism and of Chaucer with artistry, potential, and futurity, in their own works and in current scholars' appreciations of these men and their compositions. Chaucer's writings scorned the understanding, represented by Gower, that poetry was a vehicle of social engineering, all the while offering a more effective means than Gower's texts for reproducing the social formation in late medieval England and in the subsequent history of English letters.

I

CHAUCER'S AND GOWER'S EARLY READERSHIP EXPANDED

ohn Sharnebrok, a chandler and citizen of London, owned "Clensyngsyne," valued at 8d. in 1376. Nearly two decades later, Gilbert Prynce, a London painter, left a missal to the church of St. Giles without Cripplegate, London. John Clifford, a mason and citizen of Southwark, willed one book to his parish church in Southwark in 1411 and two books to a convent of Franciscan nuns. Upon his death in 1443, a York glover named John Newton bequeathed two books, one of which seems to have been Ranulf Higden's *Polychronicon*. Richard Person, an armorer of London, willed his grandchild a Psalter in 1446. John Cadeby, a mason of Beverley, possessed a pair of writing tables and six English books, the latter valued at 10s. at the time of his death, around 1450.[1] All these men were from the nonruling classes. Nonetheless, they owned books. Examining social practices surrounding education and literacy, along with a constellation of legal records, this chapter demonstrates that substantial portions of the upper strata of nonruling urban classes, including men like these testators, possessed the ability to read the vernacular, and occasionally Latin, in late fourteenth- and early fifteenth-century England. Deploying similar types of evidence, I argue that significant portions of these strata owned and consumed books and that these men and women were among the readership for Chaucer's and Gower's vernacular poetry prior to 1425, strata that had produced substantial numbers of rebels in the English Rising of 1381.

Delineating Groups

Before turning to the literacy of these strata, this chapter explains the formulation the "upper strata of nonruling classes," discusses the significance of these ranks, and positions this readership in relation to other lay groups Middle English scholars have envisioned among Chaucer's and Gower's early readership. Maintaining that the Ricardian period ushered in vernacular poetry (such as the writings of Chaucer, Gower, and Langland) concerned with common profit and the public good, Anne Middleton has argued that early readers of Chaucer's poetry included "New Men," resembling the Canterbury-bound Man of Law, Franklin, Monk, Clerk, and Squire, a readership that Chaucerians have frequently reiterated.[2] Middleton grounds her demographics in Paul Strohm's scholarship, scholarship that has helped structure how most literary scholars conceptualize Chaucer's and Gower's early readership. Strohm argues that Chaucer's primary reading circle for his poetry during his lifetime consisted of his fellow knights and esquires in Richard II's household and of civil servants and lawyers in the London-Westminster area, men in social situations close to the poet's. Strohm adds that this circle may have included educated women at the court and wealthy London merchants prior to the fifteenth century. Identifying Chaucer as part of a "middle social grouping," Strohm locates the poet's primary reading circle among the "middle class," "the middle strata," or the "ill-defined middle ranks of society," which he conceptualizes as excluding royalty, ecclesiastical orders, peasants, wage laborers, and the highest levels of the aristocracy.[3] Replicating the amorphousness of this category, it is common for Chaucerians and Gowerians to conceptualize what were in fact the protobourgeoisie and portions of the aristocracy as occupants of a "middle class" or "middle strata" when discussing these groups as readers and/or audience members for Chaucer's and Gower's poetry.[4]

Kathryn Kerby-Fulton and Steven Justice's scholarship on Langlandian reading circles has also been enormously influential on understandings of Chaucer's and Gower's early readership. Pointing further down the socioeconomic ladder, Kerby-Fulton and Justice argue that Chaucer, Gower, Langland, and, later, Thomas Hoccleve shared a ready, central readership of bureaucrats, consisting of sergeants and justices of law, civil servants, and legal scribes, in London, Westminster, and Dublin from 1380 to 1427.[5] Although Kerby-Fulton and Justice do not pursue questions surrounding the socioeconomic origins or alignments of these men, the higher echelons of these London-Westminster circles emerged from the ranks of the landed gentry and the merchant class, an example being Chaucer himself, often classified as a high-ranking civil servant.[6] The lower ends of these London-Westminster circles, however, are of greater interest in my project. Kerby-Fulton and Justice point out that the lower levels, among whom they place Langland, included anonymous legal scribes, some of whom worked for hire outside their regular posts, often setting up shops near Paternoster Row or occasionally "moonlighting in the literary booktrade in order to keep body and soul together (as in fact Hoccleve did)."[7] Hoccleve, a clerk of the privy seal, intermittently contracted piecemeal to copy manuscripts, including a deluxe version of the *Confessio*.[8] *Piers Plowman* was copied in the same small workshops on Paternoster Row and, in some cases, by the same scribes as those who transcribed the poetry of Chaucer and Gower.[9] Kerby-Fulton and Justice explicitly locate Thomas Usk on the lower ends of Langland's and Chaucer's bureaucratic reading circles and view him as representative of these occupational rungs. Beginning his career as a scrivener hired by Mayor John of Northampton and possessing sufficient legal knowledge to later work as a deputy, undersheriff, and attorney, Usk, the son of a hurer (a maker of fur hats) and hence seemingly from what I call the "upper strata of nonruling classes," is referred to in legal records as a "*clericus*," although he is unlikely to have taken more than the minor orders and hence offers an example of the kind of career that literacy furnished for clerks in minor orders at the time.[10] Kerby-Fulton and Justice believe that Usk's borrowing, in *Testament of Love*, of Chaucer's most recent poetry before 1388 suggests how quickly Londoners in the legal clerical community could access Chaucer's poetry.[11] Keeping in mind Kerby-Fulton and Justice's study, and subsequent work by Simon Horobin and Linne Mooney on London scriveners, I place the lower levels of the Westminster-London reading circles alongside London's network of guilds, while taking seriously Kerby-Fulton and Justice's understanding of the rapid dissemination of the vernacular literary texts being copied by scriveners in the late fourteenth- and early fifteenth-century London area.[12] I provide a larger socioeconomic contextualization of the cadre of men and women who produced and sold books in this period, a contextualization that clarifies the demographics of some of the adjacent readers who benefited from this rapid dissemination, demographics toward which medieval English literary scholars have not yet turned their attention.

Before offering a more precise alternative to the amorphous categories "middle strata" and "middle class" that Chaucerians and Gowerians often employ, it is necessary to outline the socioeconomic categories structuring this study. The ruling classes in late medieval England consisted of the landed aristocracy (i.e., the nobility, the landed gentry, and the ecclesiastical landowners) and the mercantile governing oligarchies of the chartered boroughs. Rural areas were dominated politically and economically by the aristocracy, whose most important characteristic was not income size but the means through which this income was obtained: the bulk of an aristocrat's regular revenues came from land, typically from rents, dues, and taxes.[13] Rural esquires were usually aspirant knights or men who had every necessary quality to acquire a knightly title but who decided against doing so. According to Christopher Dyer, late medieval English gentlemen typically enjoyed considerable incomes (a minimum of £10 per annum, often much more) and generally ascribed to the larger aristocracy's values but sometimes lacked the lordship of a manor, living instead on lease-hold land, the rents of urban property, or entirely on fees and payments for administrative or legal services,[14] with this third category including higher-ranking members of the Westminster-London bureaucratic circles. Chris Given-Wilson argues that the wealthier aristocracy harnessed the support of the gentry and the protobourgeoisie to a program of continual expansion of governmental power in late medieval England by allowing the gentry and the protobourgeoisie to employ the government's judicial power to further their social and economic interests, an expansionist project in which parliament and justices of the peace were key, both drawn from the same social groups.[15] In numerous ways, the aristocracy and wealthy merchants shared interests and strong alliances in late medieval England. With income on a comparable scale, wealthy merchants generally identified with rural lords, shared many of their tastes and interests, and intermarried with them. Successful merchants frequently purchased enough land to become country landowners, and some secured noble status for their descendants. Merchants often trained the sons of gentry as apprentices, who, in turn, became merchants.[16]

Mercantile oligarchies, consisting primarily of wealthy merchants who conducted wholesale trade and who typically held the highest ranks in local mercantile guilds, ruled late medieval urban areas. By the end of the fourteenth century, a developed mercantile stratum flourished in approximately thirty of the larger towns and cities. This elite's monopoly on power was derived from their economic dominance over lesser guild members and over other urban dwellers and was inseparably linked with the tendency of wealthy merchants to occupy such influential offices as the mayoralty and to serve as aldermen of guilds and jurors in the borough courts.[17] Late medieval London was governed by a mayor and twenty-four aldermen drawn almost exclusively from the highest echelons of the greater companies (namely, men who traded in wine, wool, spices, cloth, and furs as well as the fishmongers and goldsmiths), while the bulk of London's wholesale merchants either assisted in this governance or acquiesced.[18] Wealthy merchants occupied the highest ranks of the greater companies, in whose ranks practically all citizen merchants in London were enrolled. The highest-ranking members of the greater companies were primarily involved in wholesale trade, while the lower-ranking members primarily either produced goods or engaged in retail trade. These distinctions were operative among the mercers, grocers, drapers, fishmongers, goldsmiths, skinners, tailors, and vintners in the fourteenth century and also among the ironmongers, salters, and haberdashers in the subsequent century.[19]

Sylvia Thrupp argues that merchants in late medieval London were drawn apart as a superior social elite, with a consciousness of political difference from Londoners and an awareness of cultural difference which affected marriages, friendships, and daily social interactions.[20] Thrupp notes that lawyers generally identified themselves as part of the ruling groups rather than the ruled. Lawyers and high-ranking government administrators moved in the same exclusive circles as merchants, participated in the House of Commons, and often were the sons of merchants or married into prominent mercantile families.[21] In many ways, wealthy late fourteenth-century Yorkshire merchants, particularly those in York, Beverley, and Hull, resembled their London contemporaries not only because they dominated political office but because these Yorkshire merchants shared commercial interests that drew them together into an economic community that transcended town boundaries and that tied them to wealthy merchants in other English cities and towns, including London. These geographically dispersed merchants often held more in common with each other than with lower-ranking men and women from their own towns. Jennifer I. Kermode believes that wealthy merchants in Yorkshire towns "shared attitudes and ambitions, shaped by the distinctive experience of commerce and the exercise of political authority into an evolving class-consciousness" and that merchants in late medieval England more generally were differentiated by their mode of dress, lifestyle, economic and political expectations, and cultural and literary interests.[22] The merchant class, of course, included the women born into this class. If wed, women from London's merchant class tended to marry (and to remarry) within their own ranks. In late medieval London, women sometimes conducted wholesale trade themselves, particularly when carrying on a deceased husband's business.[23]

Medieval literary scholars have not infrequently identified Chaucer and especially Gower as men from the "middle class" or "middle strata,"[24] and when one argues that the poets' close associates occupy similar socioeconomic positions, one almost invariably places their primary reading circles in this middle class or middle strata as well, as Strohm has. Hence, it is important to clarify that *both men were from the ruling classes*. Chaucer was born into the merchant class of medieval London. His paternal grandfather was a London citizen and vintner, while vintners were one of the wealthiest and most powerful guilds in England, and Chaucer's paternal grandmother had three successive husbands, the last two of which, along with both her sons, were wine merchants. Chaucer's father owned substantial property in and around London, as did Chaucer's mother, whose second husband was also a vintner; Chaucer inherited at least some property from his parents.[25] Being born into the mercantile class facilitated Chaucer's successful career in the courts of Edward III, John of Gaunt, and Richard II.[26] Chaucer received years of free rent and generous, often multiple, annuities from monarchs, such as Chaucer's exchequer annuity from Richard of £20 per annum, while his wife Phillipa also received annuities. Chaucer's miscellaneous earnings gleaned through his legal and administrative posts seem to have provided him with larger sources of income, including £104 gained through a grant of wardship and marriage and £71 4s. 6d. through the seizure of an illegal exportation of wool.[27] Chaucer's administrative posts included an occupation targeted heavily by insurgents in 1381: from 1385 to 1389, Chaucer was a justice of the peace, helping to enforce labor laws and keep the peace.[28]

Gower is typically identified as "upper middle class," partially due to the John H. Fisher's ascription of Gower to this socioeconomic category, since Fisher is considered Gower's most authoritative biographer.[29] Gower's aristocratic pedigree, however, is marked by the coat of arms on his tomb, a crest that links the large landowner Sir Robert Gower as a relative of the poet.[30] In his 1532 description of Gower's funerary monument in the nave of St. Mary Overie, Thomas Berthelet explains that the ledge of the tomb had once identified the poet as "*J. Gower, arm./Angl. poeta*," with "*arm.*" standing for "*Armiger*," as in esquire. Fisher suspects that Gower remained an esquire because there may have been financial advantages in refusing knighthood and citizenship in London. Fisher also believes that Gower's writings intimate that the poet may have been a lawyer or in a civil position associated with law.[31] I believe that while Gower may have received legal training, as did many young men from the aristocracy and the merchant classes in late medieval England, the absence of records surrounding employment—coupled with the rents Gower enjoyed—suggests that Gower led a life of leisure in London, living off rental income. As Fisher explains, in 1382 "John Gower, esquire of Kent" purchased the manors of Feltwell in Norfolk and Multon in Suffolk, and immediately after acquiring the Feltwell manor, Gower leased this property for the rest of his life at £40 per annum. There are records of Gower making multiple land acquisitions (along with some divestments) over the course of his life and include documentation of his embroilment in a land-purchase scandal, where he loaned a young heir, William de Septvauns, £60. Gower is also believed to have invested in the wool trade.[32] In his will Gower bequeathed the bulk of his wealth to his wife, Agnes: £100 of lawful money and "all the rents due to me from the farms of my manors, both of Southwell in the County of Nottingham, and of Multon, in the County of Suffolk."[33] Gower fits the profile of a man from the lower levels of the aristocracy.

In this study, the "upper strata of nonruling urban classes" refers to the most affluent and powerful layers of the population, beneath the wealthy merchant class, in the approximately thirty largest cities and towns in late medieval England. Regarding London, this category refers, in part, to the rank and file of the greater companies: these demographics consist primarily of artisans and retailers, including a large body of prosperous shopkeepers. This category also refers to the master craftsmen and to other leading members of the lesser companies, along with the bulk of the membership of the lesser companies, including workers who were artisans, apprentices, and journeymen (trained employees in their respective crafts). This rubric does not include servants or waged laborers, for although some of these ranks may have been among Chaucer's or Gower's audiences, we have less evidence that they were literate than those higher in the guilds. Late medieval Southwark, with no guild companies of its own, was home to a large number of artisans and lesser merchants, some of whom were members of London companies, including the Brewers' company, while others were free of London's guild system.[34] In late medieval England, although London's lesser companies had limited political power, for they did send representatives to the Common Council, the distinction between the governing role played by the merchants and the governed role played by the artisans was notable and contributed significantly to the instability of the civic government in late fourteenth-century London.[35]

Since the distinction between greater and lesser companies did not extend beyond London, in other medieval English cities and towns, the upper strata of nonruling classes consisted of prosperous guild members excluded from the mercantile elite. The most privileged nonruling ranks were typically artisans and shopkeepers, manufacturing craft masters, and retail traders in foodstuffs, many of whom enjoyed rather substantial amounts of wealth and property.[36] In York fairly wealthy master craftsmen, though organized into strong fraternities, held only limited roles in the constitutional structure of the town's governance, while real power remained firmly in the hands of the elite.[37] In sizeable late medieval English cities and towns more generally, master craftsmen were permitted representation on advisory councils and not infrequently operated as an arm of civic administration, while the actual governance of urban areas was exercised by mayors and aldermen (or their equivalents) who were merchants.[38]

This study understands the upper strata of nonruling urban classes to be composed of men and women both. Women in late medieval English cities and towns were not infrequently artisans and traders in their own right. More commonly, women worked in the same guilds as their male relatives, especially of their fathers or, if married, their husbands.[39] In late medieval English towns, the basic unit of production for manufacturing artisans was conventionally the family household, enlarged by apprentices and journeymen, seldom more than two or three.[40]

I specify the upper strata of nonruling urban classes for several reasons. First, despite the explosion of interest in literacy and audiences in the past two decades, this readership, apart from the lower ends of the Westminster-London circles, has been largely overlooked in medieval English literary studies, even though these strata constituted a sizeable body of early readers from the nonruling classes for Chaucer's and Gower's vernacular writings and for erudite English poetry more broadly. Second, these strata produced substantial numbers of participants in the 1381 insurrection and hence provide us with concrete examples of rebels and rebel-sympathizers addressed by Chaucer's and Gower's vernacular poetry. In late fourteenth-century England, wealthy merchants and the upper strata of nonruling urban classes had structurally competing interests generally, with consequent social friction, rooted in the relations of production. Merchants strove to reduce artisans' remuneration, in an attempt to maximize their own profits, setting the terms of trade, both as dealers in raw materials and as wide-scale marketers of finished goods, acting as intermediaries in markets to which artisans, including master craftsmen, lacked access.[41] As Caroline M. Barron observes, after 1350 there were frequently conflicts among London guilds between men who were employers of labor and sellers of goods and the workers whom they employed, often the poorer members of the same craft.[42] Propelled in part by these structural antagonisms, substantial portions of the upper strata of nonruling urban classes participated in the English Rising of 1381 and in smaller uprisings around that time.

Andrew Prescott has demonstrated that support for the revolt in 1381 was broadly based in London, encompassing all classes outside the oligarchy of the wealthiest merchants, from masters of small crafts to casual laborers. The identities of some participants from the upper strata of nonruling urban classes are known, including the following: seven London weavers, one of whom was William Pygas, master of the guild of English weavers in 1391; William Cawse and Richard Skeat, men identified in 1376 as two of "the best men of the mistery of fullers," with Skeat becoming master of the fullers four months after the rising and representing the fullers in common council; Walter West, master of the blacksmiths in 1391; and John Blackthorn, one of the leatherdyers sworn to supervise the implementation of regulations for the working of calf leather in 1372.[43] Barron explains that rebels from the countryside did not fall upon a peaceful and united London in June 1381 but that the city "was exposed to almost continuous rioting during the 1370s and 1380s."[44] From the 1370s until the 1440s, numerous political events in London betray significant rifts and volatile relations between the merchant class and the upper strata of nonruling urban classes: the 1377 swearing by all members of the fifty most powerful guilds to keep the peace and put down conspiracies; the factionalism surrounding the merchant-backed grocer Nicholas Brembre and the draper John of Northampton, the latter of whom, when elected mayor in October 1381, attempted to widen craftsmen's and shopkeepers' participation in civic government; the demand for masters and keepers of guilds to provide Chancery with information about their guilds and fraternities in 1388; and the cause of the artisan tailors, led by the wealthy tailor-alderman Ralph Holland in the 1440s.[45] In Beverley the 1381 rebellion transcended all craft boundaries to create a formidable, if temporary, coalition among craftsmen, sellers of food, and laborers; exploitation by the oligarchy united members of craft guilds in opposition to the *probi homines*, with craftsmen attempting to seize the leading offices of the town from the mercantile families who typically dominated these offices.[46] Many artisans prominent in the York riots were from prosperous crafts (such as goldsmiths, armorers, tailors, and large numbers of butchers), against which the merchant class closed ranks, adopting various measures to neutralize the threat posed by master craftsmen.[47] In Canterbury, in the 1360s and 1370s, social and economic antagonisms fueled acts of violence both by the laboring population and by the middling ranks of tradesmen and craftsmen against members of the ruling group, antagonisms at the root of the conflict in June 1381.[48]

A third reason for emphasizing the upper strata of nonruling classes lies in the historical records. As a general rule, regarding late medieval England, historical records and the individuation of men and women grow sparser the further down the socioeconomic ladder one descends (at least as historical records and archival routes to information are currently formulated). Since information about poorer men and women and evidence concerning education and praxes surrounding literacy in late medieval England is typically less abundant for poorer ranks, a medieval English literary scholar who wishes to discuss literacy among nonruling classes from the laity has limited options, if this scholar wishes to respond to those ubiquitous demands for empirical proof that anyone other than the most exceptional individuals from the poorer classes could read and did so.[49] The category of the upper strata of nonruling urban classes allows us to consider a well-documented readership with divergent economic and political interests from those who ruled.

Fourth, this study highlights the upper strata of nonruling urban classes because of their significance in the late medieval English social formation. Economically, these strata were strategic to win over to the social order for obvious material reasons, one being that these men and women were crucial for trade in late medieval England, since a large portion of them generated most goods on which the wholesale merchants relied for business. More broadly, these strata were strategic to recruit, not only so that they would no longer obstruct the ruling classes, either through future insurrections or through the numerous other conflicts in which these strata engaged with the ruling classes, but so that they might be subjected to greater economic, political, and social control and surveillance by the ruling classes. Furthermore, once won over, these ranks could, in turn, facilitate the control of poorer urban dwellers. The upper strata of nonruling urban classes were available for recruitment because they lacked a sense of themselves as a group, as evidenced in part by the lack of cohesiveness among a prominent sector of its group, namely, artisans, as Heather Swanson's *Medieval Artisans: An Urban Class in Late Medieval England* has demonstrated.[50] The larger upper strata of nonruling classes were riven by internal divisions: in London, York, and numerous cities and towns, some sectors of these strata formed intermittent alliances *with* the merchant class, against members of their own ranks and/or against less privileged urban dwellers, while at other times some sectors formed coalitions among members of their own strata and with the urban ranks beneath them *against* the merchant class.[51] The English Rising of 1381 attests to the divisions within the upper strata of nonruling classes, for although large numbers of them rebelled in given towns, in the same towns it seems that many did not, indicating that constituents of this group as a whole did not understand themselves to share universally the same political interests. Such internal fractures meant that the upper strata of nonruling urban classes were available for mobilization and social redefinition.

Finally, this study foregrounds these strata because Chaucer's and Gower's vernacular poetry is structured by an address to these strata. The upper strata of nonruling urban classes constituted one of the principle recipients of address for Chaucer's and Gower's vernacular poetry, not the *only* recipients, but significant ones, a key readership for investigating the new poetry as political discourse and for demonstrating ways in which an English rendition of learned literature in its nascence participated in socioeconomic struggles. These strata represent an important site for examining the relation between the emergent vernacular poetics and readers from the nonruling classes. Although the rest of this chapter caters to medieval English literary studies' conventional demands for empirical evidence regarding readership, the larger book, with its emphasis on address, represents a different way of knowing a readership: via an ideological address speaking through texts or a set of texts, an address that the subsequent two chapters investigate at length. Chaucer's and Gower's English writings involved addresses to other ranks as well, most obviously, to groups of readers from the ruling classes, engagements this study also considers, but not as extensively.

Literacy Among the Upper Strata of Nonruling Urban Classes

Substantial portions of the upper strata of nonruling urban classes possessed the ability to read the vernacular, and occasionally Latin, in late fourteenth-

and early fifteenth-century England. The first place to find evidence of such literacy is in the late medieval English educational system. Between 1380 and 1425, large numbers of men and women from these strata typically received training in the ability to read in English—frequently combined with writing in English—and sometimes training in Latin as well. Elementary and grammar schools were common in English towns by the end of the fourteenth century, with schools in London being particularly numerous by the start of the fifteenth century.[52] Prior to the late fifteenth century, aristocratic boys were not usually educated in the grammar schools and never in local parish reading schools. Because most aristocratic boys and girls were educated in the households of their parents, of other privileged families, or of ecclesiastics (or, in the case of some girls and very young boys, in nunneries), the aristocracy, including the gentry, had little impact on the history of elementary and grammar schools until the end of the fifteenth century. Instead, guilds' impositions of literacy requirements on apprentices were one of the motivating forces behind the growing availability of education in towns. Simultaneously, the church helped propel this increase in education, in part due to a growth of elementary education at the parish level and an increased demand for lower-level clergy.[53]

Regarding secondary-level educations, the chief aim of most grammar schools was to provide a good general grounding in Latin, with a special focus on language structure and on literature, especially poetry. Students were taught how to read, write, speak, and understand Latin language and texts, both classical and medieval, as well as how to engage in literary interpretation.[54] Many grammar-school children had not attended parish elementary schools but had been tutored privately, meaning that grammar schools tended to cater to higher social classes than elementary schools, including high-ranking townspeople and, intermittently, the lower ranks of the gentry. The most widespread, prominent and best-attended of the late medieval English grammar schools were the fee-paying institutions of the town, which were not restricted to any particular class,[55] but which were open to all who could afford to attend them, a requirement that included not only tuition but also sufficient release from labor. Fortunately for children from less affluent households, in the fourteenth century and especially the fifteenth century, education became a major charitable preoccupation of the pious and wealthy. In many places, local arrangements were made for supplying poor scholars with at least their basic meals. Some schools had provisions for paying stipends to young scholars or for funding room and board, particularly for boys who expressed interest in becoming priests. By the late fourteenth century and especially in the fifteenth century, subsidized education was reasonably commonplace, which helped bring education into the reach of the poorer ranks. There were endowed free grammar schools, some under clerical governance (particularly monasteries and university colleges) and others under lay governance (including London city companies and religious guilds consisting of urban merchants or urban yeomen). The master of an endowed school was expected to give lessons in grammar, and often in reading and plainsong, to all comers gratis. Small endowed schools, whether grammar or reading and song schools, starting in the 1380s, were dedicated to providing free education to outsiders rather than boarding students and hence had strong connections to the surrounding vicinity that these schools served.[56] Even when not free, tuition was inexpensive: grammar schools usually cost 8d. a quarter during the fifteenth century, while an unskilled London laborer earned about 4d. to 5d. daily.[57] Children dwelling in towns and cities had an advantage over those in rural areas or small villages because the former need not pay room and board to attend a school, which was the largest impediment to a poorer child obtaining education. Education was financially within the reach of the upper strata of nonruling urban classes, and there was likely to be a fee-paying grammar school in any substantial town.[58]

Even more than secondary-level educations, it was elementary educations that helped propel the noticeable increase in literacy rates in England after 1350. Many elementary schools were parish schools, and those most affected by growing parochial education in the late fourteenth and in the fifteenth centuries were the less wealthy merchants and the artisans, yeoman, and well-to-do-husbandmen, many of whom supported parish scholars and sent their children to these schools.[59] There were large numbers of reading schools in late medieval England, where children learned to read the vernacular, to read introductory Latin (with the degree of training in Latin varying considerably), and likely to write in the vernacular.[60] In song schools, children learned to read Latin aloud, to read and understand English, and probably to write English. In practice, the boundaries between curricula in reading versus song schools, on the one hand, and reading and song schools versus grammar schools, on the other, often blurred.[61] The degree of Latin comprehension taught in song schools has been the subject of debate, with Katherine Zieman arguing that song-school children likely learned a considerable amount of Latin grammar and comprehension and that song schools were continuous with grammar schools.[62]

Cathedral song schools were not confined to the choristers and others who ministered in the church but were open to the locality, and most secular cathedrals had grammar and song schools. But the only recipients of free education at secular cathedrals were the choristers, who received free board, lodging, schooling, and often payments in return for their services in the choir. A chorister's post was therefore analogous to a scholarship for a boy who lacked resources for education. Once a chorister's voice broke, he became eligible for promotion as a secondary, a post offering daily meals, a stipend, and more advanced studies. Some secondaries acquired sufficiently strong knowledge of Latin to become local schoolmasters or to attend university. For a few choristers, their posts were intended as a charitable means to provide access to university study.[63] Notably, according to Nicholas Orme, the minor clergy, among whose ranks vicars, annuellers, choristers, and secondaries are counted, originated from the ranks of artisans and husbandmen.[64] In the late Middle Ages, several song schools were attached to London parish churches and religious houses, including one at St. Mary Overie Priory, from which Gower rented his London house and in which Gower sponsored a chantry.[65] Most chantry schools, several founded specifically to provide free education for the poor, offered free education to all comers. Some monasteries, especially Benedictines houses, maintained and educated a small number of almonry boys, typically poor children from nearby parishes, who received educations, usually in small reading and grammar schools, in Latin grammar at the monks' expense, with the expectation that many of these boys would eventually join the monastery. Free education was also available through other foundations, including hospital and almshouse schools and occasional schools held in the friaries, with friars perhaps viewing the boys as potential future novices. In short, in late fourteenth- and early fifteenth-century England, a child could obtain an elementary education from a variety of institutions: song schools of the cathedral cities and other towns, chantries and colleges, hospitals and almshouse schools, parish schools, and less-common guild schools.[66] Plenty of elementary schools in late fourteenth- and early fifteenth-century English towns offered affordable educations. The ranks of artisans and lesser merchants were among the primary demographics who attended such schools, particularly at the elementary level, and hence learned how to read and write in English and, not infrequently, learned some basic Latin as well.

One could also obtain an education from informal sources, a social practice that has been much more difficult to document. The most infamous clandestine sources of education in late fourteenth- and early fifteenth-century England involved Lollards. The London parchmener John Coddeshulle was tried in Norwich in 1429 for keeping a school for heretics.[67] A blacksmith from Leicester named William Smith, said to have taught himself to read and write, formed a school; at his inquisition for heresy in 1389, Smith handed over books he had written out in English, including selections from the Gospels, the Epistles, and theological texts.[68] Less notorious informal elementary education was being provided in most late fourteenth- and early fifteenth-century English cities and towns. Barron explains that most boys and girls in late medieval London would have attended small, informal schools, some run by chantry priests and some by scriveners. Others of these informal schools were run by women.[69] Two of the most common sources of informal, private elementary education in England were ordinary chaplains and parish clerks (the latter being clergy in minor orders who assisted parish priests to sing the divine office, celebrate mass, and administer occasional offices such as baptisms and burials). It was generally acknowledged that a clerk had the right to teach boys from his own parish, although such teaching occasionally met with resistance when it clashed with the rights of an established school.[70] Informal educations offered by members of the church are intermittently documented through complaints and prohibitions against them. In 1367, for example, the precentor Master Adam of York complained to Archbishop Thoresby that "various chaplains, holy water carriers and others were maintaining song schools in parish churches, houses and other places in the city of York."[71] In 1395 the chapter of Lincoln Cathedral summoned a local chaplain named John Austin to explain why he kept a group of boys in the exchequer of Lincoln, teaching them singing without license from the cathedral song schoolmaster. In 1408 one of the vicars choral of Lincoln was accused of teaching three boys and made to pay a small fine for the offence.[72] In 1423, unlicensed teachers in Walden were teaching English and Latin.[73] Clandestine teaching occurred at higher educational levels as well. Around the time of the English Rising of 1381, enough London law students were informally offering training (in such tasks as the writing of documents, clerical procedures, and the handling of writs) to elicit a prohibition from the chancellor.[74] In fifteenth-century York, priests were teaching writing, perhaps free of charge, and selling the resulting texts. York's Scriveners' guild responded by making it illegal for any priest with an annual salary above seven marks to teach writing to any apprentice, hired man, or servant to write texts for profit. Regardless, some of the priests, presumably the poorer ones, apparently continued to do so.[75] The only area of teaching absolutely restricted to priests was in the small endowed schools. London, apart from its authorized schools, supported several private teachers in the later Middle Ages. Similarly, Bristol had freelance masters, apparently without official sanction, and there were many lesser towns lacking schools where a visiting master could likely set up his own informal school. Some schoolmasters taught temporarily, with other goals in mind, such as becoming ordained and assuming a benefice or saving sufficient funds to attend a university. Notably, Nicolas Orme believes that schoolmasters, both the professionals and the temporary ones, appear to have come from modest burgess families, from the yeomanry of the countryside, and from even lower socioeconomic ranks.[76]

Various sources indicate that large numbers of the upper strata of nonruling urban classes in late fourteenth- and early fifteenth-century could read English and, intermittently, Latin. Official records of the men who joined the clergy are revealing. In her analysis of the York *Register of Freeman*, Swanson counted 806 artisans' sons who took out the freedom by patrimony from 1387 to 1534. Appropriately half these sons kept their fathers' trades; approximately one quarter moved into some other form of manufacturing or victualing; and 7 percent took out the freedom as merchants or chapmen. Of the remaining artisans' sons, virtually all secured the freedom either as clergy or, in a small number of cases, as members of the legal professions. A far greater proportion appears to have joined the church, either as religious or secular clergy, without wishing to be freemen of the city.[77] The proportion of boys from artisan ranks becoming secular clergy and, to a lesser extent, joining legal professions, is noteworthy.

Swanson's statistics are interesting for a more convoluted reason as well. Medieval English children undertook educations with different motivations, some planning to enter the church, others to lead lay lives. Not all those who undertook a grammar-school education with the stated intention of becoming priests completed their courses of study. Some unknown proportion of boys who undertook a grammar-school education to become clergymen either failed to successfully complete as much as all nine years of grammar school or ultimately decided, after completing their programs, not to take up the cloth. In the late Middle Ages, approximately one half and possibly as many as two-thirds of secondaries, for example, remained among the religious clergy when they reached adulthood.[78] The rest returned to lay lives, with considerable literacy in hand. From the mid-fourteenth century, candidates normally received major orders at the average age of twenty-four, and significant numbers of men failed to take major orders, because they were unable to find a benefice, because they wed, or because they chose alternate careers that required literacy.[79] Men with substantial clerical educations who failed to take up major orders can be found among the types of civil servants discussed by Kerby-Fulton and Justice.[80] Many young men who received educations, whether partial or significant, also decided against clerical careers altogether, sacred or lay. Given the large numbers of York's artisan boys becoming religious or secular clergy or joining the legal professions, it is reasonable to assume that many artisan boys who received clerical educations of varying degrees decided in the end to follow their fathers' trades, even after benefiting from free or subsided educations.

Some children received formal educations explicitly as part of their training as future craftsmen, craftswomen, and merchants. Legal documents indicate that, by the late fourteenth century and the first quarter of the fifteenth century, some future guild members were expected to possess an education before their apprenticeship began or to receive or improve their education during their apprenticeship. In a formal apprenticeship, the placement of children in the households of merchants, shopkeepers, and craft masters was accompanied by written contracts specifying duties, discipline, maintenance, instruction, and sometimes schooling or language teaching. Many contracts specified educational requirements (i.e., schooling and training in languages) that craft masters were required to grant to their apprentices during the period of indenture, since a certain amount of teaching, excluding technical training, was frequently expected.[81] Some extant wills and contracts document obligations by various guild masters to have apprentices specifically taught to read and write during their apprenticeships.[82] Similarly, the wills of laity who bequeathed money or books to their children or relatives for schooling occasionally indicated that the inheritors were being educated into crafts.[83] For example, a 1391 will specified that John Yssak, son of chaplain Robert att Hall, was to go to school until he had learned to say his Psalter, at which point the boy was to enter a craft.[84] In 1349 Matilda de Myms, widow of an image maker named John de Myms, made various bequests to an apprentice named William, including the provision that William was to be delivered for three years into the care and teaching of Friar Thomas de Alsham of the priory

33

and convent of Bermondeseye.[85] Not surprisingly, there are legal cases in which apprentices charge masters of failing in their legal responsibility to have apprentices learn these skills.[86] In 1415 John Holand from Norfolk complained to the mayor of London that the barber to whom he had been apprenticed was so poor that he could not feed and clothe him appropriately, nor keep him in school until he could read and write, as per their agreement in Holand's indentures.[87] The nature of the business affairs of late medieval English merchants, shopkeepers, and prosperous craftsmen required the ability to read and write, tasks that included making contracts; keeping records of stock, orders, and sales; and possibly corresponding with suppliers outside the immediate vicinity.[88] Likewise, according to Barron, late medieval Englishwomen who conducted businesses or who ran workshops must have acquired basic literacy skills to keep control of their accounts. After contemplating what books artisan women may have read, Barron remarks that it is time to stop being surprised when we find fifteenth-century English women in towns reading and writing.[89] The same can be said of artisans and lesser merchants in late fourteenth- and early fifteenth-century England.

The abstract book of London's Brewers' guild provides testimony of literacy among its members. Guild members' literacy in English was the impetus for the well-known 1422 entry explaining that the guild decided to keep future records in "our mother-tongue, to wit the English tongue . . . the common idiom," because "there are many of our craft of Brewers who have the knowledge of writing and reading in the said English idiom, but in others, to wit, the Latin and French, before these times used, they do not in any wise understand." Although the proclamation is recorded in the Brewers' Abstract Book in Latin, with a translation provided, the Brewers kept subsequent records in English, only occasionally lapsing into Latin or French.[90] The Brewers were not anomalous, since in the 1420s other guilds also switched their record keeping to English.[91] It is important to point out that the Brewers' guild was one of London's lesser misteries.[92] At least one brewer is named in the more than a dozen extant legal records for the trials of participants in the 1381 insurrection: Walter atte Keye was indicted for bringing fire with him on June 14, 1381, to burn down the London Guildhall and to incinerate the book called "Le Jubyle," a book concerning the city's constitutions. As part of his quest to destroy the "Book of Jubilee," Walter reportedly led rebels to the king's Compter in Milk Street, where he was one of the chief malefactors in breaking into and despoiling the property.[93]

The history of the benefit of clergy provides evidence of the ability to read Latin among some men from the upper strata of nonruling urban classes. The benefit of clergy permitted men accused or convicted of secular crimes by secular courts to be transferred for trial and judgment to an ecclesiastical tribunal, which was typically more lenient. This benefit could be claimed by clerks of any level, whether in major or minor orders and even if they had received only the first tonsure. As Leona Gabel explains, after the beginning of the fourteenth century, the benefit of clergy was a simple literacy test: a prisoner was handed a Latin service book and asked to read two verses aloud. The last two decades of the fourteenth century saw a noticeable increase in the numbers of men claiming this privilege, with numerous examples of merchants, craftsmen, and peasants claiming to be clerks and establishing their status by passing the literacy test.[94] Gabel writes,

> It has been shown from cases of criminous clerks from the Gaol Delivery Rolls that every variety of occupation is represented among the prisoners who establish their clergy by reading. Selected at random from rolls dating from 6 Richard II to 1 Edward IV, there appear literate clerks described as "quondam serviens" [former servants], "mercer," "serviens," "taillour," "spicer," "fysshemonger," "hosyer," "smyth," "fyssher," "shipman," "chapman," "yoman," "bucher," "husbandmen," "masun," "walker," "webster," "couper," "vestmentmaker," and relatively numerous instances of literate laborers. The term "laborer" meant the poorer, unskilled worker as contrasted with the better paid workman or artisan.[95]

Although some of these occupations likely indicate members of the proto-bourgeoisie, specifically the chapman, the spicer, the fishmonger, and the mercer, other occupations are more ambiguous and could signify wealthy merchants, rank-and-file guild members, or independent craftsmen, including the tailor, hosier, weaver, butcher, and "fisher." Similarly, a "yeoman" could be a merchant-in-waiting or a peasant. Several occupations listed are those of common craftsmen, such as the mason, cooper, garment maker, blacksmith, and walker (a fuller of cloth, one who beats woolen cloth to cleanse or thicken it). Other occupations fall into even lower ranks, including a servant, a former servant, and several laborers. Moreover, since in the educational system a child learned to read English before Latin, one can assume that these men also read English.

Lists of witnesses in ecclesiastical and secular legal cases document the relative commonplaceness of literacy in late medieval England. As Richard W. Kaeuper explains, a legal case in Canterbury in 1334 records a list of 33 witnesses, noting each man's age and status and whether he is *litteratus* or *illitteratus* (Kaeuper defines *litteratus* as possessing "some Latin and probably some Latin learning").[96] A total of 5 men were in major orders and 25 were laymen; in three cases it is difficult to determine the witnesses' occupations. It is unlikely that any of the 33 witnesses were men of high status. Of the men without a stated clerical vocation, 13 of the 28 (or 45 percent) are classified as *litterati*. Kaeuper also discusses an inquiry in Norfolk in 1466 concerning Sir John Falstaff's will, where 44 percent of the lay witnesses were literate, including a mariner, a husbandman, and an agricultural laborer.[97] Thrupp explains that of the 116 male witnesses who between 1467 and 1476 gave evidence before the Consistory Court of London, 48 (or 40 percent) were literate (which Thrupp assumes in most cases meant the ability to read a little Latin), a proportion that tallies with that of two much smaller groups of witnesses in 1373 and 1466. The witnesses from 1467 to 1476 include a wide variety of artisans. The professional groups (e.g., lawyers, physicians and surgeons, scriveners, and lay schoolmasters) are not included, but if these occupations had been included, the percentage of the lay witnesses that were literate would have been higher. Thrupp conjectures that 40 percent of the lay male Londoners of this period could read Latin and that 50 percent could read English.[98]

Predictably, with such significant literacy among the upper strata of non-ruling classes, these ranks owned books. Extant legal records provide glimpses into their book ownership from the 1380s through the mid-fifteenth century. An inventory of the belongings of John Sharnebrok, a chandler and citizen of London, includes the manuscript "Clensyngsyne," assessed at 8d. in 1376.[99] In 1395 Gilbert Prynce, a London painter, bequeathed a missal to the church of St. Giles without Cripplegate. In his 1411 will, John Clifford, a Southwark mason, left to his parish church of St. Olave in Southwark his best Psalter, probably written in Latin, and a "librum de Euangeliis dominical' in Anglic' uerborum transpositum," which appears to be the English-language translation of the sermon cycle *The Mirror*. To a convent of Franciscan nuns, Clifford bequeathed *Legenda Sanctorum Liber* and the *Recti Diligunt Te* (which was a copy of *Ancrene*

Riwle), although the language of either text is not indicated.[100] In 1431 the rector of Arncliffe in West Riding left a "librum Anglicanum de Exposicione Evangeliorum" to Robert Forest, who was probably a member of an artisan family in York.[101] John Newton, a York glover who died in 1443, bequeathed a book of "devynyte qui sequitur regulam a.b.c.d. de anglico" and a second book called "Ponecronakyll," most likely Ranulf Higden's *Polychronicon*.[102] In 1446 Richard Person, an armorer of London, bequeathed his grandson, Richard, a Psalter.[103] According to the inventory made after his death around 1450, John Cadeby, a mason of Beverley, possessed a pair of writing tables and six English books, the latter valued at 10s.[104] Roger Elmesley, a wax chandler's servant, and hence from lower levels in the crafts than the ranks emphasized in this study, left a primer to his godchild in 1434.[105] As various medievalists have noted, for sundry reasons most books owned by late medieval Englishmen and women were not mentioned in wills, and wills were much more apt to specify religious books rather than literary ones.[106]

London parish fraternities, which were predominantly artisan and female, according to Barron, also owned books: during Richard II's reign, the guild of St. Katherine in St. Botolph Aldersgate owned a mass book worth ten marks, while the guilds of SS. Fabian and Sebastian in the same church owned a missal.[107] Communal ownership of poetic texts was a possibility writ large in the guildhall of the Armourers, a lesser mistery in London that in 1429–30 commissioned John Lydgate to compose poetry used in a tapestry to adorn the walls of their new guildhall. The guild also commissioned Lydgate to compose the narrative poem *The Life of St. George*, thought to be performed in the Armourers' hall on the feast of Saint George.[108]

Malcolm Parkes has argued that the burgeoning of "pragmatic literacy," the ability to read and write in English for business purposes, among the protobourgeoisie in England from the thirteenth through the fifteenth century led to a corresponding growth in "cultivated" reading among the laity, such as reading to improve the soul, to multiply accomplishments, and to increase knowledge of cultural information. This cultural reading included the recreational consumption of literary texts, such as Chaucerian poetry.[109] The same logic holds for those men and women one step further down on the socioeconomic ladder. The increase in literacy among the upper strata of nonruling urban classes in late fourteenth- and early fifteenth-century England coincides with an expansion of book production, which suggests that the upper strata of nonruling urban classes were among those men and women engaged in "cultivated" reading. A comparison of the number of extant manuscripts attests that the early years of the fifteenth century in England saw a dramatic increase in vernacular book production: there are approximately thirty extant manuscripts of vernacular literature from 1325 to 1400, while approximately six hundred manuscripts of vernacular literature from 1400 to 1475 survive, with the turn of the century seeming to have been a watershed.[110]

The substantial growth in book production at the end of the fourteenth century and at the beginning of the fifteenth century is reflected in the growth of book-trade artisans in London. The decade 1380–89 shows the first sizeable group of London book artisans appearing in archival records. The subsequent two decades saw large increases in the number of book artisans in the capital, numbers that remain fairly stable after 1410, until they drop at the beginning of the sixteenth century.[111] The growth in manuscript production is also reflected in the changes in the constituent membership of the relevant craft guilds that in 1403 amalgamated London's Textwriters and Illuminators into a book-artisan guild, known by the 1440s as the Mistery of Stationers.[112] Between 1390 and 1410, book production shifted from isolated and scattered manufacturing in different parts of the country into the beginnings of routine, commercial production in London. The expansion, centralization, and commercialization in the production of vernacular manuscripts from the end of the fourteenth century reflected the increase in demand.[113] York witnessed a similar growth in book production at the end of the fourteenth century and the first quarter of the fifteenth century, with guilds both of text writers and of parchment makers emerging between 1376 and 1420.[114] By 1425 the scriveners, flourishers, and illuminators of York had formed themselves into a guild, although a substantial amateur trade often came into conflict with the guild.[115]

The insistence on professionalization by book-artisan guilds, and the repeated battles in which they engaged against those who encroached on their territory, attests to the ubiquitous presence of clerks, religious and secular, to copy manuscripts, quires, booklets, or pamphlets to supplement their incomes. Linne R. Mooney's study of scribes from fourteenth-and fifteenth-century London demonstrates that a sizeable cadre of lay scribes, who are responsible for copying a large number of vernacular literary manuscripts, lived on the outskirts of London, working independently of the Textwriters' guild. Some scribes freelanced full-time, although more did so part-time, likely copying books after completing the demands of their regular day jobs, as canons, as vicars or schoolmasters, as legal scriveners, or as clerks in governmental offices in London and Westminster.[116] The skill level of this army of scribes ranged greatly, from the highly trained, such as Thomas Hoccleve and Adam Pinkhurst, to the minimally trained, an end of the spectrum toward which perhaps Margery Kempe's first priestly transcriber veers. The lower end of the spectrum blurs into the innumerable amateur scribes who copied works for themselves and for their friends, including the sixteen-year-old son of a burgess who made himself a copy of the *Canterbury Tales*.[117]

In part because of the large pool of professional, semiprofessional, and amateur labor available, books were often inexpensive in late fourteenth- and early fifteenth-century England. The price of books varied dramatically, with the opulent end of the spectrum represented by Edward III's book of romance, for which he paid more than £66.[118] The expensive side of a more normative range includes such items as a finely illuminated mass book, typically worth up to £10 in the late fourteenth and early to mid-fifteenth centuries,[119] and the "Corpus Legis Canoni" and an illuminated "Book of Romaunce of King Alexander," worth £10, two of the most expensive books listed among the records of the mayor's court of London. By contrast, the mayor's court of London also lists among an ironmonger's property two Psalters and a gradual valued at 3d.[120] The 1397 inventory of the goods of the youngest son of Edward III, Thomas of Woodstock, duke of Gloucester, itemizes numerous manuscripts valued at a few shillings or even pence, including "un rouge livre de Barlaham & Josephath" at 6d. and "un petit livre Fr3uceys del Reclus de Melans" at 1s. An inventory of the books of John Scardeburgh, rector of Tichmarsh in Northamptonshire, recorded in 1395, contains mostly inexpensive books: a *Bruyt* in French, worth 2s.; a "libellus cum causa T. Cantuariensis, et aliis," worth 18d.; a "quaternus continens forms dictanda," valued at 2s.; a "quaternus cum diversis narrationibus," valued at 20d.; a French "Maundevile in paupiro," rated at 2s.; "quaternus de arte dictandi, cum quibusdam Epistolis Blesencis," valued at 2s.; and a "dogma filosoforum" and a "textus Clementinarum," each worth 12d.[121] In 1430 the inventory of books of John, abbot of the monastery of the Blessed Mary of Graces, contained three books assessed between 8d. and 20d. each.[122] Among the belongings of an Oxford scholar named Simon Beryngton were twelve books (their titles and subjects unidentified), collectively valued by a stationer in 1448 at 4d., while in the same year, three books of another Oxford scholar were valued at 2d.[123] In 1445 William Furnyvale's possessions included five quires collectively valued at 12d.[124] Two of the best-known bankruptcy lists from late medieval England are those of London merchants. In 1361 among the goods of Roger Chalket, citizen and pepperer, were four "libros de romaunc'," adjudicated at 6s. 4d. for the group. William Cost, a London grocer, whose inventory was drawn up in 1392, possessed two "libros de Englyssh," valued jointly at 8d., a primer worth 16d., a calendar worth 8d., and a second primer worth 4d., the primers being, as Ralph Hanna notes, books of hours. The large presence of paper and parchment among Cost's inventory suggests that he was also a stationer, bookseller, practicing scribe, and/or a supplier of materials for scribes.[125] For those interested in copying their own selections, after 1400 a quire of eight sheets (sixteen pages) of paper cost only between 1d. and 4d., depending on the size and quality.[126]

As these book inventories imply, books were often sold as previously owned goods. The second-hand book trade was well established in the first half of the fifteenth century in London and also appears to have been established in more provincial areas by this time. How large a portion of the book market the sale of older manuscripts represented is unclear, but it was not insignificant.[127] As some of these book inventories also indicate, texts were being sold in rudely written, unbound copies, such as quires, and otherwise as products of inexpensive production.[128] Texts, including literary ones, were sold in booklet and pamphlet formats, and possibly as bifolia and single leaves.[129]

A comparison between such prices for books (and quires) and the earnings of the upper strata of nonruling classes at the time makes it is clear that these ranks had the ability to regularly purchase such goods. For masons, 6d. per day was the most common wage outside London from 1370 until the sixteenth century, while in London, masons' wages were 2d. per day greater. There are cases of masons hired throughout the fourteenth and fifteenth centuries for even higher rates of compensation, for weekly and annual periods, for multiple years, and occasionally for life.[130] Masons' wages of 8d. per day were likely comparable to those of carpenters and others in the building trades in late fourteenth-century London.[131] Wages for craftsmen more generally in the late fourteenth century ranged from 4d. to 6d. per day.[132] Many sectors of the upper strata of nonruling classes enjoyed greater earnings than 4d. to 8d. daily, including the master crafts-men who employed waged craftsmen and the shopkeepers who sold their goods.[133] One day's wages at the lower end of a craftsman's pay scale, namely at 4d., could have purchased the twelve books belonging to the Oxford scholar Simon Beryngton; half a day's earnings could have gained the three texts from an anonymous Oxford scholar; and two days' wages would have secured some of the grocers' former holdings (the two books written in English or the calendar) or some of the romances previously owned by Richard II or by his uncle. Two to three days of a skilled craftsman's wages would have paid for tuition for an entire semester of grammar school throughout most of England.

Readership in late medieval England was not, of course, reducible to ownership: a person need not own a manuscript to have access to it. The opening of the fifteenth century has been called "the age of library building" for secular cathedrals.[134] In fourteenth-century London, the choristers of St. Paul's Cathedral were bequeathed several dozen books, ranging from grammar and poetry to logic, law, and medicine.[135] Upon his death in 1414, John Newton, treasurer of York, donated forty books for the founding and development of a library for all parishioners at York Minster, and by 1421 the minster had a new building to house Newton's books, which were chained on lecterns, a collection that included a volume of historians and a volume of Petrarch.[136] Parish libraries were also developing at the time. Some parishes had small collections of nonliturgical books, bequeathed by clerics and laity alike, which were placed in the public domain and chained in the church.[137] Although ownership of sacred books, including compilations of saints' lives, were common, records of parish churches' ownership of less obvious books occasionally surface, including Higden's *Polychronicon*, Peter Lombard's *Textus Sententiarum*, Bartholomaeus Anglicus's *De Proprietatibus Rerum*, John Lydgate's *Fall of Princes*, and Giles of Rome's *De Regimine Principum*.[138] Several London churches in the fifteenth century had small chained libraries of books; Barron wonders what literate artisan girls might have read there.[139] Other institutions also opened their collections to the public. For example, the library of the Preaching Friars (Blackfriars) in London was what Barron dubs "the recognised 'public library'" before the Guildhall Library was built between 1423 and 1425.[140] Many monastic libraries were open freely to members of their respective districts. The Carthusians, Cistercians, and Benedictines loaned their books under certain conditions or upon receipt of sufficient pledges.[141] Gower bequeathed a missal and a *martilogium* to St. Mary Overie Priory and made monetary bequests to four parish churches (including St. Olave), two of which belonged to St. Mary Overie Priory.[142] One wonders if Gower gave copies of his own writings to these parish churches, whether informally upon his death or during his lifetime.[143]

Literate members of the upper strata of nonruling urban classes could have read a range of books owned by various institutions, or they could have borrowed books from friends and relatives. The loaning of books among individuals was commonplace in late medieval England, as evidenced by the frequency with which testators bequeathed books to friends and relatives who already had the books in their possession.[144] The most obvious sectors of the upper strata of nonruling urban classes from which to borrow books or quires were the scriveners, stationers, and book artisans (which included skilled craftswomen).[145] C. Paul Christianson explains that in late fourteenth- to fifteenth-century London, professional bookmakers and sellers formed a closely bound community professionally and personally, attested by the frequency with which they name each other as executors, overseers, witnesses, and beneficiaries of their wills.[146] One could employ the same logic to argue that this community of professional bookmakers and sellers also had strong bonds with the larger body of artisans and retailers in late medieval London, men and women who occupied the same socioeconomic ranks. These bonds are evident in the sizeable number of extant legal documents in which stationers and book artisans name people from London's sundry crafts to be executors of their wills or in which craftspeople act as executors of the wills of stationers and book artisans. Similarly, book artisans and traders often appear, alongside craftsmen outside the bookproducing guilds, as mainpernors for craftsmen and occasionally otherwise acting as surety for them.[147] With such close friendships, it would not have been unusual for book artisans and traders to loan books and quires, to informally bequeath them, or to give them as gifts to their friends in crafts outside book production.

The sense of community between London's book artisans and stationers and the larger body of craftspeople and retailers in London is also evident in their fraternities. Large numbers of book artisans and traders had associations with various fraternities in late fourteenth- and early fifteenth-century London, with membership in the fraternity of SS. Fabian and Sebastian being especially common.[148] Parish fraternities, as explained earlier, were predominantly populated by artisan ranks, especially by women; in joining these fraternities, book artisans and traders were part of large social networks of various craftspeople. The membership of book artisans and traders in a given fraternity increased the chances of the fraternity owning manuscripts or pieces thereof, with the ownership of a missal by the Fraternity of SS. Fabian and Sebastian being a case in point.

Having book artisans and traders in a given fraternity also increased the chances of a reading of current poetry at a fraternity's social events. In late medieval England, reading aloud was, of course, a common practice. Margaret Aston's studies on Lollardy and literacy have demonstrated that texts were frequently read aloud among varieties of domestic groups, which included relatives and servants, and that reading groups extended beyond domestic gatherings into neighborhood clusters formed around shared political or ideological interests.[149] Justice's *Writing and Rebellion* illustrates that it was possible to have access to the written word without reading it oneself, when members of one's family or community were literate, including, for example, a scenario where "the literacy of one family member could be a delegated literacy for the entire family,"[150] a model particularly useful when thinking of artisans' sons who received educations in Latin but who declined to take major orders.

Joyce Coleman's *Public Reading and the Reading Public in Late Medieval England and France* argues that poetry in the Middle Ages was communally read aurally (which she defines as the "shared hearing of written texts"), that aural reading was the dominant way of experiencing texts in the Middle Ages, and that most recreational literature seems to have been read publicly.[151] Coleman believes that Chaucer's poetry was directed primarily at listeners who were literate, educated members of the upper classes. Likewise, according to Coleman, Gower's *Confessio* contains extensive verbal cues indicating that it was designed primarily to be read aloud, with Gower probably intending the poem to be read aloud by a household clerk to his literate royal or upper-class masters, with Coleman's understanding paralleling Alastair J. Minnis's vision of an extremely well-educated speaker reading aloud a section of the *Confessio* to small audiences of aristocrats.[152] "As for the more general middle-class audience," Coleman writes, "we may suppose that those without a clerk on staff would have formed the clientele for that group of later *Confessio* manuscripts that sharply reduced the amount of Latin in the text, some substituting English translations or summaries, and other abstracting favorite stories."[153] Coleman remarks, "lower middle-class people like Alisoun of Bath" might have listened to texts, "if they had someone literate to read to them."[154] Assigning the term "middle class" to the protobourgeoisie, Coleman engages in the commonplace slippage of class positions discussed earlier in this chapter and mistakes as "lower middle-class" a highly skilled craftswoman who may also be a lesser merchant.

While I support Coleman's understanding that the *Confessio* and Chaucerian poetry were frequently, maybe even predominantly, read aloud, I understand the post of what Coleman calls the "prelector" to have been at least intermittently occupied by people from the upper strata of nonruling urban classes. More importantly, I believe that prior to 1425 the literate auditors and/or solitary readers of the *Confessio* and of Chaucerian poetry frequently included men and women from the upper strata of nonruling urban classes. Many, perhaps even most, men from the upper strata of nonruling urban classes and significant numbers of women from these ranks possessed the ability to read English and engaged on a regular basis with written texts in the late fourteenth and early fifteenth centuries. Hearing the poetry of Gower or Chaucer would not have been an exceptional, fortunate event for a person from these ranks, occurring only in the company of someone from higher ranks who decided to have the poem read aloud. Rather than being the beneficiaries of a trickle-down literacy, large sectors of the upper strata of nonruling urban classes read, owned, and sometimes even produced texts, including literature, in late fourteenth- and early fifteenth-century England. If members of these strata wished to read the poetry of Chaucer or Gower, many options were available to them, especially if they lived in or around London: if they themselves were not scriveners, book artisans, or stationers, they could borrow manuscripts or sections thereof from their friends in the book trade; they could borrow full or partial manuscripts, booklets, quires, or pamphlets from relatives, from their colleagues in their parish fraternities, or from sundry friends in their socioeconomic circles; they could pay one of the countless number of professional, semiprofessional, and amateur scribes to write out material for them; they could purchase collections, quires, or individual tales from stationers, including secondhand stock; or they could borrow the manuscripts, booklets, or quires from those religious institutions that granted access to locals.

The number of extant manuscripts, and fragments, of Chaucer's poetry and of Gower's *Confessio* are unusually large compared to most medieval English texts. There are fifty-five relatively complete manuscripts of the *Canterbury Tales* and an additional eighteen segments in miscellanies and nine more fragments. The dream visions and shorter poems circulated in numerous collections of the mid-fifteenth century. *Troilus and Criseyde* exists in sixteen fifteenth-century manuscripts, while the *Legend of Good Women* exists in twelve.[155] The *Confessio* survives in forty-nine manuscripts and approximately one dozen fragments and excerpts.[156] When tallying the Middle English works with the largest numbers of extant manuscripts, the *Canterbury Tales* and the *Confessio* rank fourth and fifth respectively, with a particularly large number of extant *Confessio* manuscripts from the beginning of the fifteenth century.[157] After discussing the production of copies of *Confessio* manuscripts near the end of Gower's lifetime (d. 1408), A. I. Doyle comments, "Once a work was being fairly frequently copied and offered through the metropolitan book-trade, the courtier's advantage had gone, for members of other classes had equal access to it."[158] Similarly, Kerby-Fulton and Justice remark that Usk's use of both Langland's C-text and Chaucer's *Troilus* "points to a rapid and highly organized system of dissemination" of these texts among London vernacular reading circles.[159] Ultimately, given their substantial levels of literacy, given the availability and cheapness of texts, and given their proximity to those involved in book production, it is evident that significant portions of the upper strata of nonruling classes, in addition to book artisans and traders, were among those who read Chaucer's and Gower's vernacular poetry prior to 1425.

Because large sectors of the upper strata of nonruling urban classes were immersed in textual and literary culture, not only could these men and women access this new vernacular poetry, but they were available to be addressed by this literature more thoroughly than if they had not been literate and had not regularly engaged with written texts. Sustained interactions with written texts made possible a type of interpellation of these ranks, not unlike the interpellation theorized by Louis Althusser.[160] The literacy of large portions of these strata made highly literate vernacular poetry an effective site at which to engage politically with at least one important sector of the nonruling classes, a sector that had produced large numbers of rebels in the English Rising of 1381 and that were poised to advance their cultural pursuits autonomously. The rest of the book explores the ways in which Chaucer's and Gower's poetry attempted to speak to, and about, these strata and about the larger population of subordinate groups as part of Chaucer's and Gower's negotiations over the roles vernacular poetry would play in the late medieval English social formation, ultimately positioning vernacular literature to be a powerful participant in processes of social control in late medieval England—and beyond.

AGAINST THE GREYNESS OF THE MULTITUDE:
POETRY, PRESTIGE, AND THE *CONFESSIO AMANTIS*

n the wake of the Black Death, workers in England consumed. Wage increases in the ensuing several decades provided better food, clothing, and housing for many laborers, peasants, and artisans. With new consumer goods available, including a wider range of fashionable garments and various manufactured products, consumption habits by subordinate classes frequently mimicked those of the elite.[1] Because manuscripts were not insulated from the prestige attached to consumer goods in late fourteenth- and early fifteenth-century England, some of the laity perceived manuscripts as objects that conferred cultural cachet. In his study on manuscript producers and owners in fifteenth-century Yorkshire, J. B. Friedman notes that decorated books were markers of status, combining portability, durability, and sound investment for practical, upwardly mobile people.[2] Similarly, Carol M. Meale believes that one may understand the possession of a Chaucerian manuscript in late medieval England as a gauge of fashionable tastes, irrespective of the owner's socioeconomic position.[3] Accordingly, in his *Prologue,* the Man of Law attempts to impress his fellow pilgrims by listing the Chaucerian poetry that he has consumed. Anne Middleton argues that the Man of Law illustrates the principle that narrating stories represents "a way of reaffirming one's possession of the tastes and qualities that assure one's membership in polite society." Middleton locates the Man of Law within a now heavily discussed coterie of Chaucer's "New Men," whose views, she maintains, represent literary theories with little coherent vernacular articulation in England before Chaucer.[4]

Linked in numerous ways with Gower and the *Confessio,*[5] the Man of Law points to a nexus of issues structuring Gower's text. In the *Introduction to the Man of Law's Tale*, the fictional lawyer gratuitously mentions Ovid's poetry (2.53–55, 91–93), enumerates the contents of Chaucer's oeuvre (2.47–76), and cites two tales from the *Confessio* (2.77–86).[6] By flaunting his familiarity with Ovidian and vernacular English literature, for which he clearly anticipates admiration, the Man of Law reveals his assumption that conversance with English poetry is prestigious. Recalling Elizabeth Allen's conclusion that the Man of Law and his tale reveal that "Chaucer read and understood Gower's moral and aesthetic aims" in the *Confessio Amantis*,[7] one could argue that Chaucer's Man of Law foregrounds one of the *Confessio*'s key projects: coding knowledge of vernacular literature as a version of cultural capital, a project this chapter investigates at length. Through the Man of Law's errors in his textual recollections, Chaucer announces, as do his pilgrims' overall responses, that some readers of the new English poetry will not master the material but will glean only cultural lessons half-learned.[8] As this chapter demonstrates, that different groups of *Confessio* readers gained different gradations of access to its literary riches was important to the poem's political strategies. After Harry Bailley's discussion of time and wealth and his insistence on efficiency (2.1–32), the Man of Law expends considerable time demonstrating his literary prowess. He then declares, "Bet is to dyen than have indigence" (2.114) and reiterates part of Pope Innocent III's *De Miseria Condicionis Humane*, adding a warning against poverty, depicting the poor as abject, and substituting a denunciation of riches for praise for wealthy merchants (2.99–130).[9] By flanking the lawyer's wanton display of literary knowledge with discussions revering wealth, Chaucer aligns an extravagant spectacle of vernacular literary knowledge with respect for affluence. In short, the Man of Law points to some of the *Confessio*'s central logic.

This chapter examines this logic, and a much more complicated nexus, in Gower's tome. The *Confessio* helped refashion a largely learned, predominantly Greco-Roman tradition into the basis of a new English heritage. Forged when authoritative texts were not typically composed in the language of England's commoners, the *Confessio* attached prestige to the vernacular tradition it conveyed, while the poem engaged in the very process of founding that tradition, granting this emergent heritage and familiarity with it a weight not unlike what Bourdieu identifies as "cultural capital."[10] The *Confessio*'s portrayal of the acquisition of this cultural knowledge is heavily mystified, an enchantment not unlike what Bourdieu and Jean-Claude Passeron describe as an "ideology of 'gifts.'"[11] The poem extends a similar gift to readers and forwards conversance with its textual legacy as the signifier of transformation, evidence of intellectual, moral, and spiritual superiority over the populace. Familiarity with this legacy is the mark of election by which readers and other inheritors of these cultural riches— who, given the social practices surrounding literacy in Gower's England, were predominantly members of ruling classes—could recognize one another against the greyness of the multitude. Deploying this standard of adjudication, the *Confessio* elevates enlightened men above the populace and polices debates about England's welfare, determining who constitutes suitable participants in such discussions. Exemplifying hegemonic deployments of tradition—where, as Raymond Williams has argued, a selective tradition is powerful in processes of social and cultural definition and identification and where a tradition, at its inscription, seeks to ratify power relations[12]—through this cultural heritage, the *Confessio* promotes identifications between readers and higher ranks and encourages a sense of superiority over the lower ranks. Despite inviting all readers to be inheritors of this bequest, the *Confessio* deems some readers more deserving than others, pronouncing certain audience members full inheritors of this legacy, while positioning less seasoned readers as only limited beneficiaries. The poem teaches audience members alienated by the text to differentiate between their deficient selves and the more deserving heirs and to defer to the latter as the sole legitimate producers of knowledge. After scrutinizing these strategies in the *Confessio*, this chapter situates this discussion vis-à-vis social relations in late fourteenth- and early fifteenth-century England, examining how the terms of the poem's conferral of this new heritage addressed readers who had rebelled in, or sympathized with, the English Rising of 1381. This address to select readers who had supported the insurrection attempted to reorganize political alliances in the aftermath of this dramatic crisis of authority.[13]

It is not unusual to argue that the *Confessio* authorizes itself as an English-language poem. Some Gower scholars have demonstrated how the *Confessio* heavy-handedly legitimates itself through explicit borrowing of conventions of academic textual apparatuses and discourses. According to Rita Copeland, Gower employs the techniques of exegetical translation and appropriates "the discourse of academic exegesis" to advance the *Confessio*'s claims to *auctoritas*. Alastair J. Minnis believes that the form of the poem's Prologue is indebted to the "sapiential prologue," which introduced commentaries on biblical and philosophical texts and Latin treatises, while the

Confessio's Latin apparatus recalls academic textual apparatuses. As Siân Echard points out, the *Confessio*'s Latin prose commentaries self-consciously connect the poem to the academic tradition and invest the text with the trappings of authority.[14] What is innovative, however, is to understand the *Confessio* as legitimating itself by investing its contents with a cultural authority akin to Bourdieu's formulations of cultural capital and to argue that the *Confessio* attached a version of cultural capital to English literature in its embryonic moments.[15]

Not surprisingly, the overwhelming majority of the *Confessio*'s sources are learned. Although impossible to enumerate all the book's sources here, a thumbnail sketch follows. The most influential source is Ovid's poetry, especially the *Metamorphoses* but also *Ars Amatoria*, *Fasti*, and *Heroides*.[16] Alain de Lille's *De Planctu Naturae* and *Anticlaudianus* are sources as well.[17] Through Alain de Lille's writings and Bernardus Silvestris's *Cosmographia*, Boethius's *De Consolatio Philosophiae* had an impact on the *Confessio*.[18] Gower borrowed materials surrounding the Troy story from Guido delle Colonne's *Historia Destructionis Troiae* and Benoît de Sainte-Maure's *Le Roman de Troie*, both of which drew on Statius's *Thebaid*.[19] The "Mirror for Princes" genre provides material (especially in book 7), most notably the pseudo-Aristotelian *Secretum Secretorum*, *De Regimine Principum* of Giles of Rome, and *Li Livres dou Tresor* of Brunetto Latini.[20] Nicholas Trivet's *Chronique* is the primary source for Constance's saga.[21] Several Christian-centered writings are sources: sermons, ecclesiastical writings, the Bible, exempla (especially by Jacques de Vitry and Isidore of Seville), *The Book of Vices and Virtues* (a translation of *Somme le Roi*), Peter Riga's *Aurora*, Robert Mannyng of Brunne's *Handlyng Synne*, and the larger penitential manual tradition.[22] Amans is derived from medieval French writers, including Guillaume de Machaut, Jean Froissart, and especially Jean de Meun and Guillaume de Lorris, while the larger poem borrows from various celebrated medieval European vernacular poets, such as Dante Alighieri, Giovanni Boccaccio, and Andreas Capellanus.[23] Other sources include *Epitome Rerum Romanarum* by Florus, *Ab Urbe Condita* by Livy, *Le Roman de Toute Chevalerie* by Thomas of Kent, *Le Roman de Marques de Rome*, writings by Walter Map, *Pantheon* by Godfrey of Viterbo, *Speculum Stultorum* by Nigel of Longchamps, *De Naturis Rerum* by Alexander Neckham, *Disticha Catonis*, *Poetarius* of Albericus of London, *Gesta Romanorum*, and *Policraticus* by John of Salisbury.[24]

As this partial list makes clear, the *Confessio* is heavily indebted to learned texts. Although the poem demonstrates significantly less interest in the culture of the populace, Arthurian characters strategically appear during Amans's conversion scene. This scene is paramount because it is the poem's climax, transforming the dim-witted Amans into the visionary John Gower—the goal of the fictive narrative—and because it offers the *Confessio*'s most pointed explanation of how to acquire familiarity with the textual legacy that the tome imparts, a key to unraveling the poem's nexus of issues surrounding the connections between vernacular literature and cultural capital. The drama unfolds as follows. After Genius narrates his final tale, the pathetic protagonist remains uncertain what to do. Genius admonishes Amans, advising him to abandon love. Dissatisfied, Amans asks Genius to present a supplication to Cupid and Venus (8.2029–309). When Venus appears, Amans sues for grace (8.2310–17). Venus asks the protagonist his name, to which he replies "John Gower" (8.2318–21), the first identification of the narrator as "Gower" in the body of the poem, although he is identified as "Iohannes Gower" in the first Latin gloss (at Prol.22). When Venus shows Amans a mirror, he is startled by his advanced years. She informs her disciple that nature has deemed him unsuitable for her court, and he swoons (8.2322–449).

Amans has a lengthy vision in which Cupid appears with a parliament of gentle folk who had been lovers. Lusty Youth leads joyful lovers: Tristram and Isolde, Lancelot and Guenevere, Galahad and his lady, Jason and Creusa, Hercules and Iole, Theseus and Phaedra, Telamon and Esiona, Hector and Pantaselee, Paris and Helen, and Troilus and Criseyde. Youth's company includes dissatisfied amorous men: Narcissus, Pyramus, Achilles, Agamemnon, and Menelaus. There is a contingent of disgruntled women as well (Dido, Phyllis, Ariadne, Deianira, Medea, Deidameia, Cleopatra, Thisbe, Procne and Philomela, Canace, Polixena, Circe, and Calypso). The most revered sector of the entourage consists of four faithful wives: Penelope, Lucrece, Alcestis, and Alcyone (8.2450–665).

Eld's procession follows, featuring David and Bathsheba, Solomon and his hundred wives and concubines, Samson and Delilah, Aristotle, Virgil, Socrates, Plato, and Ovid (8.2666–719).[25] A language of "grace" pervades this scene. Seeing the parade, the narrator thinks, "And thus I lay in hope of grace" (8.2725). The "olde men with o vois alle" petition Venus for Amans's sake (8.2728–29). Venus lets pity come to her ear and prays to

Cupid, Amans recalls, that "Me wolde thurgh his grace sende / Som confort, that I myhte amende" (8.2735–36). Cupid approaches Amans, while a great crowd draws nigh (8.2745–91). "Bot he [Cupid], which wolde thanne yive / His grace, so as it mai be," Amans recollects (8.2792–93). Cupid removes the fiery dart from Amans's heart and departs (8.2794–807). Amans emerges from his swoon, reason returns, and the former lover receives absolution (8.2808–901). Venus places black beads, inscribed with "*Por Reposer*," around his neck (8.2902). Addressing him as "John Gower" (8.2908), Venus tells her erstwhile disciple to abandon love and to pray for peace (8.2909–23). "Tarry no more in my court," Venus commands,

> "Bot go ther vertu moral duelleth,
> Wher ben thi bokes, as men telleth,
> Whiche of long time thou hast write."
>
> (8.2925–27)

In the Ricardian *Confessio*, Venus tells Gower to greet Chaucer, her clerk (8.2940–41*).[26] In both the Ricardian and the Lancastrian renditions, the narrator recalls how the beads were given to him to "bidde and preie" (8.2960–61), and he heads home to pray (8.2962–70). A short Latin prayer follows: the Ricardian version offers a prayer for Richard, while the Lancastrian text beseeches Christ to keep England from suffering and to correct all estates. Following the respective prayers, the didactic voice from the Prologue resumes and reprises the Prologue (8.2970–3172). The *Confessio* concludes with an elaborate Latin finale. Of the forty-nine extant complete *Confessio* manuscripts, more than thirty have a Latin *Explicit Iste Liber*, commending Gower's book to readers and to eternity (8, after 3172). In twenty-nine manuscripts, the *Explicit* is followed by the *Quam Cinxere*, a poem allegedly sent to Gower by "a certain philosopher," announcing that England praises Gower. In twenty-two manuscripts, the *Quam Cinxere* is succeeded by the *Quia Vnusquisque*, a Latin prose colophon, declaring that Gower received stewardship of a gift from God—a gift Gower is obligated to impart to others—and outlining the poet's three major works.[27]

Amans's transformation from a dim-witted failure into the visionary poet is facilitated by a predominantly Greco-Roman tradition. Eld's troupe petitions Venus on Amans's behalf, and the intercession of Plato, Aristotle, Ovid, David, and Solomon is a literalization of Amans being led to greater intellectual heights by revered philosophers and authors. The lover's cure entails further immersion in a textual tradition, for Venus tells Gower to go where his books are. A pronounced difference between Gower the narrator/poet and Amans is that while Amans cannot comprehend literature, Gower narrates scores of tales. The mark of transformation is conversance with this literary heritage. But while the presence of a Western scholarly tradition structures Amans's conversion, there is notable participation by the vernacular. Unlike most figures in Youth's and Eld's tropes, the first three couples do not reprise tales in the *Confessio*: Galahad and his lady and Guenevere are not mentioned before this point; Tristram and Isolde are only briefly referenced earlier as an example of love drunkenness (6.467–475); and Lancelot is cited in a lesson on sloth (4.2035). The appearance of these Arthurian characters in Youth's entourage is significant because they are products simultaneously of written and oral traditions and are strongly associated with vernacularity. It is equally significant that most of the other figures in Youth's company appear in Chaucer's *Troilus and Criseyde* or *Legend of Good Women* and that the *Legend* and Amans's conversion scene echo each other emphatically.[28] These Greco-Roman figures are also featured in another monument of vernacular English literature: the *Confessio*, namely, as dramatis personae of previous sections. Amans goes through the process of withdrawing from Venus's court while flanked by these revenants. Therefore, Amans's transformation results from his immersion in a learned, literary milieu, one capable of comingling with the vernacular, more precisely, one for which the vernacular acts as the conduit, a role symbolized by the Arthurian couples ushering in figures from learned traditions and by the incarnation of characters and authors present in Chaucer's and Gower's vernacular poetry.

The mark of transformation that the protagonist bears is one that members of early *Confessio* audiences will also enjoy after reading the poem. The text anticipates an alteration for readers, claiming that they too will possess higher understanding after encountering the cultural legacy the *Confessio* bequeaths. Readers are promised insight into how to effectively address social conflict, a promise implied through the poem's structure. The Prologue and the *Confessio*'s closing English lines focus on conflict in late fourteenth-century England (8.2971–3172). Because there must be *some* continuity between this frame and the tales enveloped therein, the poem's structure indicates that its contents will educate readers and thereby improve England's welfare. Gower the narrator/poet makes such a claim when he announces in the Lancastrian version that he writes this book "for

Engelondes sake" (Prol.24).[29] This formulation implies that information in the *Confessio* will improve England's well-being; familiarity with the poem's cultural treasures will equip readers to deal more effectively with England's domestic conflicts. This promise is literally enacted on Amans, who, aided by a textual heritage, becomes the sagacious John Gower who comprehends how to end strife in England.

Knowledge of the cultural legacy transmitted by the *Confessio* is also equated with good morality. This association is pronounced in Venus's command to Gower to "go ther vertu moral duelleth, / Wher ben thi bokes . . . [that] thou hast write" (8.2925–27). In this formulation, the place of moral virtue is the locus from which Gower the narrator/poet composes, meaning that the *Confessio* necessarily promotes moral virtue. This alignment of Gower's poetry with morality has been immortalized by Chaucer's epithet "moral Gower," in *Troilus and Criseyde* (5.1856), an epithet reifying the link between Gower's verse and moral goodness.[30] The association between the *Confessio* and morality is fortified through the poem's structure as a sermon on the seven deadly sins, a framework modeled after penitential guides.[31]

The seven deadly sins framework also associates knowledge of this cultural inheritance with piety, an alignment confirmed by the protagonist's postconversion plans. The beads Venus bestows resemble a rosary, and she gives her former devotee the beads to "bidde" and "preie." Appropriately, the narrator announces that he is heading home, now shriven, to pray during the remainder of his life (8.2959–61, 67–70). But the protagonist is also returning to his books, meaning that the *Confessio* is a product of his life of prayer. The penitent protagonist is devout, illustrated by the prayer discussed earlier in this chapter and by the insistence throughout the narrative frame that men must turn toward God.[32] The frame's persistent evocations of God create the impression that the cultural treasures contained therein are blessed by God himself. The seven deadly sins paradigm as the framework supporting the tales conveys that this legacy is transcendent, valent across time and space, just as this classificatory system for sins prevailed throughout Christendom for generations.

The *Confessio*'s alignment of its literary legacy with superior understanding, morality, and piety codes vernacular literature as a version of cultural capital. In so doing, the poem grants this literature a spiritual dimension, transforming this material into an incarnation of the sacred. Bourdieu's comments about sacred and profane culture illuminate the *Confessio*'s strategy: "The denial of lower, coarse, vulgar, venal, servile—in a word, natural—enjoyment, which constitutes the sacred sphere of culture, implies an affirmation of the superiority of those who can be satisfied with the sublimated, refined, disinterested, gratuitous, distinguished pleasures forever closed to the profane. This is why art and cultural consumption are predisposed, consciously and deliberately or not, to fulfil a social function of legitimating social differences."[33] Through the example of its protagonist, the *Confessio* pronounces a lack of appreciation of literature to be coarse, low, and servile: when Amans cannot comprehend the art presented to him, he is immured in sin and lust; he is venial, servile, and undistinguished from the multitude. Amans must renounce his vulgar interests to appreciate the cultural treasures spread before him. Dubbed "Amans"—which translates from the Latin as "one who is loving" or "a lover" and which includes an English pun on "a man"—the protagonist bears the burden of representation. He is Everyman. His amorous persona encapsulates the state of being of men and women oblivious to riches like those preserved in the *Confessio*, while the poem represents the initiated (particularly the enlightened incarnation of the protagonist as the poet John Gower) as sublimated, refined, distinguished, and sacred. The linkage to sacredness is, in part, buttressed by the poem's deployment of conventional Christianity, including the association of this literary knowledge with piety, the poem's insistence that men turn to God, the text's classification of its tales under the rubrics of the seven deadly sins, and the borrowings from the genre of penitential manuals.

Rites of Passage

Although the *Confessio* dramatizes the miraculous conversion of Amans and promises a similar transformation for readers, the logic of such impressive metamorphoses is unclear. Bourdieu's discussions of rites of passage illuminate the murky nature of the transfiguration of Amans and the anticipated improvement of readers. Bourdieu explains that one essential function of a rite of passage is separating those who have undergone this ritual, not from those who have yet to undergo it, but from those who never will. Rites of passage are social magic that create differences or that exploit preexisting ones, reinscribing constructed properties in a way that makes them seem like properties of nature. An act of consecration attaches the chosen one to a place and status socially distinguished from the commonplace, producing sacred beings by getting everyone to recognize the arbitrary boundary separating them from the masses. Such rites are effective because they are almost always performed on converts, confirming privilege that the elect receive because of their socioeconomic station.[34] Through consecration, Bourdieu continues, an ordinary being purifies and sanctifies himself, detaching himself from the trivial matters that debased his nature. The actions performed on the novice modify his conception of himself and his function, while transforming the understanding others have of the consecrated one and their behavior toward him.[35]

Amans undergoes such a transfiguration.[36] The procession of authorial figures, who plead on behalf of Amans, and the bestowal of a rosary constitute symbolic acts that ratify the protagonist. The ceremony is sacred, for divinity (a goddess and her powerful son) officiates over a magical transformation. The ritual produces a decided break between who Amans is and who he becomes, since the purified Amans abandons his base existence, as his movement from *cupiditas* to *caritas* testifies. The goddess presides over an act of nomination, where an admirable title is conferred on the narrator: the title of "poet," indicated by Venus's public recognition of the protagonist as an author and by her public admonition to him to return to his books. The mirror that Venus holds up to the would-be lover not only confirms his identity as an old man but since, as Simon Meecham-Jones points out, Venus's mirror recalls the title of Gower's earlier *Mirour de l'Omme*,[37] the looking-glass confirms the protagonist's identity as a writer. The sanctification of Amans is symbolized by the loss of the undistinguished title "a lover" or "a man" and the adoption of the appellation "John Gower," the poet. This title confers a social destiny on him whom it distinguishes, for following the public ceremony in which he is renamed, the protagonist returns home to compose (more) poetry. Just as the demarcation between the fictional Amans and the fictional Gower is clear, the final distinction of Gower the narrator (and poet) from the populace is evident. Unlike Everyman, the protagonist is deserving of the company of ancient philosophers, great authors, and deities—and of their efforts to save him. Venus declares the narrator (and poet) gifted, one of the few who can inhabit the locus of moral virtue.

The *Confessio* functions as a public consecration for Gower the narrator and historical personage in that, through the *Confessio*, he demonstrates that the textual inheritance has instituted him as its inheritor. Derek Pearsall maintains that Gower's use of Latin in the *Confessio* is a way of confirming his reputation as a serious writer and of committing himself to posterity as a poet worthy to stand beside his classical forbears.[38] The ritual over which Venus officiates emphatically stakes Gower's claim as their heir. Surrounded by great authors and philosophers from the past and recognized as deserving of their company, Gower grandly accepts his patrimony. Even physically Gower belongs among them, for, as Meecham-Jones notes, Venus's mirror reveals the protagonist to have reached a physical state comparable to that of "these olde men" so that he fits into their company.[39] Just as the vernacular writer is endorsed by these renowned cultural producers, the presence of characters from vernacular literature commingling with classical figures in the conversion scene implies the patriarchs' acceptance of the English language as a suitable vehicle for the continuation of their legacy. Gower is the anointed guardian of these cultural treasures, and his English poetry is an appropriate repository and means of its transmission.

Unwrapping the Gift

The rite of passage Amans undergoes to become the renowned poet John Gower intersects with the ideology of gifts structuring the conversion scene. As Hugh White notes, Amans's swoon means that the end of love comes while his rational faculties are suspended, and during the swoon crucial things happen to Amans rather than being achieved by him.[40] Bourdieu and Jean-Claude Passeron's discussion of "gifts" illuminates Amans's pronounced passivity. According to "the ideology of 'gifts,'" the ability of a privileged student to easily grasp knowledge related to dominant culture is explained as a result of grace or giftedness. The student is perceived to be naturally talented, and his ability to converse in dominant culture is understood to reflect his gift of grace from a higher power. The student is credited with an extraordinary natural ability and a keen intellect, while the cultural legacy granted because of his socioeconomic privilege tends to be erased. The privileged student, however, is acclimatized to this culture not primarily through the educational system but through family. Although the essential part of a cultural heritage is passed on discretely and indirectly, without explicit effort, its casual introduction is typically forgotten in favor of an enchanted experience of its acquisition, which does not bear the vulgar mark of work and effort.[41]

Amans does not toil to achieve the wisdom that he ultimately possesses: his labor of patiently listening to Genius's litany of tales proves futile. Rather, it is solely through the grace of higher powers that Amans learns anything (or recalls what he once knew). After Amans listens at length but remains unrepentant, tradition—in the form of mythological figures, literary characters, authors, and philosophers—miraculously appears and rescues Amans, facilitating his epiphany. The language surrounding the conversion underscores the gift of grace, for, as detailed earlier, there are several explicit references to Amans receiving grace from higher powers. "Grace" denotes a gift from God, fate, fortune, or Providence.[42] A recipient does not *earn* grace; grace is granted because a supernatural force has deemed the recipient suitable to receive this beneficence. Accordingly, Amans does not develop intellectually, spiritually, or morally as the poem unfolds.[43] Rather, he remains consistently erratic in the levels of insight that he demonstrates following Genius's sundry tales and moralizations. The *Confessio* conveys that one cannot learn its textual legacy and acquire the attendant superior understanding, morality, and spirituality through intellectual work: these qualities are bestowed by higher forces.

The *Confessio* occasionally contradicts this stance, however. The poem is a weighty tome, which required great effort to compose and which takes considerable effort to consume. In the first Latin prose commentary in the Ricardian version (at Prol.34), Gower speaks of the intense labor he expended to compile this text, from sundry chronicles, histories, poems, and philosophical texts. As Pearsall points out, this prose passage emphasizes "the painful, almost superhuman work of compilation, at the same time that the language constantly erases the writer, making him the vessel of a higher purpose, his infirmity transcended."[44] This Latin passage betrays an ambivalent stance in the *Confessio*: recognition of the toil required to generate such a volume, yet the disavowal of labor by positioning Gower as a vessel. The English verse more readily denies effort, for in the poem's opening lines Gower explains that authors who "al of wisdom writ . . . dulleth oft a mannes wit / To him that schal it aldai rede" (Prol.12–15); consequently, he decides to "go the middel weie / And wryte a bok betwen the tweie, / Somwhat of lust, somwhat of lore" (Prol.17–19). There is also a feigned casualness in the delivery of the *Confessio*'s tales. The narrator nonchalantly recounts a little springtime occurrence, where he encounters a priest who freely narrates stories in a nonacademic context. Because the body of the poem primarily features pleasant stories, the *Confessio* obscures the labor audience members expend perusing its contents. This labor is further eclipsed through the rite of passage paradigm for readers: they do not *learn* the legacy the *Confessio* offers but gain what they do after reading the text because reading the poem constitutes a form of preparation.

Hence, the *Confessio* is structured by this contradiction: the poem is a monument to hard work in that it attests to the years Gower spent mastering this scholarly tradition and composing his tome, and the text demands a considerable commitment from a reader who wishes to consume the entire volume; yet the ideology of gifts insists that knowledge and understanding of this tradition come naturally. How does the poem negotiate this contradiction? The text argues that effort proves futile unless one is already a member of the elect. As the example of Amans testifies, once an audience member has experienced this poem, if the right type of man—and the masculine noun is not unintentional—he is a suitable recipient for grace and, by extension, for superior understanding, morality, and piety.[45] The character Genius reinforces this paradigm, because although he may be conversant with a litany of Greco-Roman stories, as his misguided *moralitates* indicate, Venus's minion does not truly understand this literature; Genius possesses limited comprehension and demonstrates neither impressive piety nor morality. He lacks the gift.

Ultimately, the poem goes to great lengths to teach readers a predominantly learned literary tradition but covers over its transmission, insisting that either one possesses grace and therefore has a knowledge of this tradition and the accompanying understanding or one is not blessed and possesses no such heritage or insight. This logic reinforces the social order in late medieval England, for this stance refuses to acknowledge that class position and gender were the primary determinants of who held such knowledge: who received grammar-school educations, where, as chapter 1's discussion of curriculum makes clear, students learned many of the tales that the *Confessio* borrowed; who was exposed to this legacy informally, including in family settings; and who otherwise had access to literature like the *Confessio*.

Against the Greyness of the Multitude

Gower claims the great task of transmitting an impressive cultural legacy to its new and rightful heirs. The *Confessio* works to make readers become participants in a common culture, shareholders in a lofty civilization, and to generate a sense of community around that culture of which the poem declares them guardians. Interestingly, most of this "common" culture is not indigenous to England. The poem does not reify an English literary heritage that Englishmen and women organically share, but a culture that is artificially introduced and cultivated, as the discussion of sources demonstrates. Showing little interest in the culture of the English populace, the *Confessio* maintains that to be a participant in one's own literary heritage in late fourteenth-century England, a reader must be conversant predominantly with Latin, European, and Greco-Roman texts, texts that in medieval England had traditionally been the preserve of the ruling classes, texts that Gower and Chaucer were transforming into the basis of a new English literary tradition. The structure of the poem as a penitential manual naturalizes this heritage, promoting the illusion that this corpus is an inevitable, immutable part of the literary landscape, while working to create this new cultural arrangement that seems already fixed.

The poem codes conversance with this literary tradition as the litmus test by which men and women in Gower's England are adjudicated to be enlightened. The poem offers this legacy, and its attendant stamp and guarantee of enlightenment, to establish membership in a select coterie: those familiar with this tradition—before or after reading the poem—are separated from those who are not. The *Confessio* encourages the chosen to recognize their election, and conversance with this legacy is the mark of distinction: it helps the initiated recognize one another against the greyness of the multitude. It also helps them recognize their mission, which is to be few in number and to keep the populace in check—particularly those who do not understand England's best interests. Knowledge of the canon, as outlined in the *Confessio*, allows readers to certify their entitlement in the face of others, to cultivate their spiritual selves, and to manage groups lacking this mark of election. Given social practices surrounding literacy in late fourteenth- and early fifteenth-century England, the *Confessio* could not have addressed nonruling classes widely to inculcate in them a feeling of inferiority and instead worked to encourage a sense of superiority in its readers.

Book 1 of Gower's *Vox Clamantis* is vitriolic in its account of the English Rising of 1381, virulently opposing rebels' seizure of consumable goods, physical spaces, and political power reserved for the wealthy and displaying contempt for rebels' efforts to redistribute goods and to empower themselves. As explained in the introduction, in 1381 significant numbers of insurgents emerged from the upper strata of nonruling urban classes, strata that included lesser merchants and prosperous artisans, strata immediately beneath the urban ruling classes and largely excluded from political and economic power in late fourteenth-century England. As chapter 1 demonstrates, significant portions of these strata possessed the ability to read English in the last quarter of the late fourteenth century and the first quarter of the fifteenth century. Furthermore, some readers from these strata were consuming English vernacular literature, including the *Confessio*, from the 1380s through 1425. In the wake of the English Rising of 1381, the *Confessio* clearly included this sector of nonruling classes among its inheritors of the new English literary legacy. Through dissemination of its cultural treasures, the poem appeared to redistribute the possessions of the affluent to the less privileged. The *Confessio* offered to supplement impoverished lives with culture, shares in the immaterial, in part to decrease demands for shares in the material. The poem addressed rebels' desires for fuller lives by offering them cultural capital, thereby appearing to facilitate the sharing of privileged lives and pastimes.

As Bourdieu explains, China's Great Wall was intended not only to prevent foreigners from entering but also to stop the Chinese from leaving their homeland, which is the function of all magical boundaries: to stop those inside from leaving the prestigious group.[46] The *Confessio* tells readers that they are more gifted than average people, that they are the select few, encouraging readers to police boundaries between themselves and lower ranks. Audience members may believe in their own giftedness and may dwell in the company of the elect and thereby relinquish ties with the lesser orders, although as Bourdieu and Passeron note, when lower classes are acculturated into privileged culture, they rarely express their training as renunciation and repudiation of their socioeconomic origins, because the knowledge they have to master is highly valued by society and because this achievement symbolizes entry into the elite.[47] Although the *Confessio*'s Prologue claims that the poem can help end divisiveness in Gower's England, the tales do not resolve in any obvious manner the social issues decried in the Prologue: political inefficacy, papal schism, insurrection, war, heresy, and social conflict. In fact, stressing the importance of culture worked to defer adequate analyses of, and suitable responses to, these and other difficulties in late medieval England; an emphasis on largely Greco-Roman tales deflected sincere scrutiny from the conditions producing discontent, poverty, and strife. Instead, the *Confessio* proposed to reduce social conflict by distinguishing the upper strata of nonruling urban classes symbolically from lower ranks.

The anointment of readers as heirs to a great heritage attempted to create a disparity between the cultural experiences and references that the upper strata of nonruling classes enjoyed compared to their poorer counterparts. By slightly initiating readers into privileged culture and its values, the poem worked to introduce a break with the worldviews of the populace and thereby drive a cultural and political wedge between readers and poorer ranks.[48] The mark of distinction for the upper strata of nonruling classes may ultimately have been illusory, but as long as these strata *perceived* themselves to be superior to lower ranks, the effects would have been the same. The acculturation that the *Confessio* offered attempted to exacerbate differences between the upper strata of nonruling urban classes and lower ranks, symbolically distancing the two echelons. The promotion of respect for high levels of formal education could have strained their alliances. Lower ranks were less likely to have access to the literary traditions that the *Confessio* conveys, and therefore the poem bequeathed to readers—to varied degrees—a cultural heritage largely denied to the poor, encouraging readers to appreciate different cultural legacies, values, and expectations than those possessed by underlings. Fracturing identifications between these two groups would have decreased support from the upper strata of nonruling classes for poor ranks in future uprisings. Furthermore, charisma ideology in the *Confessio* argued that powerful groups controlled England because they were the most enlightened, moral, and pious; disempowered groups were disenfranchised because they deserved to be, because they were less enlightened, moral, and devout. Hence, the distribution of power reflected the natural allotment of gifts. By implication, because nature decreed the social order, it was futile to strive to change this order.

Because, according to the *Confessio*, conversance with learned texts is an index of the attributes necessary to discuss England's best interests, this mark of election separates those enlightened thinkers fit and able to participate in informed debates about England's welfare from those who are not, an assumption upon which Gower, the character and poet, clearly operates. By setting up such knowledge as proof of intellectual, moral, and spiritual fitness, the *Confessio* works to police the field of debate, authorizing certain people to speak and deauthorizing others. While excluding poorer ranks from discussions about England's welfare, rank does not *appear* to be a determining criterion for participation. Intellectual, moral, and spiritual health appear to constitute the prerequisites so that those unable to participate in these debates seem to have excluded themselves by being immoral, sinful, and anti-intellectual. The text hides its true principles of selection for those certified capable of advising others about England's welfare— wealth and leisure and the access to texts that wealth and leisure provided. By dividing appropriate from inappropriate participants and by privileging the point of view of the former, the poem legitimates the political positions of the consecrated elite, meaning that the elite's interests could more easily dominate, reducing visible conflict among competing groups and legitimating social relations in England.

As Bourdieu explains, all aristocracies must expend considerable energy to convince the chosen few of the need to accept sacrifices required by privilege, such as public service.[49] Through the narrator's example, the *Confessio* works to foster in readers a sense of duty toward the common good. The protagonist's consecration exemplifies such duty, for once sanctified he pontificates about how various estates must change to improve society. Likewise, the Prologue is replete with advice for common profit, which, as Russell A. Peck has demonstrated, is a structuring motif in the *Confessio*, and, as mentioned earlier, in the Lancastrian version the narrator announces that he composes his book "for Engelondes sake" (Prol.24).[50] Evidently, Gower, the narrator and poet, believed that he possessed special insight into England's social conflicts and that it was his *duty* to share his perceptions. The *Quia Vnusquisque* in the *Confessio*'s Latin finale confirms this sentiment:

> Quia vnusquisque, prout a deo accepit, aliis impartiri tenetur, Iohannes Gower super hiis que deus sibi sensualiter donauit villicacionis sue racionem, dum tempus instat, secundum aliquid alleuiare cupiens, inter labores et ocia ad aliorum noticiam tres libros doctrine causa forma subsequenti propterea composuit. (2:479)

> [Because each man is obliged to impart to others as he has received from God, John Gower has, therefore, concerning those things with which God has perceptibly endowed the account of his stewardship, while time hastens on and desiring to elevate in some respect, composed, between labors and leisures for the attention of others, three books for the sake of doctrine.][51]

Apparently, God has entrusted Gower with a great gift, and the poet had a moral and spiritual responsibility to disseminate his perceptions of social problems. The *Confessio* offers readers a perspective from the ruling classes on the causes of conflict in late fourteenth-century England, and Gower's example, as protagonist and author, demonstrates that those with an enlightened perspective on England's failings must speak out and advise others—the rich man's burden. One sacrifice demanded by privilege is to advise the lower orders, those lacking gifts, so that all Englishmen can live in harmony, harmony without equality, that is. Ultimately, the *Confessio* worked to reduce conflict by urging readers to participate more heavily in political debates and by attaching significantly more weight and authority to these voices than to the voices of those excluded from prestigious literary pursuits. The poem simultaneously attempted to decrease conflict by encouraging readers to adopt a stance of what the *Confessio* codes as benevolent paternalism, a perception that those conversant with a learned literary tradition understand what is in the best interests of all and are obliged to guide the less enlightened.

Anxiety

While the Latin apparatus bespeaks Gower's desire to make his vernacular poem appear scholarly, this apparatus also betrays the poet's anxiety about the democratizing potential of transmitting a scholarly tradition in the vernacular. Gower, a member of the gentry, was well educated in Latin, Anglo-Norman French, and English, with English being the language of commoners. In book 1 of the *Vox*, Gower displayed unabated contempt for disobedient men and women lower in the socioeconomic hierarchy, portraying them as beasts lacking rational capacities. To quote David Aers, Gower "writes with moral outrage and an unselfreflexive [*sic*], violent hatred of those lower-class people whose actions are seen to be conflicting with the traditional ideal of the social order."[52] Gower must have been ambivalent at best about sharing his beloved cultural inheritance with the nonruling classes. Translating this erudite tradition into English opened up the possibility of more widespread access to this material and to the authority it conferred than English men and women had yet known. By anglicizing this legacy, Gower perhaps unwittingly facilitated the erosion of the traditional preserves of culture and enabled the dissemination of cultural authority. Commoners no longer needed the highly educated to dispense this knowledge or to interpret it for them. In rendering this tradition into English, Gower risked watching the populace become too familiar with his prized inheritance, a populace who might sully this treasure: these ranks could generate new meanings from this corpus of knowledge or assimilate this largely Greco-Roman material into their oral folk traditions, appropriating this material as they saw fit. Nonruling classes with access to this legacy might be empowered to produce knowledge and values, in short, to authorize culture. Gower railed at length in book 1 of the *Vox* about nonruling classes consuming exclusive foods and wines and sullying with their filthy limbs the beds of the wealthy (1:359–74). One wonders how the poet felt about commoners consuming, and especially transmuting, the literary tradition that he expended such great effort to master and to translate into the vernacular.

To some degree, the Latin in the *Confessio* abates the potential dissemination of cultural authority that the poem facilitates. Although the *Confessio's* alignment of its proffered knowledge with superior morality, intellect, and piety than that possessed by Everyman proclaims all readers potentially fit and able to participate in political debates, the poem's Latin makes finer distinctions. In providing a Latin apparatus for the *Confessio*, Gower thwarts newer readers from becoming full inheritors of the legacy he transmits. The poem's Latin works to circumscribe the democratization of literature that the *Confessio* facilitates. The Latin apparatus consists of several elements: an indexing tool with incipits, explicits, and running heads; speaker marks, indicating which character is speaking; prose passages (also called "commentary," "glosses," "notes," and "marginalia");[53] the two or three final Latin poems discussed earlier; and elegiac couplets, comprising sixty-eight sets of verses, that appear within the English poetry.[54] In Echard's examination of forty-seven of the forty-nine extant manuscripts of the complete poem, thirty-eight offer a full Latin apparatus, six offer some Latin, and three contain no Latin.[55] Pearsall explains that Latin is granted special status visually, for the Latin verses and prose commentaries, especially the verses, are written in a more formal hand than the English and are often underlined.[56] Furthermore, Echard notes that in more than two-thirds of the manuscripts, Latin verses and glosses are red, while English letters are black, not uncommon in medieval English manuscripts. Glosses in *Confessio* manuscripts tend to migrate from margins into text columns, which is not unusual in glossed manuscripts. Of forty-three *Confessio* manuscripts containing Latin, eleven locate the Latin commentary in the margins; twenty-five place them in the text columns; and seven offer a combination. In several manuscripts, Latin verse and gloss visually merge, making it difficult to tell them apart. Moreover, Latin often claims the space of the English, impairing the ability of either to function. Glosses are frequently distinguished by large initials or markers, with the placement of these glosses often obviously disrupting the progression of the English narrative.[57] The Latin marginalia are particularly striking because Gower scholars believe that the poet wrote them himself.[58] It is not unheard of for late medieval vernacular authors to supplement their own poetry with glosses, as Boccaccio's *Teseida* and Christine de Pizan's *Letter to Othea* attest.[59] Such glosses, however, are typically written in the poem's vernacular. As Ardis Butterfield points out, Gower's decision to add Latin glosses to his own authorial compilation is rare and distinctive within medieval English writing and even within the broader context of European vernacular texts.[60]

The presence of such copious Latin contradicts efforts to recruit the largest audience possible, an effort evident in Gower's decision to compose the *Confessio* in English, unlike his *Vox* and *Mirour*. All audience members could read or at least listen to English, but only a portion of early *Confessio* audiences understood Latin; as chapter 1 demonstrates, the upper strata of nonruling urban classes were much less likely to be trained to read Latin than the vernacular. Only those conversant with both languages had access to the entire poem, meaning that while the *Confessio* invites all readers to be inheritors of the tradition it helps found and legitimate, Gower extends the invitation more fully to readers conversant with Latin. But even among the Latin readers, the *Confessio* makes distinctions. While the prose glosses consist of fairly straightforward Latin, the Latin couplets are technically difficult and evasive. The difficulty of the couplets places them largely beyond the grasp of readers with modest levels of training in Latin, although those with higher levels of Latin mastery can more readily construe them. Hence, *Confessio* readers with training in Latin possessed gradations of access to the poem's extensive Latin apparatus. Since, as chapter 1 demonstrates, educations in Latin in late fourteenth-century England were typically more advanced the further up the socioeconomic ladder one investigates, the ruling classes (especially men) were more likely than readers from nonruling classes to possess the training to construe difficult Latin.

Gower scholars have offered dramatically different assessments of the usefulness of the *Confessio*'s overall Latin program at the denotative level.[61] The presence or absence of substantive meaning in the Latin glosses and larger apparatus is not necessarily important, as long as the Latin is *perceived* to be valuable. Readers unable to decipher Latin, or to decipher it well, may have assumed that the Latin apparatus, especially the glosses, held the key to the numerous gaps in logic with which the *Confessio* is riddled. There are many non sequiturs in the *Confessio* to confuse inexperienced readers. The disparity between the Christian framework of the seven deadly sins and the largely Greco-Roman tales creates what Meecham-Jones perceives to be a hybrid text, "constantly seeking to reconcile the opposing claims of two incompatible systems of value."[62] The exempla are unsettling because of chronic disjunctions between the *narrationes* and their *moralitates*, a convention seasoned medieval readers knew well. The Prologue announces that the ensuing material demonstrates how to resolve conflicts in England, but the text does not appear to do so. Therefore, less skilled readers may have felt unsettled, expecting concrete instruction never delivered. Because the Prologue implies that there are correct readings, that the clever reader, upon completing the *Confessio*, will understand how to solve England's maladies, the text may have generated anxiety in inexperienced audience members unable to glean pragmatic knowledge. The extensive Latin apparatus creates the illusion that those conversant in Latin are privy to the poem's full meaning. The motif of divine intervention implies that, although many may hear the tales, only a select few emerge with the insight the narrator ultimately possesses. Charisma ideology seeks to elicit a sense of hopelessness in frustrated audience members, a sense that if they do not understand the *Confessio*, they never will. Those distanced from the *Confessio* may blame themselves for this alienation, as charisma ideology insists that failure results from—and is proof of—a lack of gifts.[63]

There is a concurrent narrative that a reader's failure results from his immorality. The representation of the dim-witted Amans—who, when mired in lust and sin, lacks understanding—implies that those who do not glean substantial wisdom from the *Confessio* must be sinful, a logic buttressed by the figure of Genius, whose service to Venus clouds his intellectual and spiritual capacities, rendering him incapable of fully grasping the meaning of the tales he narrates and ill-equipped to provide spiritual guidance to his pupil. Alienation from the text is not represented as the consequence of one's social position and level of formal education. Instead, through claims of carnality and immorality, a reader is blamed for his/her distance from the poem. To add insult to injury, an ignorant reader is parodied through the figures of Amans and Genius. The overwhelmed may feel himself/herself to be the brunt of the joke, the stupid reader that more educated audience members are invited to mock. While the poem worked to create a sense of community from a sharing of celebrated culture, it simultaneously worked to create a sense of partial to complete exclusion for others. Although the *Confessio* invites all readers to be inheritors of the cultural legacy it bequeaths, the extensive Latin apparatus separates fuller inheritors from partial ones. Rather than pronouncing all readers authentic cultural stewards, through its extensive use of Latin the *Confessio* implies that readers without expansive educations deserve to be excluded from the inner sanctum of its rarefied world of culture because they remain too ignorant and inadequate. Their minds are ill-equipped to sincerely appreciate this glorious legacy. Lacking cultural prerequisites for full membership in the cultural elite, such readers have only themselves to blame. By extension, because of their intellectual and spiritual shortcomings, they deserve only partial enfranchisement and peripheral positions in politics and government. Hence, the Latin in the *Confessio* promotes cultural distinctions, as well as the class divisions underwritten by those distinctions.

The *Confessio* positions all readers as bearing the mark of distinction, set off against the undistinguished multitude but not necessarily sufficiently refined to enter the inner sanctum of the cultural world the poem presents. Just as the *Confessio* instructs readers to recognize a metonymic chain between learned texts and higher understanding, superior morality, and greater spirituality than the average man, the poem's Latin teaches audience members to employ a classificatory system where readers from the upper strata of nonruling classes occupy a range of positions of knowledge and entitlement superior to the multitude but generally beneath wealthier classes. Although all audience members may recognize one another against an unenlightened populace, only those who can read the *Confessio* in its entirety are full inheritors of the most valuable treasures the text imparts. After encountering the *Confessio*, audience members deemed incomplete inheritors should have gleaned invaluable lessons: presumably they could make distinctions among types of cultural knowledge and could recognize gradations of cultural authority. The *Confessio*'s classificatory system encouraged the underinitiated to distinguish those who possessed the markers of knowledge "beyond" them.

As Bourdieu explains, educational qualifications strongly contribute to the sense of full membership in the universe of legitimate culture and politics, which includes a sense of belonging to the "legal nation," of being a full citizen, entitled and duty-bound to participate in politics and to exercise a citizen's rights. While education functions as a principle of selection, it is insufficient to consider the capacity to understand, reproduce, and even produce political discourse, which is guaranteed by educational qualifications; it is imperative to consider the (socially naturalized and encouraged) sense of being entitled to participate in politics. Political choices involve the more or less explicit and systematic representation an agent has of the social world, of his position in it, and of the position he "ought" to occupy. Capacity, Bourdieu points out, is inseparable from feeling competent, that is, socially recognized as entitled to deal with political affairs, to express an opinion about them, or to be able to modify their course. The authorized speech of status-generated competence is answered by the silence of the equally status-linked incompetence, with the latter experienced as technical inequality and leaving no choice but delegation, a misrecognized dispossession of the allegedly less competent by the allegedly more competent. The propensity to delegate responsibility for political matters to others recognized as technically competent varies in inverse ratio to educational capital, Bourdieu continues, because the educational qualification, and the culture it helps to guarantee, is tacitly regarded, by its holder and by others, as legitimate title to the exercise of authority.[64]

While defining conversance with literature as a prerequisite for participation in political debates, the *Confessio* further refines these standards, pronouncing Latin a competency required for access to political authority. Promoting Latin as the standard of adjudication, the *Confessio* encouraged audience members versed only in the vernacular to view themselves as deficient, as lacking the ability to fully participate in discussions about the social body and about England's problems, while the poem encouraged readers possessing only minimal skills in Latin to perceive themselves as less inadequate but as still lacking. The poem insists that the economically and culturally less advantaged readers rely on "experts" and attempts to restrict legitimate opinions to authorities selected for their presumed intelligence and competence, since the capacity to understand and to produce political discourse is guaranteed by educational qualifications. Through the use of Latin, the *Confessio* attempted to discourage the *illiterati* of the upper strata

68

of nonruling classes from feeling entitled or authorized to talk about politics—and to proceed as actors on the political stage. Similarly, through the varied degrees of difficulty of the elements of its Latin program, the *Confessio* sought to discourage those minimally trained in Latin from feeling sufficiently authorized to participate in the political sphere. The Latin acts as a mechanism to solicit the self-exclusion, or at least marginalization, of those whom this elite selection would exclude or marginalize anyway.

Although there is no record of him holding political office, Gower clearly understood himself to be competent to discuss political affairs, and he decidedly understood himself to be entitled to express opinions about them and able to modify their course. In the spring and summer of 1381, large numbers of the upper strata of nonruling classes had also felt entitled to participate in English politics, as their substantial involvement in the insurrection attests. In the wake of the English Rising of 1381, the *Confessio* worked to erode this sense of entitlement. In the *Vox*, Gower's vitriolic depiction of rebels as sundry beasts making animal noises betrays his pronounced belief that nonruling classes, especially those men and women who rebelled, were inherently incapable of intelligibly discussing political issues. Through its classificatory system, the *Confessio* pronounced subordinate classes inept at political affairs, however these groups might have conceptualized their agency in 1381. If these readers accepted the *Confessio*'s message and began to understand themselves as ill-equipped to participate in political affairs, they would no longer seek to assertively shape England's political landscape. Persuading the upper strata of the nonruling classes that they were incapable of dealing with the political sphere, of espousing reasonable opinions about this sphere, or of modifying its terrain would have decreased the likelihood of their involvement in future rebellions. For this sector, the poem attempted to enact a process of mystification, alienation, and ultimately pacification.

Persuading the economically and culturally less possessed ranks to recuse themselves from the political sphere would have generated similar effects as convincing them to fracture their alliances with poorer groups, since both routes decreased the likelihood of their contributions to subsequent rebellions. Through its classificatory system, the *Confessio* implied that these ranks needed to resign the field to the better educated and "more qualified," encouraging these ranks to submit to those with "superior" knowledge and with more extensive formal educations. By preventing the *illiterati* and those possessing only modest conversance with Latin from enjoying full access to the poem, the *Confessio*'s Latin creates a need to administer it, making its contents available only to the cherished few and keeping readers with less extensive educations dependent on others to mediate the language for them. Those with more extensive formal educations were positioned as the guardians of knowledge, guardians with the prerogative of exposing the less learned to the amount that the former deemed appropriate. Promoting these relations of dependency, the *Confessio* reinscribed the ruling classes as the locus of legitimate knowledge production in England and reasserted the authority of their views, while constructing the basis for a cultural institution that would become English literature. The *Confessio* constructed a metonymic chain where suitability for political participation was guaranteed by conversance in erudite English poetry. Nonruling urban groups were pronounced unfit to participate alongside the ruling classes in the governance of society. Readers deemed incompetent in politics might have pursued the path outlined by Bourdieu and might have chosen the learned as their spokesmen. If not actively choosing these ranks as their spokesmen, allegedly inept readers may have been persuaded, at least, to respect the intellectual accomplishments of the well educated.

Establishing a vernacular tradition in English in the late Middle Ages meant that members of the upper strata of nonruling classes inevitably gained access to literature. The birth of English literature involved poetry's expansion into the circles of precisely those people deemed incapable of truly appreciating it. At the founding moments of this literary heritage, the *Confessio* proclaimed the comprehension of relatively inexperienced readers limited. The overall logic is not unlike that which Ania Loomba outlines regarding the institutionalization of English literary studies in nineteenth- and twentieth-century India:

> A central feature of hegemonic ideologies is their projection of the dominant viewpoint as universally true, transcendentally valid and non-political. In this way, they claim to represent all humanity and fix their "others" as inferior and finally non-human. . . . Thus also white racism implies not only that European culture is superior but that it is the only kind of culture there can be; by exclusion from it the non-European is necessarily non-human, barbaric and animalistic. . . .
>
> The primary contradiction engendered in this situation involves the fixing of English literature and the Indian reader into positions

that imply a permanent and inherent inability of the latter to comprehend the truths enshrined in the former. At the same time such a
comprehension is posited as a *requirement* for knowledge and a *measure* of ability. . . . The elitist nature and civilising mission of English
studies was established through a strategic inclusion as well as exclusion of certain categories of people. . . . The institutionalisation of
English literary studies in Britain involved an inclusion of the uncul-
tured into the "boudoir" of knowledge, where their inferiority would
become apparent and their subservience ensured.[65]

In many ways, the institutionalization of English literary studies in India,
as outlined by Loomba, parallels and repeats the terms of the *Confessio*'s
project of founding a new literary tradition. The poem fixed less experienced readers into positions that implied a permanent and inherent inability to comprehend the truths enshrined in the text, while such
comprehension was posited as a requirement for knowledge and as a measure of ability. The *Confessio* invited new readers into the enclave, the store-
house of cultural treasures, and proclaimed these readers more gifted than
Everyman, while simultaneously informing inexperienced readers that they
remained inferior to the more formally educated and that they must turn
to higher ranks to mediate the cultural legacy and to provide wisdom and
insight. While this bequest became a *referent* for all *Confessio* readers, it
remained the *property* of only a select few. The poem encouraged readers
from the upper strata of nonruling urban classes to recognize an inheritance
either not belonging to them or pronounced ill-suited to them, thereby
fixing them in the social hierarchy. Ultimately, the *Confessio*'s gems were
not made *for* nonruling ranks but primarily *against* them.[66] During the
founding of the English literary tradition, the *Confessio* attempted to circumscribe the democraticizing potential of this new knowledge to ensure
that the ruling classes maintained leverage in public affairs and control over
poorer men and women.

Conclusion

Encouraging readers from the upper strata of nonruling urban classes to
support higher ranks and to perceive themselves as being reasonably similar
and as sharing interests, the *Confessio* worked to produce disparities—real
or imagined—between these readers and lesser ranks, threatening bonds

between them. The text discouraged audience members from identifying with lower ranks, from supporting the interests of their underlings, and from aligning with the populace in future insurrections. The *Confessio* attests that, at the nascence of what is now the English literary canon, this embryonic corpus was ascribed something akin to cultural capital, deployed as an attempt to reconfigure identifications, particularly those of readers from ranks that had not previously enjoyed significant access to erudite texts. The *Confessio* offered to initiate these strata into this rarefied realm, in part, to solicit submission to their socioeconomic superiors. The poem responded to the crisis of authority in the wake of the English Rising of 1381 by constructing a literary legacy, the terms of which instructed readers to recognize their assigned positions in the social hierarchy and to subject themselves accordingly. The *Confessio* bears witness that increased access to literary troves in late fourteenth- and early fifteenth-century England was mobilized, at least intermittently, to produce consent for the social formation. The production of this new knowledge enabled new forms of governance and a palatable, even tasteful way to make unruly bodies more docile.

TIME AFTER TIME: HISTORIOGRAPHY AND
NEBUCHADNEZZAR'S DREAM

In the Prologue to the *Confessio Amantis*, the narrator recounts Nebuchadnezzar's dream from the Book of Daniel. As Nebuchadnezzar slept, he dreamed of a wondrous image formed in the shape of a man. The head and neck were forged of fine gold; the breast, shoulders, and arms were carved of silver; the stomach and thighs were molded of brass; the legs were made of iron; and the feet were composed of an unstable mixture of iron and clay. Without warning, a boulder rolled down a nearby hill and landed on the statue's feet, causing the entire body to crumble (Prol.595–624). Daniel explained that the king's dream foresaw the history of the world, anticipating how the world would grow increasingly less valuable until it becomes worthless. As the mixture of earth and iron and as the separation of the feet indicate, in its final stages the world would be divided and humankind would sin incessantly. God would then overthrow the human race, and the world would end (Prol.625–58). Amplifying Daniel's exegesis, the narrator explains that the world has already passed through most of the stages envisioned by the seer. Babylon lived the golden age. Persia saw the age of silver. The height of Greek civilization comprised the brass age, while the Roman Empire forged the reign of iron (Prol.670–848). Speaking of late fourteenth-century England, the narrator laments, "And now upon his olde ton / It [the world] stant of brutel Erthe and stiel" (Prol.876–77).[1]

Nebuchadnezzar's dream provides an important site for mapping the *Confessio*'s political discourse because this divine vision contains one of the poem's most pointed discussions of history as a process. Nebuchadnezzar's dream enjoys a prominent place in the *Confessio*: this vision and its exegesis occupy nearly half the Prologue. The importance of this dream is reflected in the colophons to the *Confessio* and *Vox Clamantis* that describe Gower's three major works, for in these descriptions of the *Confessio*, references to Nebuchadnezzar's vision are particularly prominent.[2] Similarly, although Gower manuscripts are not heavily illustrated, the most common illustration in *Confessio* manuscripts depicts Nebuchadnezzar's dream of the tiered statue.[3] On the surface, Nebuchadnezzar's dream offers a coherent narrative about the history of "great empires," the progression of history, and the resulting social order in late fourteenth-century England. Upon closer examination, however, Nebuchadnezzar's statue becomes a nexus of contradictory ideologies about historical processes. Competing models of history structure the metallic statue and its accompanying exegesis: Nebuchadnezzar's vision simultaneously represents history both as a teleological progression into ruin and as a homogeneous, static mass. Through these competing histories structuring this biblical tale, the ideologies speaking through the poem addressed early *Confessio* readers from the upper strata of urban non-ruling classes, offering to alter the ways in which they understood how history happens and experienced their own relation to the past and future. Through these histories, the tale worked to reshape how readers understood their relation to the English Rising of 1381 and to insurrection in general. In doing so, the poem proposed to change how readers conceptualized their agency, interests, enemies, and allies.

Teleological History

The structure of Nebuchadnezzar's statue forms a teleological history. A "teleological history" denotes a series of events or traits, attributed to past epochs, that unfold in an observable pattern. In a teleological model of history, there is a perceived continuity within the movement of events so that prior moments form a constant, unified process. Events are typically related in a causal manner, with one leading inevitably to the next. The terms in which a teleological history is conceptualized frequently have organic overtones, employing such metaphors of development and wholeness to interpret previous occurrences or eras. In such a history, the past continues to exist in the present; it animates the present, having imposed a predetermined form on all its fluctuations. Prior events validate the necessity of the moment, and the present becomes the aim or cumulative meaning of the past. Later stages of history are anticipated by earlier ones, with later history functioning as a goal or as the destiny of previous moments.

In Nebuchadnezzar's dream, the age of gold becomes the age of silver; the age of silver leads into the epoch of brass; the epoch of brass turns into the era of iron; and the era of iron ends in the days of iron and clay. History begins with a golden age and gradually proceeds in a linear movement through a progressive degeneration, indicated by the association of each subsequent epoch with an increasingly less valuable metal. As Daniel explains, the statue in Nebuchadnezzar's dream "Betokneth how the world schal change / And waxe lasse worth and lasse, / Til it to noght al overpasse" (Prol.628–30). The unfolding of time fabricates a coherent narrative of progressive deterioration. According to the logic of Nebuchadnezzar's statue, the depths to which late fourteenth-century England has sunk are the inevitable end product of the unfavorable path that man has followed for centuries.[4]

This developmental understanding of history is amplified through the statue's allusions to the Greco-Roman formulations of the ages of man.[5] As John H. Fisher explains, in medieval renditions of Nebuchadnezzar's dream, the history of empires commonly intersected with Ovid's four ages of man.[6] This intersection is evident in the *Confessio*'s version of this biblical tale through the statue's shape, for world history is inscribed on a body that resembles that of a man. Similarly, stages of world history are equated with stages of human life through anthropomorphic metaphors, evident, for example, in this description of the metallic figure:

> Of Bras, of Selver and of Gold
> The world is passed and agon,
> And now upon his olde ton
> It stant of brutel Erthe and Stiel,
> The whiche acorden nevere a diel; . . .
>   Thapostel writ unto ous alle
> And seith that upon ous is falle
> Thende of the world; so may we knowe,
> This ymage is nyh overthrowe,
> Be which this world was signified,
> That whilom was so magnefied,
> And now is old and fieble and vil,
> Full of meschief and of peril,
> And stant divided ek also
> Lich to the feet that were so,
> As I tolde of the Statue above.

(Prol.874–78, 881–91)

This passage anthropomorphizes the moment in which Gower wrote (and, by implication, the past and processes of historical change): the world stands on its old toes and is now aged, feeble, and vile; the world is full of mischief and peril; and, just as the statue's feet are split apart and composed of incongruous elements, the world stands divided. Like a human life, history grows, develops, and finally reaches an end. This is a continuous history whose stages form an observable pattern of maturation and degeneration, with earlier moments anticipating later ones and with final events as the cumulative effects of all preceding occurrences.

What messages might this conception of history have conveyed to early *Confessio* readers who had supported the English Rising of 1381? The teleological model structuring this rendition of great empires invests the past with an inherent law of development; events had to unfold as they did, and this trajectory led inevitably to Gower's England. The inevitability of this development ratifies the social order and social relations in late medieval England. This ratification is buttressed by the contradictory claims for homogeneous history in Nebuchadnezzar's statue, namely, representations of the present order as eternal. History, invested with a teleological law of development, acts as the counterpart of natural law, doubly legitimating the social order as well as its precarious divisions. Both models of history naturalize the social order and social relations in late medieval England.

By representing history as subject to some teleological design produced by God, destiny, or natural law, Nebuchadnezzar's dream positions medieval men and women as more or less helpless objects of grand forces. This understanding of history teaches readers that events occur in spite of human volition, that readers are only *subject* to history, not active *producers* of history. By obfuscating human agency from the past, this tale denies that people might continue to shape events. Similarly, the metaphor of the ages of man portrays history as an accretion, where the most recent manifestation of society is the cumulative result of all that has come before; as the end result of all preceding epochs, the political and economic structures of medieval England were thousands of years in the making and could not have turned out differently. Nebuchadnezzar's dream thereby implies that the effort required to change society would have to be commensurate with the pressure of thousands of years of history and, of course, mustering such a force at one moment in time is impossible. By implication, political action is futile. These messages likely resonated strongly for late fourteenth- and early fifteenth-century readers in the aftermath of the English Rising of 1381, if many medieval historians are correct in their assessment that the 1381 insurrection did not facilitate any significant political or economic changes.[7] It may have appeared to early *Confessio* readers that despite tremendous amounts of energy and even social upheaval, such as the efforts of thousands of rebels in 1381, social relations could not be altered. This understanding of how history happens encourages resignation and accommodation, which diminish readers' confidence about creating their own history.

The claims the *Confessio* makes about history through this teleological model, however, are dramatically at odds with the ideological assumptions on which Nebuchadnezzar's dream operates politically. While denying that people can influence history, the text, through this biblical vision, encourages readers to actively shape political forces in England. While maintaining that humans cannot alter social relations, the poem's rendition of this biblical tale still invites readers to participate heavily in the production of social relations and of history. Despite explicit pronouncements to the contrary, the *Confessio* addresses readers as having agency, and because of the threat that large portions of the upper strata of nonruling classes posed to the social order in the English Rising of 1381, the Prologue's version of Nebuchadnezzar's dream works to properly harness and direct this sociohistorical agency.

Strikingly, the poem works to channel this agency through the same teleological model that denies that readers have volition. The linear model of history locates late medieval England at the end of a chain of great empires and, consequently, at the end of history. In the passage quoted earlier illustrating the anthropomorphism in Nebuchadnezzar's statue, the narrator indicates that his era is at the end of history: he announces that brass, silver, and gold are gone from the world, "And now upon his olde ton / It [the world] stant of brutel Erthe and Stiel" (Prol.876–77). He also laments, "Thapostel writ unto ous alle / And seith that upon ous is falle / Thende of the world" (Prol.881–83). Similarly, in the lines immediately preceding the passage quoted earlier, the narrator locates late fourteenth-century England at the end of time:

> Bot in this wise a man mai lere
> Hou that the world is gon aboute,
> The which welnyh is wered oute,
> After the forme of that figure
> Which Daniel in his scripture
> Expondeth, as tofore is told.
>
> (Prol.868–73)

The placement of Gower's England at the end of history creates several effects. First, this placement works to generate a sense of crisis, a sense that readers are living in a desperate time and that society is on the verge of collapse. This message is underscored by the image of the stone descending the hill, landing on the statue's toes, and grinding the figure into powder. This is the fate that threatens Gower's England. The apocalyptic tone accompanying this image and the subsequent sense of imminent destruction position late medieval England at the end of a long line of history, tottering on the edge of the abyss.[8] By locating society in such an undesirable predicament, the text prompts readers to support conservative groups in society, namely, groups who attempt to conserve or maintain social relations and the distribution of wealth and power, as opposed to those who might attempt to change the social order. According to the dream's logic (reflected in the shift from a golden age to a silver age, to a bronze era, to an epoch of iron mixed with clay), the passing of time represents a movement into an increasingly less glorious, less desirable state of existence. Therefore, movement into the future holds little in store but further decline. It appears that the only hope for the continuation of Gower's society lies in the stabilizing measures offered by conservative forces. The best strategy is to fight change, to reinforce the social order, and to align with conservative groups in society. The imperativeness of joining such forces, and of doing so quickly, is underscored by the ominous promise, embodied in the images of the old toes, the threatening boulder, and the crumbling feet, that if change continues, England has no future.

The ideologies at work in Nebuchadnezzar's dream encourage early *Confessio* readers not only to fortify the social order but also to endorse a repression of the lower ranks. The kingly vision invites this response by claiming that the lower orders imperil the rest of society, an accusation embedded in the statue's form. Nebuchadnezzar's statue is structured by both a diachronic and a synchronic model of time: the figure relates a serial history of great empires and simultaneously reflects a cross-section of one moment in time, namely, England in the 1390s. In its representation of one moment in time, the statue specifically depicts the socioeconomic hierarchy in Gower's England. The Platonism in Nebuchadnezzar's statue is facilitated through this link with the status hierarchy. As Fisher explains, in the Middle Ages, the model of social hierarchy offered by Plato's Socrates in the parable of the metals in book 3 of *The Republic* was occasionally embedded in Nebuchadnezzar's statue, where its tiered metals symbolized the various echelons in the socioeconomic hierarchy, a Platonic tradition on which Gower draws when discussing Nebuchadnezzar's dream at the close of the *Vox*.[9] This tradition continues into the *Confessio*'s Prologue, where Nebuchadnezzar's statue is formed of a graded series of metals, with the statue's feet being the least stable part of the body, consisting of an unreliable mixture of iron and clay. Notably, it is the feet that crumble when the boulder descends, and their fragmentation produces the collapse of the entire figure. By analogy, according to this prophetic vision, the weakness of the lower orders will cause the entire body to implode. Because the lower strata are the least stable part of the social body, they will be the conduit for—or the primum mobiles of—society's destruction.

How would this ominous vision contribute to the production of consent among the upper strata of nonruling urban classes for more repressive rule against lesser ranks? If the lower orders will be the immediate cause of, or at least the most obvious contributors to, society's impending demise, higher ranks should monitor these groups more closely—control these groups, if necessary—to thwart their opportunity to hasten the prophesied end. Such surveillance might stave off disaster for a little while. Claims about the magnitude of the crisis invite support for the restoration of order through imposition. Threats of the abyss place late fourteenth-century England in an unusually desperate situation, and desperate times call for desperate measures. Because England is on the brink of collapse and because the lower ranks pose the greatest menace, for society to survive, the text implies, ruling classes must closely oversee the actions of the poor. This logic encourages the upper strata of nonruling urban classes to back coercive means of rule against less powerful urban dwellers.[10]

According to late fourteenth- to mid-fifteenth-century chroniclers Jean Froissart, Henry Knighton, and Thomas Walsingham, following the English Rising of 1381, Richard II and his impressive army scourged English towns and countryside, beheading, hanging, quartering, disemboweling, and otherwise prosecuting hundreds of rebels.[11] Official legal records, however, indicate that surprisingly few prosecutions followed the insurrection.[12] If the legal records are correct, then Richard II and his council might have been lenient with punishments because of lingering volatility: harsh punishments could have ignited further risings. By attempting to provoke a sense of crisis to create a demand for repressive rule, the *Confessio*'s rendition of Nebuchadnezzar's dream seeks to decrease resistance against the repression of rebels; the dream legitimates the need to crush subversive actions, to save society from destruction. By claiming that less powerful ranks pose the greatest danger to society, Nebuchadnezzar's vision ultimately threatens to fracture alliances between the upper strata of nonruling classes and their underlings in late fourteenth- and early fifteenth-century England and to turn the highest members of urban nonruling classes aggressively against the less powerful ranks with whom many had had strong alliances in the spring and summer of 1381.

By positioning Gower's England at the end of history, the teleological model constructs the relation between late fourteenth-century England and the past in contradictory terms: on the one hand, Gower's England is the repository of all that has preceded it; on the other, late fourteenth-century England differs radically from the past. The dramatic disparity between past and present is created through a trajectory that locates Gower's England at the end of history because "the end of history" implies "out of history." Late fourteenth-century England is positioned outside history because, unlike previous epochs, this era is not a temporary stage in an endless chain of historical periods nor one of the many products of continually changing historical processes. Instead, Gower's England is the end result of history, the culmination of everything that has come before, the moment all preceding history was destined to reach. As the end product of history, this era inevitably differs starkly from every period before this point and thus represents a rupture, a break with what has come before. By arguing that the current moment differs radically from all preceding moments, the teleological history structuring Nebuchadnezzar's dream works to render impotent the knowledge that readers had gleaned during the past and about the past. This past-present gulf discounts practical knowledge of the past because the present differs so dramatically from everything coming earlier: what happened in the past is relevant only to the past, not to the present, constituting a change of course.[13] Because the poem isolates prior moments as completed and finished, personal experiences and memories are delegitimated, and past injustices are best forgotten.

The stakes of such erasure are tremendous, and Walter Benjamin's warning about the importance of the past points to one of those stakes. Benjamin explains that the oppressed class is the depository of historical knowledge. In Marx, Benjamin writes, the oppressed class "appears as the last enslaved class, as the avenger that completes the task of liberation in the name of generations of the downtrodden." When the working class adopts the role of redeemer of future generations and thereby abandons its role as redeemer of past generations, "the sinews of its greatest strength" are cut. Forgetting oppressed grandparents makes the working class "forget both its hatred and its spirit of sacrifice, for both are nourished by the image of enslaved ancestors rather than that of liberated grandchildren."[14] By claiming that the present is unlike anything before, the *Confessio* buries generations of the downtrodden. The poem renders unintelligible histories of nonruling classes so that no evidence can back claims about systemic violence against them. Should commoners point to a history of oppression, Nebuchadnezzar's dream argues that this past is irrelevant because previous events have nothing to do with the new context, new rules, or the current state of emergency.

This erasure of the history of subordinate classes is not confined to the placement of Gower's England at the end of time; it is also more explicitly at work in Nebuchadnezzar's vision. The histories of Babylon, Persia, Greece, and Rome encapsulated in the statue are the histories of the *rulers* of these empires. Babylon prospered until the world became diverse, that is, until King Cyrus of Persia and his son seized Babylon, and the former King of Babylon was slain (Prol.677–86). Persia fell when Alexander overthrew Darius's rule (Prol.690–700). Greece reigned supreme until the last monarch divided his land among his knights, an act that produced fighting among the new rulers of the fragmented kingdom. These divided kingdoms fell under siege by Julius Caesar (Prol.710–26). Rome's demise consisted of conflicts between Emperor Leo and his son Constantine, on the one hand, and Charlemagne and Pope Adrian, on the other (Prol.738–68).[15] In all these accounts, each ruler bears a synecdochical relation to his empire: the demise of a ruler equals the demise of an empire.[16] Entirely overlooking the populace, on Nebuchadnezzar's stage, history is the drama of princes.[17] This pattern is repeated throughout the *Confessio*. The tales that form the bulk of the poem revolve around deities and semideities, kings and various royal family members, emperors, earls, knights, lords and ladies, popes and high priests, and sundry other characters from ruling groups. These stories do not center on shopkeepers, artisans, and peasants. Such ranks are rarely present in Gower's *Confessio*, and when they are, they typically provide the mise-en-scène in which members of ruling groups act. The histories preserved through these tales are the dramas of the privileged.

The erasure of the histories of nonruling classes and the placement of Gower's England at the end of history have a similar effect: ordinary men and women are irrelevant to historical transformation. Although both strategies erase the histories of nonruling ranks, they do so in very different ways. Positioning medieval England as a radical break with the past renders all ancestors irrelevant, both those from dominant and those from subordinate classes. Recounting the history of only dominant classes renders specific ancestors irrelevant, namely, those of subordinates. This lesson conveys to readers that just as subordinate classes were irrelevant to the production of the past, these ranks will be irrelevant to the production of the future.

The terms this teleological model of history offers readers from the upper strata of nonruling urban classes for thinking about their identities threaten their political effectiveness in yet another way. Because Nebuchadnezzar's statue draws on a Platonic formulation, according to which the statue's body of tiered metals symbolizes various echelons in the socioeconomic hierarchy, the divine dream argues for an essentialist understanding of the social order. In *The Republic*, Plato's Socrates offers a Hesiodic allegory of metals, claiming that citizens in the ideal city-state should be taught that the several natural castes that comprise society are determined by the sort of metal—gold, silver, brass, or iron—the gods have employed in their composition. A man's inner substance determined the caste to which he belonged and, by extension, decided his range of possible occupations. In Socrates's scheme, those deemed to possess superior inherent qualities conveniently correlated with those who occupied the highest socioeconomic positions.[18] Because a Platonic model of the social body is embedded in Nebuchadnezzar's statue, the figure argues for an essentialist understanding of the social order, one in which people occupy different ranks because they are inherently composed of varying qualities of inner metal, some more valuable than others. Moreover, the intersection of an essentialist model of the status hierarchy with a teleological history reinscribes such biologism by implying that social position is an inheritance, an acquisition that descends through generations: a biological legacy from one's ancestors (albeit a tarnished legacy because of teleological deterioration throughout history).

One obvious message this model of the status hierarchy conveys to readers who participated in or sympathized with the English Rising of 1381 is that the social order cannot be changed. Since rank is determined by inner substance, the status hierarchy in Gower's England reflects nature's allotment of gifts; therefore, it is futile to try to alter the inequitable distribution of wealth and power, a claim that discourages rebellion. Such naturalizing claims about rank in Nebuchadnezzar's dream are reinforced by the larger

Prologue. Twentieth- and twenty-first-century editors of the poem have viewed the *Confessio*'s Prologue as structured by the paradigm of the three estates, demarcated by G. C. Macaulay as "Temporal Rulers" (Prol.93–192), "The Church" (Prol.193–498), and "The Commons" (Prol.499–1088), with the same sections delineated by Russell A. Peck as "The State," "The Church," and "The Commons."[19] The conventional medieval estates model decrees that there are those made to rule, pray, or toil. This paradigm naturalizes status, insisting that some folks are inherently suited to rule or to be ruled, to lead lives of leisure or of labor. Evidently, in Nebuchadnezzar's status hierarchy and in the Prologue's larger structure, rank is essentialized, represented as inherent and inexorable. Of course, the three estates model needed buttressing after the English Rising of 1381. As Christopher Dyer explains, the insurrection suggested that a significant number of peasants felt no obligation to toil for the benefit of others who, in the peasants' view, had dramatically failed to provide military protection and effective prayers and that these peasants could not accept that such an inequitable contract had ever existed in the first place.[20] The theme of John Ball's sermon at Blackheath, as recorded in Thomas Walsingham's *Historia Anglicana*, bespeaks this incredulity: "Whan Adam dalf, and Eve span, / Wo was thanne a gentilman?"[21] Clearly, the three estates model did not enjoy widespread consent when Gower composed the *Confessio*, and hence it is hardly surprising that an address to former rebels or rebel-supporters insisted heavy-handedly on the propriety of the three estates model, despite its inappropriateness even as a basic description of Gower's England, given the significant numbers of merchants, lawyers, artisans, and secular clerks.

Claims about the naturalness of rank in Gower's England obviously work to thwart future insurrection, but there are also more nuanced ways in which this essentialist understanding of the status hierarchy works to undermine insurrection. In Nebuchadnezzar's dream and in the larger Prologue's representation of the three estates, rank is conceptualized as an objective and unambiguous social fact and as steadfast and unchanging. The poem's claims for stable status convey to readers that the terms in which they currently understand their interests are the terms in which they should always be understood. After all, if a given rank never changes, presumably a specific set of interests naturally corresponds to that position; these interests are the position's inevitable, necessary accompaniment.

By conceptualizing rank and, by extension, interests apart from ongoing political struggles, the poem discourages readers from rearticulating their needs in relation to a shifting ideological climate. If early *Confessio* readers from the upper strata of nonruling urban classes who had participated in or supported the uprising internalized the proffered message here—that the interests that accompany a given rank are stable—the effects could be profound, for readers who were convinced that interests were stable would lose their political effectivity. As Antonio Gramsci and Stuart Hall have demonstrated, interests are continually reconstructed, metamorphosing as the political terrain shifts. Because interests shift, for an ideological address to be compelling to auditors, it cannot be outdated: to recruit people to a position, one must tap into their *current* desires, fears, and fantasies. One must intersect with auditors' common sense to shift it into a new direction.[22] Readers who had supported the insurrection and who clung to static formulations of their needs would be disadvantaged in recruitment. Their fossilized formulations would no longer speak to the ways in which potential recruits understood their lives and would no longer be compelling. Moreover, a stagnant agenda might be viewed with suspicion, for, as explained earlier, many historians believe that the uprising did not produce any significant social or economic changes; therefore, a potential recruit might wonder why or how the same agenda would succeed the next time. Similarly, for early *Confessio* readers to continue to support resistance, this resistance must be conceptualized in terms that continued to intersect with their perceptions of the world. If readers who had participated in or endorsed the insurrection believed that their interests must remain steadfast, their commitment to goals articulated by rebels in 1381 would decrease, as such goals inevitably became incongruous with how readers understood the rest of their lives. In short, by representing interests as stable, the *Confessio*'s rendition of Nebuchadnezzar's dream sought to thin the ranks of future insurgents, discouraging new recruits and former rebels alike.

By representing interests as stable, Nebuchadnezzar's dream threatened to decrease the number of future rebels in related ways as well. First, readers who were convinced that interests did not change would deny that groups could recruit new members into identifying with them and would conceptualize rebel forces in static terms: either one supports the English Rising of 1381 or, because one is of a certain rank, one does not; there is little chance of making a future insurgent of someone who opposes insurrection. Of course, as Gramsci and Hall demonstrate, political groups continually shift, in their parameters, self-definition, identifications, and membership. But rebels who believed that their forces could not change in composition would be disadvantaged in recruitment, for they would not attempt to win converts to the rebel cause to swell the numbers of future insurgents. Second, readers who believed that each rank possesses a specific set of interests that naturally corresponded to that rank might think that men and women of a specific socioeconomic status would inevitably rebel, as it is in their interests to do so. But, as Gramsci and Hall explain, alignments between one's social position and one's interests are much more fraught: a person does not necessarily hold a given set of wants and needs dictated by his/her social position but is often recruited into identifications with other social positions, especially higher ranks. Hence, readers could not assume that a participant in the 1381 insurrection would inevitably continue to self-identify as a rebel; a participant's commitment to rebels' goals must be continually regained and reaffirmed. Readers who assumed that commitments to insurgency were steadfast would not work to maintain the rebel body's active membership, as men and women lost interest in rebellion or were recruited elsewhere, including into identifications with proestablishment forces. In short, by representing interests as static, Nebuchadnezzar's dream worked to decrease support for further insurrection.

Ultimately, there is a dramatic disjunction between several claims that Nebuchadnezzar's dream makes and the ideological processes functioning therein. The dream disavows that readers have the capacity to change the social order, yet the vision works to channel readers' agency into fortifying social relations in Gower's England. The apparition denies that members of a given rank have the ability either to reformulate their interests and agendas or to recruit new allies, yet the tale works to reshape the interests of early readers from the upper strata of nonruling urban classes and to produce identifications between these strata and rulers. Because the divine dream makes the claims that it does about agency, interests, and the social order, while evidently operating under a different set of assumptions, the tale offers to alter readers' identifications, agency, interests, and alliances without appearing to participate in social conflict. The narrative naturalizes social position, insists that the status hierarchy is ordained by God and nature alike, and erases the constructedness of the social order. By doing so, in this instance, the tale camouflages its own participation in the construction of that social order.

The teleological model of history structuring Nebuchadnezzar's statue facilitates the illusion that the tale does not participate in power struggles among competing ranks. By positioning England at the end of history and outside history, the poem renders the past entirely static. The past is finished, constituting a dead inheritance. Therefore, the *Confessio*, by implication, functions in a mere curatorial role: the poem *preserves* the rich traditions of the past; it does not *construct* these traditions. By rendering the past static, the Prologue's rendition of the biblical tale erases the political nature of its version of history, denying that its representation of the past participates in power struggles among competing groups in late medieval England.

Similarly, by claiming to occupy a position at the end of history and outside history, the *Confessio* claims not to exist *in* history. Nebuchadnezzar's dream is positioned as a recollection not from a place where history is still in the making, but from a place where history is finished or where history never occurs. Consequently, the divine vision is presented neither as operating within a network of social relations nor as supporting one group's interests against another's. The dream's promotion of ruling-class interests in Gower's England is erased, and the tale appears to exist in a realm divorced from worldly affairs.

Homogeneous History

Homogeneous history also structures Nebuchadnezzar's dream. "Homogeneous history" refers to a version of history featuring an eternal image of the present; the present is projected onto the past, transforming the past into a mirror image of the present and creating the illusion that the present order is timeless. This illusion of constancy is facilitated through an erasure of historical differences, where only superficial changes remain visible in an otherwise uniform past. Perhaps the languages, customs, and geographical locations of an array of societies may differ, but such variations are merely inconsequential trappings. What truly matters—such as morals, God, and what it means to be human—remains steadfast throughout time.

Homogeneous history is evident in the elaborate systems of equivalence embedded in the striped statue. In this investigation, a "system of equivalence" is a verbal structure in which each term has meaning primarily in relation to other terms within the same system rather than deriving meaning from an anchoring in material existence. The ages of gold, silver, brass, iron, and iron and clay structuring Nebuchadnezzar's statue operate as one system of equivalence. What are the qualitative differences between an age of gold and an age of silver: more murders annually per capita, worse land inheritance laws for women? The disparities between the golden and silver ages in the divine statue are unclear, with the poem offering no criteria by which to distinguish one age from its successor. Similarly, the text provides little or no specific historical information about each era, an absence that will become clear in a moment. The vagueness of what a golden age entails and the absence of almost all historical information about each epoch means that the golden age is golden in Nebuchadnezzar's dream not because of intrinsic qualities that golden eras possess or, more importantly, because of specific historical conditions markedly superior to those of a silver age (if it were possible to make such comparisons). The age of gold is golden because it is not silver, brass, iron, or clay. These terms do not possess stable meaning outside this closed system of rating; referentiality is inward looking and relational, not grounded in material history.

Just as various epochs are defined only in relation to one another, rank exists in Nebuchadnezzar's statue through a system of equivalence. The narration offers no concrete signifieds for the body parts that comprise Nebuchadnezzar's statue. It is not clear to which exact positions in late medieval England these body parts refer. Does the head refer to England's royal family, archbishops, bishops, archdeacons, abbots, aldermen, or knights? Do the thighs represent artisans, squires, franklins, vicars, yeomen, husbandmen, or laborers? Nebuchadnezzar's dream is devoid of correspondences to precise socioeconomic positions. Rank is defined relationally, the belly of the social body, for example, gaining meaning alongside its head, shoulders, breast, arms, legs, and feet, all parts existing in an insulated system of signifiers.

The litany of empires forms a third abstract system of equivalences in Nebuchadnezzar's dream. The *Confessio* emphasizes the relational value of ancient Babylon, Persia, Greece, Rome, and medieval England, rather than the unique history of each realm, as an examination of the information provided about any of the empires illustrates. This is the description of Persia, the briefest account of any of the five empires:

> And in this wise it goth aboute
> In to the Regne of Darius;
> And thanne it fell to Perse thus,
> That Alisaundre put hem under,
> Which wroghte of armes many a wonder,
> So that the Monarchie lefte

With Grecs, and here astat uplefte,
And Persiens gon under fote,
So soffre thei that nedes mote.
And tho the world began of Bras,
And that of selver ended was.

(Prol.690–700)

The brevity of this discussion and paucity of detail indicate that the *Confessio* is not overly concerned with Persian history. Persia is defined not through its unique history but in relation to Babylon, Rome, Greece, and England: as the analogy with silver indicates, Persia was less valuable than the golden Babylon but more valuable than the brass Greece, the iron Rome, and the iron and clay England. Persia is not exceptional in its mode of definition: all realms are defined primarily in reference to one another, not through their own specific histories, with the exception of the alleged reasons for their respective demises.

These three abstract systems of equivalence (ages, ranks, and empires) buttress one another, with all three systems forming an elaborate series of tautologies that mutually point to one another to reinforce differences. The disparities between Babylon and Persia are the disparities between gold and silver, which parallel the differences between the highest-ranking groups and groups slightly below. This series of verbal relationships sustain one another, and while each series guarantees the meaning of the other series, all terms are mystified, where these free-floating, unanchored signifiers construct a verbal structure detached from references beyond itself, existing in a sealed and inward-looking enclosure. Within such closed systems of verbal exchange-values, there is no room for history. The insulation of these free-floating signifiers from a grounding in material existence produces an eternal, homogeneous history, creating the illusion that eras, ranks, and empires somehow exist apart from history, with historical change having only superficial effects on any of these terms.

These series of equations further produce homogeneous history through the gradations within each series. As a necessary precondition, a system of equivalence requires a leveling of differences. To be ranked in a series, items must occupy similar categories, share common denominators. In these litanies of ages, ranks, and empires, difference exists only in degree, not in kind. Incongruities among empires or ages (such as ancient Greece having a slave economy, while fourteenth-century England did not) are not part of the history recounted in Nebuchadnezzar's dream. Past empires and ages are reduced to similar categories so they can be rated against one another. The teleological history structuring this statue—as with any version of teleological history—is ultimately a type of homogeneous history, for a teleological understanding of the past requires an erasure of historical differences, flattening out disparate elements, to form a unified trajectory. As differences in degree, not in kind, these greater and lesser empires and ages form a homogeneous history, where contrasts are only superficial. Despite apparent variations, common denominators underpin all human history.

Evocations of an eternal present and common denominators provide a favorable backdrop for claims in Nebuchadnezzar's dream that the social order has remained steadfast across time. The representation of rank as existing outside history is particularly relevant here, for it announces that the status hierarchy is not a product of a specific society at a particular moment but instead is timeless and inevitable. The *Confessio*'s Platonic paradigm produces a homogeneous history through its conflation of several different social bodies into *the same* social body, implicitly equating the political and socioeconomic structure of late fourteenth-century England with that of a potential Greek city-state from the fourth century B.C.E. There is no mention of profound disparities between the two social bodies: Socrates's envisioned Republic is premised on the large presence of slave labor, for when Plato wrote *The Republic*, substantial portions of the populace in Athens were slaves. Evoking a caste system devised in Plato's Greece to discuss England's social hierarchy, the poem communicates that ancient Greece and late medieval England possess the same political and economic system. Moreover, the stasis of the status hierarchy structuring Nebuchadnezzar's statue does not acknowledge the changing nature of socioeconomic relations throughout an empire's history: for example, Rome's socioeconomic order was not the same before the establishment of the empire (753–509 B.C.E.), as it was as an imperialist power (264 B.C.E.–44 C.E.), or as it was after the empire split into east and west (395–476 C.E.). The *Confessio* lumps the diverse social relations enacted at various moments in ancient Rome into the "age of iron," which, in turn, is camouflaged behind a late fourteenth-century English appropriation of Plato's model of an ancient Greek city-state. Not surprisingly, the changing nature of social relations is not acknowledged in any of the four realms. Instead, social bodies from Greece, Rome, Babylon, and Persia are metamorphosed into a likeness of the social body in Gower's England, reducing a range of political and socio-economic systems to the same system.[23]

This conflation produces a homogeneous history, where the past provides an eternal image of the present, creating the illusion that social relations have been structured in the same way for thousands of years. Through the evocation of an eternal present, Gower's England floats in time, unencumbered by any understanding of how the distribution of wealth and power at that moment came into being or was sustained. Products of history appear as the consequences of unalterable, eternal laws of nature. Nebuchadnezzar's statue thus acts as an apologia for the existing order and offers proof of its immutability. The obvious message for readers is that the social body cannot be altered; it is futile to attempt to change what is inexorable. The social order in late medieval England, the *Confessio* assures readers, represents the only way to organize social relations.

By insisting on the steadfastness of the social body, Nebuchadnezzar's dream circumscribes debates about societal problems and parameters of future unrest. Universalizing England's social order instructs insurgents and their sympathizers to conceptualize social problems in limited terms. Insisting on the inevitability of structural arrangements in England encourages readers to view myopically the shortcomings of the social relations in which they participate and to understand various social maladies as isolated problems rather than as the effects of structural inequities. Readers who viewed the effects of structural inequities in isolation would not launch structural attacks but would articulate grievances in less comprehensive, local terms, rendering their attacks less effective. Rebels who conceptualized their oppressions as unusual incidents rather than as the products of larger institutional arrangements would not see fit to challenge the institutions that organized society but would set more modest agendas and pose weaker threats.

The naturalization of England's social order through homogeneous history encourages readers to underestimate their power to alter social relations. Fossilizing the social order and veiling the mechanisms that sustained the distribution of wealth and power in medieval England, the poem obscures the real nature of socioeconomic institutions. History, as Georg Lukács explains, is an intractable problem for bourgeois thought, one remedy for which is to abolish the process of history and to regard the social institutions of the present as "eternal laws of nature." When this erasure occurs, Lukács writes, it ceases to be possible to understand the *origin* of social institutions. The objects of history appear as the objects of immutable, eternal laws of nature. History becomes fossilised in a *formalism* incapable of comprehending that the real nature of socio-historical institutions is that they consist of *relations between men*. On the contrary, men become estranged from this, the true source of historical understanding and cut off from it by an unbridgeable gulf. As Marx points out, people fail to realise "that these definite social relations are just as much the products of men as linen, flax, etc."[24]

The *Confessio*'s rendition of Nebuchadnezzar's dream enacts a similar strategy of reification. The history in the dream obscures the ways in which the present emerged from the past, working to fragment readers' understanding of how history is produced: that the seemingly fixed and eternal structures in society emerged from the struggles of earlier moments and are sustained through ongoing struggles among competing groups and that institutions and social relations have been continually remade in the past and that they therefore can be changed again. Working to fragment readers' historical consciousness, the biblical dream denies that readers' own actions shape history. By challenging the social order, readers can change it; by being compliant about the status quo, they reproduce it. Nebuchadnezzar's dream encourages readers to dramatically underestimate their ability to alter the socioeconomic arrangements in which they live.

Nebuchadnezzar's dream, however, announces that readers have a specific type of agency, at a site conveyed through the dream's mise-en-scène. As Diane Watt points out, in the biblical source a mountain grows from the boulder and fills the entire earth (Dan. 2:35). A conventional Christian understanding of the dream and its interpretation, derived from Saint Jerome, is that the boulder refers to Christ's first Advent, while the mountain symbolizes the church. Gower, however, interprets the dream as an eschatological prophecy concerned with the end of the world, with the stone evoking Christ's Second Coming and the tone recalling Revelation 21:1 ("for the first heaven and the first earth were passed away"). With no reference to the mountain, the emphasis in Gower's rendition of Nebuchadnezzar's dream is on judgment (as in Prol.1032–44) rather than redemption, on the ending of the old world instead of the arrival of the new.[25] In Gower's apocalyptic dream, there is nothing outside the tiered metal body except the threat of its extinction. This bleak proposition is symbolized by the dream's stark landscape, where the striped figure stands on a stage, accompanied only by a boulder perched menacingly on a hill, threatening to destroy the statue. The incarnation of the social body is presented as an either/or proposition: one must either protect the status hierarchy, preventing the ominous boulder from destroying England, or one will be obliterated. The social body cannot change but can only be lost. Such a binary offers little latitude for agency: there is no agency to modify the social hierarchy, only to protect it. In other words, readers possess the power to reproduce social relations but lack the corresponding power to alter them. The kingly vision warns readers that to change the social order is to propel the boulder down the hill and to thereby destroy the very grounds of their agency; in other words, agency that seeks to alter the social body destroys itself.

The barren mise-en-scène of Nebuchadnezzar's dream also implicitly claims that identity exists *only* through the current social body. If men and women alter the social formation, they risk losing everything, for nothing exists outside the tiered statue except the means of its annihilation. No new social bodies stand on the horizon, waiting to take the place of the first structure. The fragility of the statue hides new possibilities for social formations, just as the reduction of various political and economic systems from past empires into the same structure insists that it is impossible to organize social relations otherwise. A less monolithic rendition of the past might point out that each realm witnessed various ways to organize its social relations, that the social structures dominating at various points in these respective empires represent selections from numerous alternatives. But Nebuchadnezzar's dream insists that there never were, and never will be, any other ways to organize social relations beyond that which existed in Gower's England. Through these erasures, this vision discourages readers from imagining alternate social bodies—past or future—that differ from those in which they are immersed.

Just as the social order is a common denominator throughout past and present societies, according to Nebuchadnezzar's dream, the same reason for the demise of societies underlies all human history. The *Confessio* insists that Babylon, Persia, Greece, and Rome fell for the same reason, with the introductory remarks to the dream foregrounding this shared *primum mobile*:

> Whereof I finde in special
> A tale writen in the Bible,

Which moste nedes be credible;
And that as in conclusioun
Seith that upon *divisioun*
Stant, why no worldes thing mai laste,
Til it be drive to the laste.

(Prol.572–78; emphasis added)

This preamble explains that the conclusion to be drawn from the ensuing narrative is that, because of division, nothing worldly lasts. As Peck has demonstrated, division among men within England and within each man is a recurrent theme in the *Confessio*, with Gower positioning divisiveness as the enemy of common profit and as a denial of a common nature.[26] Similarly, Fisher identifies warnings about the dangers of divisiveness on the local and the national level as the *Confessio*'s central theme.[27]

Not surprisingly, the motif of division is central to Nebuchadnezzar's dream, as Daniel's interpretation of the statue's base attests:

Bot yet the werste of everydel
Is last, whan that of Erthe and Stiel
He syh the feet *departed* so,
For that betokneth mochel wo.
Whan that the world *divided* is,
It moste algate fare amis,
For Erthe which is meynd with Stiel
Togedre may noght laste wiel,
Bot if that on that other waste;
So mot it nedes faile in haste.

(Prol.641–50; emphasis added)

Daniel was alarmed about the mixture of elements in and the separation of the statue's feet, for the placement of the feet and their incongruous elements foretold of divisiveness, and hence of great woe and inevitable demise, in the world's final stages.

Accordingly, Babylon enjoyed prosperity, "Til that the world began diverse" (Prol.677).[28] Greece reigned supreme until the last monarch "schop his Regnes to divide / To knyhtes whiche him hadde served" (Prol.706–7), an act that produced fighting among the rulers of the parcelized kingdom. These competing kingdoms fell under siege by Julius Caesar

(Prol.710–27). Rome flourished until conflicts emerged between Emperor Leo and his son Constantine, on the one hand, and Pope Adrian and King Charlemagne, on the other (Prol.738–65).[29] Once the height of the Roman Empire had passed, Lombards ruled Rome until internal conflict consumed the ruling circle:

> Bot thanne upon *dissencioun*
> Thei felle, and in *divisioun*
> Among hemself that were grete,
> So that thei loste the beyete
> Of worschipe and of worldes pes.
>
> (Prol.781–85; emphasis added)

"Al only thrugh divisioun," the Lombards lost rule of their realm (Prol.799–801). "And thus for thei hemself divide," the Roman Empire fell into the hands of seven German princes (Prol.802–10). The fall of a string of empires indicates that conditions change, that history happens. But nothing *really* changes, for although the personae in each drama differ, the primum mobile of the demise of Babylon, Greece, and ancient and later Rome was invariably the same: division.

At the end of the litany of fallen empires, the text recalls Daniel's warning that the world would end after the final token appeared (Prol.821–26), that the time is nigh:

> Upon the feet of Erthe and Stiel
> So stant this world now everydiel
> *Departed*; which began riht tho,
> Whan Rome was *divided* so:
> And that is forto rewe sore,
> For alway siththe more and more
> The world empeireth every day.
>
> (Prol.827–33; emphasis added)

Not only are competing groups in Gower's England engaged in conflict, but, the text continues, man has difficulties at the personal level (Prol.849–55). As Peck and Elizabeth Porter point out, such spiritual confusion, according to the Prologue, results from the division between man's reason and his will. The text discusses this internal division for the last 239 lines of the Prologue, repeatedly insisting that divisiveness engulfs late medieval England and continually ascribing England's social problems to division, both within individuals and among different groups in England.[30]

How might such a homogeneous representation of both the demise of former realms and the cause of England's problems have spoken to early *Confessio* readers who had participated in or sympathized with the uprising? A blatant message behind the narrative that Babylon, Greece, and Rome fell because of divisiveness and that England is tottering on the verge of collapse because of division is that discord annihilates a society, that conflict can never be productive. Although it survived widespread risings in 1381, England might not be so fortunate the next time, a possibility implicit in claims by Jean Froissart and in the *Vox* that rebels nearly destroyed England in the uprising. Such threats are corroborated by the Prologue's generation of a sense of crisis, a sense that contemporary society is on the verge of collapse. On a more nuanced level, the reduction of forces that ended the former realms into the vague formulation of "division" encourages a monolithic understanding of political interests. Because divisiveness is credited with destroying each civilization, by implication, aligned interests are the key to the prosperity (or at least to the continuation) of society, and history demonstrates what happens when groups in a given society do not support the same interests. These examples argue that dissent and struggle are not inevitable effects of economic and political structures in which groups have unequal access to wealth and power, but aberrations, with multiple interests being an index of social decay and immanent danger. Gower's conceptualization of conflict was commonplace at the time among medieval social theorists, who, as Hilton explains, recognized that society was differentiated into social strata with unequal wealth and power but who nevertheless insisted on the allegedly harmonious interrelationship of these strata, with their respective and particular functions being necessary for the survival of the whole, despite the fact that medieval society was riven by social conflict, peasant rebellions in particular.[31]

Demonizing social conflict, Nebuchadnezzar's dream denies that fundamental antagonisms are inherent within feudal and protocapitalist structures, that it is impossible to align the interests of all groups. Representing unanimous consensus as the key to prosperity, the poem instructs readers from nonruling classes to compromise. When their desires are incompatible with "common profit," readers must abandon their wants and needs for unity's sake. Through the claim that multiple interests indicate imminent decay, the text encourages readers who hear different groups articulating competing demands to understand this multiplicity as proof that England is imperiled. The sense of crisis that this misrecognition fosters makes compromise appear crucial; readers must forego their demands to stave off disaster. This logic not only urges readers to abandon their needs in favor of "the greater good" but works to prevent them from articulating demands in the first place. Urging more than self-censorship, this logic encourages the censorship of men and women who articulate demands that differ from those announced to be for common profit. The insistence that only unified goals will save society from disaster teaches readers to distrust and to actively oppose those who articulate goals that differ from the declared common good; this insistence teaches readers to annihilate difference.

Whose "common" interests does this rendition of Nebuchadnezzar's dream encourage readers to support? As explained earlier, in Nebuchadnezzar's dream, the ruler of each empire bears a synecdochical relationship to society: when the ruler falls, society crumbles. This synecdochical relationship states that the prosperity of an entire realm is dependent on its leader's well-being. History demonstrates the alignment of rulers' fates with those of their respective empires. By extension, what is good for a ruler is good for every member of society. The biblical dream thus instructs readers to view their interests as coincident with those of their ruler. The statue's body argues not only for the importance of the interests of *the ruler* but also for the interests of rulers or *ruling groups*. Unclear whether the head of the social body corresponds to the king, royal family, archbishops, bishops, knights, wealthy merchants, or to other members of ruling classes, the head symbolizes an amorphous cadre of leaders. The statue testifies to the importance of the welfare of these leaders precisely because of the correspondence of rulers with the head of the social body. The literalization of the corporeal in the social body metaphor would seem to teach that all groups are essential for the continuation and prosperity of the larger social organism, since all body parts contribute to the organism's health. Not all are essential, however: if a body loses its head, it dies; if a body loses a foot, although the loss may be substantial, the body can persevere. Identity is communal, not because all body parts are essential for the prosperity of the whole organism but because the well-being of rulers in their proper posts is crucial for anyone to exist. Not only is the head the most valuable part of the body physically, but, unlike the rest of the body, the head possesses the ability to think

and hence the rest of the body should naturally obey. As the Prologue
proclaims, to emerge from England's current crisis, "unto him which the
heved is / The membres buxom scholden bowe" (Prol.152–53). Everyone
should work to ensure rulers' prosperity because such prosperity directly
correlates with the welfare of the entire body.

The correlation between obedience to ruling groups and society's prosperity is even more pronounced in the *Confessio*'s description of an idyllic
society, a discussion initiating the Prologue's examination of the rights and
responsibilities of the first estate. Apart from Nebuchadnezzar's dream, this
description entails the Prologue's only discussion of an earlier society:

> If I schal drawe in to my mynde
> The tyme passed, thanne I fynde
> The world stod thanne in al his welthe:
> Tho was the lif of man in helthe,
> Tho was plente, tho was richesse,
> Tho was the fortune of prouesse,
> Tho was knyhthode in pris be name,
> Wherof the wyde worldes fame
> Write in Cronique is yit withholde;
> Justice of lawe tho was holde,
> The privilege of regalie
> Was sauf, and al the baronie
> Worschiped was in his astat;
> The citees knewen no debat,
> The poeple stod in obeissance
> Under the reule of governance,
> And pes, which ryhtwisnesse keste,
> With charite tho stod in reste . . .
> Tho was ther unenvied love,
> Tho was the vertu sett above
> And vice was put under fote.
>
> (Prol.93–110, 115–17)

Not surprisingly, this society is located in neither time nor space: the narrator simply recalls a "tyme passed." In this elusive society, everyone prospered: the world was wealthy and abundant; humankind was healthy; there
was plenty, riches, and unenvied love; and virtue triumphed while vice

was trampled. Because of its perfection and its unlocatability spatially or temporally, this society functions as an elusive Platonic ideal. This empire contrasts starkly with Babylon, Persia, Greece, Rome, and England, because of its overall prosperity and its unity. Unlike the empires in Nebuchadnezzar's dream, there was no conflict: "The citees knewen no debat." This description of the idyllic place provides very little information about this society, except that people readily obeyed their socioeconomic superiors: the privilege of royalty was safe; all the barony was worshipped, in accordance with its rank; and commoners obeyed rulers' laws. Telling only of this society's prosperity and respect for socioeconomic position, this description argues that the two phenomena go hand in hand: to have general prosperity, to avoid divisiveness, rank must be properly acknowledged, and subordinates must obey rulers. The moral of the tale is that to ensure any society's prosperity, nonruling classes must humble themselves and follow the dictates of the ruling classes, and through such submission society flourishes. This logic assumes that what rulers deem best for society is best for all.

The Prologue takes up sectional interests and universalizes them. Although many men and women in Gower's England were dramatically disadvantaged by the inequitable distribution of wealth and power, according to Nebuchadnezzar's dream, history proves that the prosperity of the larger culture is dependent on the flourishing of rulers and that by attacking rulers one sabotages one's own prosperity. Encouraging readers to support rulers on the understanding that such support guarantees readers' benefits, the Prologue teaches readers to view their own prosperity as tied to—and as dependent on—the continuation of the specific power relations in which they are subsumed. Through such logic, Nebuchadnezzar's dream encourages capitulation of the upper strata of nonruling urban classes to their rulers.

While working to forge identifications between the upper strata of nonruling classes and their rulers in the aftermath of 1381, the *Confessio* simultaneously threatens current and future alliances between the highest strata of urban nonruling classes and the less powerful ranks by representing the lower orders as inherently divisive or prone to divisiveness. This essentialism is evident in the composition of the statue's feet, consisting of an ill-mated mixture of iron and clay, rendering the feet divisive and unstable by nature, while higher ranks are not guilty of the same charge, since the metals of which they are composed are pure. Because of the unstable coexistence of elements in the feet, contrariness structures the very constitutions of the lower ranks, evident also in the separation of the feet. Although the human body has numerous locales on which to posit divisiveness, including arms, legs, and hands, the separation of sundry parts from their respective mates is overlooked in this dream's exegesis. Only the separation of the feet is mentioned and pronounced an ill omen (Prol.642–725). Divisiveness, it seems, is exclusive to the lower orders. Gower is not unique in making such claims in late medieval England. As Stephen Knight explains, in late medieval English literature, medieval laborers were routinely characterized as argumentative and combative, a cliché demonstrated by the personification of Gluttony in *Piers Plowman*.[32]

This representation of the lower orders encourages readers to rethink where the culpability for the English Rising of 1381 lies. Since the poor are inherently contrary, while ruling classes enforce the social relations that are best for society, the interests of the poor that conflict with those of ruling classes are inevitably suspect. When the interests of lesser ranks oppose those of the highest ranks, the lesser ranks are being divisive ipso facto. By implication, responsibility for acquiescence lies solely with the nonruling classes. The interests of those who reinscribe the social order are the normative standard from which there can only be destructive deviations. Positing divisiveness as inherent in the poor, the text delegitimates the reasons that the lower orders had for rebelling in 1381 and any grievances these ranks might articulate in the future. Inherently contentious, the lower orders will always find reasons to complain, and therefore their complaints should not be taken seriously. The *Confessio* instructs readers not to countenance insurgents' rationales because their actions were not motivated by legitimate grievances but were the product of the poor's inherent instability and quarrelsomeness. Such claims discourage the upper strata of urban nonruling classes from supporting the causes of poorer ranks or from uniting with them in the future. Ultimately, Nebuchadnezzar's dream works to threaten the base of support that the upper strata of nonruling urban classes pledged to the lower-ranking rebels during the 1381 insurrection.

Although Nebuchadnezzar's dream offers contradictory and incoherent models of history, the ideological narratives that these models present effectively reinforce each other. Both histories naturalize the social order in Gower's England, insisting that the distribution of wealth and power cannot be changed. All the while, Nebuchadnezzar's dream encourages readers to reinscribe the socioeconomic hierarchy, and in doing so the poem tacitly acknowledges that the social order is continually constructed. But the dream elaborately covers over its participation in the forging of that order. The competing models of history also converge in their portrayals of readers' agency. Nebuchadnezzar's dream explicitly denies that readers have the agency to change the social order, to win converts to a proinsurrection position, and to produce history, but the text operates under very different assumptions. The text continually acknowledges that readers can change the social order and can forge English history, and the biblical tale works to direct their agency. These competing models of history also coincide in their promotion of certain alliances over others. Nebuchadnezzar's dream represents the lower orders as the biggest threat to England's survival. The tale argues that their demands should not be taken seriously and that these groups must be controlled to ensure England's stability. Through such claims the text discourages those readers from the upper strata of nonruling urban classes from aligning with their underlings and encourages readers instead to unite with rulers, since the interests of rulers are in the best interests of all, and as history demonstrates time after time, societies prosper when subordinates willingly subjugate themselves to rulers.

History Versus a Time for l'Amour

Just as Nebuchadnezzar's dream is structured by two competing versions of history, the larger *Confessio* is structured by two competing versions of time. The *Confessio*'s narrative frame is grounded firmly in history and in the sociopolitical struggles of late fourteenth-century England, while the bulk of the poem is set in the seemingly timeless realm of love, a shift mimicking Gower's larger oeuvre, since his sequel to the *Visio Anglie* consisted, in part, of the *Confessio*'s foray into the land of amorous affairs. In book 1 of the *Confessio*, historical and sociopolitical struggles recede starkly, while the lamentations and shrift of a lover move to center stage, and the conundrum of unrequited love, the complaint of an Everyman figure unanchored temporally and spatially, dominates the narration. Likewise, Genius recounts his tales in an unchanging milieu seemingly insulated in an eternal present, a realm unregulated by the clock. The class divisions evident in the Prologue are obscured in this land of courtly love, while gender becomes the most marked divide, manifested as the frustrated courtly lover pursuing his unattainable lady.[33] The stagnation of time in this domain is exacerbated by Amans's lack of progression or development as the *Confessio* unfolds, as explained in chapter 2. In the end, however, the illusion of insulation from history is punctured, and history dramatically erupts into the narration, when Amans discovers his advanced age; when he adopts the name "John Gower," thereby becoming locatable in time and space; and when the narrator reprises his earlier discussion of sociopolitical conflicts in late medieval England. For Gower, history haunts love visions and classical tales.

Amans may have been, in part, Gower's response to Chaucer's disavowal of the political nature of poetry. It is not unlikely that Gower was unsettled by what he observed of Chaucer's readership: poetry with larger audiences than Gower's Anglo-Norman and Latin texts enjoyed and, more importantly, audiences that consumed Chaucer's work not for political or ethical reasons but for amusement and for vaguely humanist understandings of improvement. After generating Anglo-Norman and Latin texts, Gower finally shifted to the language in which his colleague had composed for decades. Gower turned (or, more appropriately, returned) to the topic of love, a subject he had considered in *Cinkante Balades* and in *Traitié Pour Essampler les Amantz Marietz*, a subject about which Chaucer had written extensively and for which the junior poet had won considerable accolades. Amans is a hypothetical reader of Chaucer's amorous poetry, a character who is leisured, who is eager to hear tales of love, and who is apathetic toward his society. At the end of the *Confessio*, Amans miraculously transforms into Gower's ideal: a politicized auditor who comprehends the need for social change and who abandons amorous engagements to reflect sincerely on societal strife in order to pursue the common good. Gower's English text stages a fantasy of recruiting Chaucerian audiences to a different version of literature than Chaucer offers and of readers acting in more explicitly politicized ways as a result.

The *Confessio* stages a recruitment fantasy not only of Chaucer's audiences but also of Chaucer himself, a fantasy articulated the most baldly in Amans's conversion scene, a scene that, as Coleman has detailed, shares specific, sustained literary correspondences with the *Legend*.[34] In the Ricardian *Confessio*, Venus relays an oft-quoted message via Amans/Gower to Chaucer:

> "And gret wel Chaucer whan ye mete,
> As mi disciple and mi poete:
> For in the floures of his youthe
> In sondri wise, as he wel couthe,
> Of Ditees and of songes glade,

The whiche he for mi sake made,
The lond fulfild is overal:
Wherof to him in special
Above alle othre I am most holde.
For thi now in his daies olde
Thow schalt him tell this message,
That he upon his latere age,
To sette an ende of alle his werk,
As he which is myn owne clerk,
Do make his testament of love,
As thou hast do thi schrifte above,
So that mi Court it mai recorde."

(8.2941–57*)

It is this passage that Elizabeth Allen believes issues "a specific challenge to Chaucer's notorious political reticence," where Gower "charges his fellow-poet to take a personal stand."[35] One can construe Venus's message as Gower's complaint that the compositions Chaucer penned in his younger days have contributed to the problem that "the lond fulfild is overal" with amorous poetry, competing with and displacing poetry with more serious agendas, even as a highly literate English poetry was coming into being.[36] Venus requests that Chaucer write more like Gower, that Chaucer's love poetry be directed to explicitly political ends, a request immediately following Venus's admonition to Gower to go where his books are, the locus of moral virtue. At this point in the narrative, l'amour becomes a pursuit outgrown by Gower, now older, wiser, and worthy of assuming his place among a pantheon of great intellectuals. According to the *Confessio*'s logic, it is precisely his abandonment of Venus's service that makes the narrator worthy of standing in the company of Plato, Aristotle, Ovid, David, and Solomon. The goddess's message implies that Chaucer has not yet moved beyond a young man's preoccupations and toward a greater calling but is arrested in an immature stage, fixated on topics that lack sufficient *gravitas*. Gower asks his friend to compose works on more stately topics, which, as the *Confessio* bears witness, a poet can do even as he speaks of love and recounts amusing tales. Venus conveys a fantasy of recruiting Chaucer to a Gowerian vision of poetry.

Chaucer likewise offers advice to Gower. As explained more fully in chapter 4, Carolyn Dinshaw has demonstrated that the *Legend* is directly tied to the ending of *Troilus and Criseyde*, since Cupid criticizes the narrator for Criseyde's falseness, to make amends for which, the narrator spins tales inverting the gendered paradigm in *Troilus and Criseyde*.[37] In an oft-quoted passage, the narrator beseeches female readers not to be angry with him for Criseyde's betrayal, asserting that he merely follows sources, that he prefers to write of Penelope's truth and of good Alceste, and that he tells the Trojan saga to warn women to "beth ware of men" (5.1779–85). In the next stanza, Chaucer sends his book to follow in the footsteps of Virgil, Ovid, Homer, Lucan, and Statius (5.1786–92). Shortly thereafter, Chaucer writes,

> O moral Gower, this book I directe
> To the and to the, philosophical Strode,
> To vouchen sauf, ther nede is, to correcte,
> Of youre benignites and zeles goode.
>
> (5.1856–59)

This passage initially appears to be Chaucer's dedication of his book to the philosophical Strode and to moral Gower, asking the latter to correct the poem, claiming that because of Gower's benignancy and goodness, the elder poet is particularly well suited to the task. But *direct* may be interpreted as "dedicate," "address," "offer," "guide" (as in conduct or procedure), or "lead"; *benignite* commonly translates as "a manifestation of good will"; and *zeles* denotes an enthusiastic striving toward an objective, a fervent commitment or resolve to obtain a result or to pursue a course of action, an ardent desire, earnest intention, devotion, or strong emotion, especially wrath or jealousy, but also passion.[38] Hence, one can translate this dedication as "O moral Gower, I offer this book to instruct you, as a guide (to conduct or procedure). . . . There is a need to correct your benignancy, your fervent commitment to good" or "your resolve to pursue a course of action," which is some understanding of Good.

The close proximity of this stanza to the passage mocking hypothetical protests by *Troilus and Criseyde*'s female readers is significant when interpreted through Cupid's concern that Criseyde's depiction could shape readers' understandings of and behaviors toward women. In effect, Chaucer advises Gower to correct his zealotry shortly after the Chaucerian narrator scorns the idea that literature affects readers' perceptions of the world. Chaucer instructs Gower to take a lesson: poetry is not about didacticism, about changing minds or shaping lives. Of course, in a typical Chaucerian contradiction, Chaucer here offers the lesson to Gower that poetry is not designed to teach lessons. Furthermore, Chaucer proclaims his Trojan tragedy continuous with a glorious literary legacy, emulating the writings of Virgil, Ovid, Homer, Lucan, and Statius, with the implication that Gower's poetry, forwarding explicit agendas, is not. Both authors claim that their respective version of poetry is the authentic inheritor and continuation of a Greco-Roman textual tradition. Both men proffer their own model of English poetry as the authoritative one to be emulated.

Chaucer's dedication condemns Gower in other ways as well. "Zele" characterizes the senior poet as overly emotional, even feminized, and, accordingly, it is a highly feminized, irrational figure such as Cupid who maintains that poetry affects hearts and minds, as chapter 4 explains. The formulations "moral Gower" and "philosophical Strode" posit a division between intellectualism and the type of poetry Gower produces. Placed in opposition to the "philosophical Strode," the epithet "moral Gower" implies that Gower does not engage in intellectualism or create sophisticated cultural material but generates material that is merely a product of a principled morality and religious zeal. The designation "moral Gower" also participates in an opposition between historicopolitical discourse and Art. Artistic poetry is conventionally understood to be capable of generating endless possibilities for new meanings, whereas moral writings are predictable or immediately knowable, offering only limited interpretative options. Great literature, such as that of Virgil and Ovid, inspires subsequent texts in later eras, unlike didactic literature, which is quickly consumed and forgotten. Chaucer's epithet works to circumscribe Gower's power as an author, encouraging readers to mistake ideological critique for moral pedantry, not unlike how Cupid's ideological critiques of the fictive Chaucer's writings are sometimes interpreted by Chaucerians as moral lamentations.[39] By thwarting readers from recognizing Gower's writings as a particular type of political discourse, the moniker "moral Gower" discourages readers from viewing poetry—and culture more generally—as an appropriate forum for political dialogues. It is only those undereducated readers, such as Cupid and Alceste, the ones who neither understand nor truly appreciate poetry, who connect literature to projects of social justice, an alignment that, as the *Legend* maintains in a complicated argument, is inappropriate to the domain of poetry.

4

IN DEFENSE OF CUPID: POETICS, GENDER,
AND THE *LEGEND OF GOOD WOMEN*

upid has been dubbed "one of Chaucer's most comically obtuse exegetes."[1] However, I propose that we listen attentively to Cupid in the *Legend of Good Women*, and at the risk of appearing obtuse, I insist that we take his understanding of literature seriously. In the Prologue to the *Legend of Good Women*, Cupid complains that the gender politics of Chaucer's poetry are problematic, that Chaucer's poetry shapes men's perceptions of women, and that men treat women worse as a result. In essence, Cupid argues that cultural artifacts help shape readers' consciousness and lives. Cupid's complaint should not seem too inane to literary scholars familiar with British cultural studies or with the past four decades of contemporary cultural theory, especially feminist, queer, and critical race theory, where the ways in which cultural artifacts shape consciousness have been an area of intense investigation. Despite the prevalence of such premises as Cupid's in current cultural theory and in much literary scholarship, Suzanne C. Hagedorn, who branded Cupid "one of Chaucer's most comically obtuse exegetes," is not wrong. How does one negotiate this contradiction? How does Chaucer take what are self-evident premises for most literary scholars now—that texts shape consciousness, that literature informs readers' beliefs about themselves and others, and that cultural artifacts help produce readers' understandings of the world—and render these propositions absurd? Remarkably, Chaucer managed to do so in late fourteenth-century England, when several of his contemporaries, most notably John Gower and William Langland, generated poetry founded on these assumptions. This chapter investigates the complex processes through which the *Legend* makes such an understanding of literature uncompelling and incoherent, processes articulated the most clearly at the site of gender.

Cupid's complaint is key to these strategies and to the poem's discussion of poetics and accountability. A central concern of the *Legend of Good Women* is the issue of art and social responsibility, a discussion instigated narratively by Cupid's grievance. This chapter argues that, in what could be viewed as a Chaucerian treatise on poetics, the *Legend* launches a full-blown investigation of the problem of poetry and accountability and conducts this investigation at the locus of gender. The poem examines the conundrum of where culpability for suspicious gendered practices in and surrounding the field of cultural production lies. Through its investigation, the *Legend* obscures inequitable gender relations in Chaucer's poetry, in the larger textual tradition, and in social praxes surrounding literature in late fourteenth-century England. Furthermore, the *Legend* helps to construct the parameters of debate regarding acceptable responses to poetry and to establish which conversations about literature could occur in late medieval England. Ultimately, the poem works to fragment readers' recognition of gender as an appropriate, or even possible, category of analysis when discussing texts. In doing so, the poem simultaneously works to disarticulate understandings that cultural artifacts shape consciousness and hence affect lives—while proceeding as if poetry can do exactly that—rendering such approaches uncompelling and incoherent.

The Complaint

Textuality and reading have been central issues in scholarship on the *Legend of Good Women* for the past three decades, discussions in which Cupid frequently looms large.[2] Regarding Cupid's complaints about the effects of literature on readers, two approaches have dominated. Among one group of Chaucerians, Cupid's concerns about effects have been deemed untenable or even derisive. Lisa J. Kiser, whose chapter on Cupid is tellingly dubbed "On Misunderstanding Texts," maintains that Cupid's claims about the effects of Chaucer's poetry reflect his incompetence as a literary critic, while Sheila Delany believes that Cupid's confidence in the effectiveness of literature, namely, "that it will change the behavior of masses of readers—can only strike us as it must have struck Chaucer, as another piece of utopian-bureaucratic comedy."[3] One could loosely align Elaine Tuttle Hansen with this camp. Although Hansen maintains that the *Legend* explores the impact of literary and social idealization on women, she is surprisingly silent regarding Cupid's comments about effects, ultimately arguing that Cupid, the narrator, and the antifeminist tradition to which both subscribe, are undercut by Chaucerian irony.[4] A second group of Chaucerians have viewed Cupid's concerns about literature's impact as part of an elaborate literary game engaging *La Querelle des Femmes*, an approach articulated particularly well by Florence Percival and Betsy McCormick.[5] It has been extremely rare for Chaucerians to take Cupid's concerns about literature's effects on real lives seriously. Carolyn Dinshaw, an exception, maintains that Cupid's complaint about the effects of Chaucer's writing bespeaks the poet's anxiety about the aftereffects of his work; she argues that the *Legend* exposes the patriarchal literary tradition and demonstrates that a literary tradition cannot be founded on the constraining of the feminine, because it will eventually silence the masculine and poetry too.[6] I revisit Dinshaw's insistence on the gravity of Cupid's complaint and push her insight in a different direction.

Poetry's potential to shape the consciousness and hence behaviors of audience members is pointedly raised by Cupid in the F-Prologue, where he immediately and insistently draws attention to the effects of Chaucer's writings. Cupid complains that Chaucer translated *Le Roman de la Rose* into plain text requiring no glosses, a poem that is a heresy against Cupid's law and that makes wise folk withdraw from his service (F 322–31). This translation, Cupid explains, hinders potential suitors and leads current enthusiasts from amorous devotions, holding it folly to serve love. "And of Creseyde," Cupid laments, "thou hast seyd as the lyste, / That maketh men to wommen lasse triste, / That ben as trewe as ever was any steel" (F 332–34).[7] Here, the god of love maintains that pejorative portrayals of women harm women because such representations help construct men's perceptions of, and behavior toward, them. Alceste's defense of Chaucer intermittently echoes her partner's language of effects, for she claims that the accused's writings have furthered Cupid's law (F 413) and made devotees delight in serving her companion (F 415–16). Through tales of faithful women, Alceste decrees, the narrator will promote Cupid, in contradistinction to the *Romaunt of the Rose* and *Troilus and Criseyde* (F 435–41). The defendant also employs the language of effects when he declares that in these texts, "yt was myn entente / To forthren trouthe in love and yt cheryce, / And to ben war fro falsnesse and fro vice / By swich ensample" (F 471–74).

F allows Cupid's complaint to stand as worthy of consideration, since explicit insistence on his lack of intellectual prowess is largely reserved until the end of the Prologue. For example, in F, Cupid is not initially loquacious, although the protagonist rambles about his springtime frolics. Only in Cupid's ample final speech (F 507–77) does his intellectual flaccidity become readily apparent, when he enthusiastically endorses Alceste's project of atonement (F 548–62), mandates that the first tale center on Cleopatra (F 566), and praises his partner's self-sacrificing, wifely devotion (F 518–34); all three stances betray Cupid's unsophisticated understandings of literature and gender. The selection of Cupid—as opposed to Athena, for instance— does, however, undermine from the beginning the gravitas of the *Legend*'s formulations of art and social responsibility, for medieval conventions hold that the god of love encapsulates a thought process antithetical to reason, symbolized by his blindness and promotion of cupiditas, with the *Legend*'s Cupid exemplifying the cupidinous reader, according to James Simpson.[8] Moreover, this particular incarnation of Cupid is highly feminized, since he advocates, however perversely, for women and is accompanied by an extensive, exclusively female entourage (F 559–60). Femininity, according to medieval conventions, is associated with emotion, fickleness, and untruth,[9] while late medieval Englishwomen, often with lower educational levels than men from comparable classes, as explained in chapter 1, were generally attributed more intellectual shortcomings than male colleagues. Aligned with femininity, Cupid's stance that gender as a category of analysis matters when assessing literature; his concern that literary texts affect readers' perceptions, actions, and lives; and his insistence that a poet bear responsibility for his writings are compromised.

While F generally defers explicit testimony of Cupid's intellectual fallibility and thereby prompts readers to consider his position, the G-Prologue immediately thwarts this possibility. G-Cupid's entrance is directly preceded by a discussion of copulating birds (G 131–40) and features what film scholars would call "graphic rhyming" or a "visual dissolve" between fornicating fowls and Cupid's outstretched wings (G 142–43). The G-narrator is less loquacious, but the inverse is true of his judge, whose diatribe balloons from twenty lines (F 320–40) to seventy (G 246–316), offering more diffuse rationales for despising his detractor, including a now belabored accusation of impotence (G 246, 258–63; cf. F 320) and anger at his nemesis' condemnation of hot, hard lovers as fools (G 253–61). Cupid's allegations in F that the defendant attacks love and its followers narrow in G to accusations that the defendant attacks Cupid personally,[10] indicating that G-Cupid is more narcissistic and less of an advocate for his followers and for women and rendering his motivations more dubious. Accusing his opponent of ad hominem belligerence, the god of love in G deploys a series of ad hominem attacks, including charges that his opponent is dim-witted (G 258, 261–62, 313–15), charges that—appearing in a mildly incoherent rant—can be easily read as projection. Cupid laments that his foe translated *Le Roman de la Rose*, a heresy against the god of love's law, both hindering supplicants from devoting themselves to Cupid and inducing wise folk to retreat (G 248–57). Cupid complains that Chaucer composed *Troilus and Criseyde*, "shewynge how that wemen han don mis" (G 266). "Why," Cupid asks, "noldest thow as wel [han] seyd goodnesse / Of wemen, as thow hast seyd wikednes? / Was there no good matere in thy mynde" (G 268–70). After all, Greco-Roman texts offer "evere an hundred goode [women] ageyn oon badde" (G 277). G-Cupid codecrees the narrator's penance (G 268–312) and issues reductive, universalizing pronouncements, including a claim that no man was as faithful as a woman in classical times (G 302–304). G-Cupid seems unable to comprehend either gender or literature adequately and is not unlike Amans, possessing cultural lessons half-learned. Moreover, relishing sundry ways in which women in classical texts died for love—self-immolation, slaying themselves, and drowning (G 288–98)—the demideity appears to glean vicarious pleasure at the specter of suffering women, compromising his motivations for requesting such tales, further discouraging readers from taking seriously positions he articulates about literature and social responsibility.[11] In G-Cupid's somewhat rambling tirade, there is no more complaint about Criseyde making men trust women less, and the social effects of the accused's writings shift from a central concern to one foregrounded initially (G 248–57) but muted thereafter. G-Cupid's reservations about the consequences of Chaucer's writings are less compelling than in F, while the heightened critique of the articulator of these concerns undermines their legitimacy, alterations that transform reasonable considerations into a diluted, highly suspicious complaint. Although Chaucerians do not know which prologue was penned first or if they were composed simultaneously, for the purposes of my argument, it does not matter, since both share the same goals but proceed slightly differently.[12]

Accountability

Though Cupid's remarks in G are less reasonable than in F, the poem pursues the issues he raises about art and accountability. The *Legend* examines where an author's responsibility for the gender politics of his poems lies, while simultaneously scrutinizing a network of forces subtending poetic production. The most obvious area of inquiry is the literary tradition. When Cupid complains that the narrator's writings disparage love and women, Alceste, Percival notes, does not dispute the charge but tacitly confirms "the antifeminist bias of the writing of 'old clerkes,'" excusing the accused as merely following sources, translating "that olde clerkes writen" (F 370; see also G 350).[13] The poem confirms Alceste's insistence on the weight of the "olde appreved stories" (F 21; see also G 21) through the pronounced presence of highly literate antecedents. Ovid and Virgil are key sources, with the narrator proclaiming himself their follower (924–29), in an homage derived from Dante.[14] Elsewhere, the poem explicitly refers to Guido delle Colonne and Ovid.[15] The Prologue echoes poetry by Jean Froissart, Guillaume de Machaut, and Eustache Deschamps, while the legends borrow from Livy, Vincent de Beauvais, and Boccaccio.[16] Alceste's defense borrows heavily from the *De Regimine Principum* tradition, including the *Secretum Secretorum* and writings by Seneca, John of Salisbury, and Giles of Rome.[17] The ubiquity of scholarly antecedents supports Alceste's contention that the textual heritage possesses a determining influence and highly circumscribes an individual poet's agency.

Alceste's stance is reinscribed through circumlocutory logic unwittingly forwarded by Cupid. His insistence that the literary legacy features "evere an hundred goode [women] ageyn oon badde" (G 277) exposes him to be an extremely poor reader. Cupid's analytical skills are further indicted by his praise of Jerome's *Adversus Jovinianum* and Valerius Maximus's *Facta et Dicta Memorabilia* for tales of admirable women (G 280–85), authors that the Wife of Bath cites from Jankyn's "book of wikked wyves" (3.669–85).[18] Cupid's comments convey that while the educated recognize that Chaucer works within ordained gendered conventions, only audience members with impoverished understandings of classical texts demand dramatically different portrayals of women. The poem demonstrates the force of these "olde appreved stories" by offering perversely unconventional narratives and character traits for renowned figures, such as the spurned Medea merely writing Jason a polite letter of grievance. The outlandishness of the adaptations insists that the lives and traits of these famed figures are so heavily scripted that an author cannot substantively alter them. A late fourteenth-century English poet working within a learned Greco-Roman and European literary legacy inherited its arsenal of tales and its hegemonic construals of gender. To be considered a legitimate student of this impressive legacy, these outrageous adaptions imply, an author had to discipline his poetry to adhere to the conventions of Greco-Roman texts and their sanctioned rewritings, especially by French and Italians authors. Because Cupid provides the poem's sole critique of gender in Chaucer's writings, the *Legend* suggests that such complaints bespeak an inadequate education, an inability to appreciate the obligation to tradition.

Insisting that an author's volition is heavily circumscribed, the *Legend* simultaneously undermines this logic. McCormick notes that evocation of Jerome's *Adversus Jovinianum* was a hallmark of participation in the scholarly debate about women, while Percival explains that Alceste reiterates Jean de Meun's specious claim to be merely translating what other men had written from their experiences of women's ways.[19] Invoking a clichéd defense, Chaucer enacts the lines of his poetic ancestors to demonstrate mastery of their texts, proclaiming himself their scion. Insisting that he cannot substantively change conventional incarnations of tales and characters, Chaucer dramatically does exactly that. His willful misreading of Cupid's complaint, his movement of Cupid's initially reasonable concerns into a parodic direction, allows Chaucer to enact brilliant misreadings of inherited tales. These emphatic reconfigurations argue that each poet makes unique decisions about his productions and that it is therefore inappropriate to hold the larger literary heritage culpable. The poem stages a conundrum: an individual practitioner cannot be held accountable for the politics of his productions because he travails within the terms of an inheritance; yet neither Alceste nor the *Legend* successfully indict the larger tradition but merely remove one individual practitioner from accountability. Accountability is lobbed back and forth from tradition to the individual talent, but both are acquitted.

More strikingly, the poem disavows that problematic gendered patterns exist in Greco-Roman literature and its later redactions. The "corrective" paradigms of women "goode and trewe" (G 272) and "wommen trewe in lovyng al hire lyve" (F 438; see also G 428) argue that harmful representations of women entail a prevalence of narrative patterns and character traits surrounding female figures. To accommodate Cupid and Alceste's mandate,

Chaucer selects a cadre of female characters whose stories are not inherently similar in obvious ways and erases important distinctions in conventional narratives surrounding these figures to make their stories reductively similar, each woman acting in variations on the same plot.[20] Chaucer also levels disparities among personalities, reducing these figures to a system of equivalences, where characters are more or less interchangeable. Chaucer's emphatic refashioning of the heroines argue that only when tales are flattened to common denominators and grossly distorted can they be compared. These bastardizations insist that the Greco-Roman literary legacy contains no gendered patterns but that such paradigms appear solely by wreaking violence on texts, reconfiguring them to fit an explicitly ideological agenda. The heavy-handedness of Alceste and Cupid's decree and the resulting cultural artifact exemplify the biases of criticism; gender in conventional renditions reveals no such pedantry. Lacking such didactic agendas, conventional tales do not promote particular understandings of gender. When differences are not liquidated under such arbitrary dictates, poetry is wonderfully diverse. The *Legend* claims that poetry is highly individuated: Alceste enumerates the contents of Chaucer's oeuvre, illustrating that each author has his own unique history of writings, and Cupid and Alceste's behest hyperbolically demonstrates that poetry is generated through specialized requests by patrons. This insistence on individuation maintains that tales are too varied to sport any systemic or coherent ideologies of gender and obscures the ways in which gender inflects and structures the poetic tradition. By providing such flat stories and by reifying Cupid's and Alceste's simplistic understandings of what constitutes good gender politics, the poem also suggests that those who critique gender in Chaucer's writings neither comprehend literature nor appreciate artistic difference.

Some of Cupid's and especially Alceste's understandings of what constitutes progressive gender politics range from slightly naive to puerile: their shared perception that celebrating female fidelity bespeaks an enlightened understanding of women and promotes women's interests is inane, and their investment in a negative/positive representation of women paradigm is simplistic. As Sabina Sawhney explains, while differences between subordinate and dominant groups are generally recognized, such differences are usually permitted to operate only within limits set by the dominant group.[21] Accordingly, Michele Wallace argues that demands for positive representations of a marginalized group are highly problematic, because such portrayals reinscribe the terms of debate set by the dominant group and neither shift the ideological terrain nor challenge the dominant group's control over representation. A temporary inversion of characteristics associated with dominant versus subordinate groups does not permanently alter associations aligned with certain groups but constitutes an ineffectual Sadie Hawkins Day reversal.[22] The supernatural duo's request for inversion acts as a red herring, a distraction from more complicated analyses. The *Legend* aggressively foregrounds Alceste's and Cupid's reductive comprehensions, impoverishing the poem's articulations of what constitutes dominant gender politics in a cluster of writings. At more nuanced levels, gendered similarities abound in conventional versions of the tales Chaucer narrates, but Alceste seems incapable of grasping such subtleties, while Cupid seems unable to remain focused on the glimmers of insight he raises. Ultimately, the poem explicitly maintains a facile discussion about gender and literature, although such simplicity was not imperative at the time, as many formulations by Christine de Pizan in the early fifteenth-century *Le Livre de la Cité des Dames* and *La Querelle de la Rose* attest. By offering an unsophisticated level of discussion, the *Legend* encourages readers to dismiss claims of gender inequity as naive and discourages audience members from meaningfully interrogating gender in the poetry of Chaucer or of other authors.

Contrasting with the inexpert comprehensions of gender and literature offered by Alceste and frequently by Cupid stands the authority of Chaucer the poet. His vast knowledge of scholarly texts saturates the *Legend*, radiating from the opening lines, in a poem replete with allusions to erudite authors and texts. Chaucer's displays of intellectual authority imply that to question the propriety of Chaucer's portrayal of Criseyde, a reader must be conversant with Greco-Roman texts and their descendants: one must know Criseyde's antecedents before talking authoritatively about *Troilus and Criseyde*. Not unlike the *Confessio*, as outlined in chapter 2, in the *Legend*, knowledge of sources determines who constitutes suitable participants in the debate, separating those entitled to engage in discussions of Chaucer's gender politics from those who are not: those familiar with this tradition form a community of enlightened thinkers fit and able to participate in an informed conversation, an assumption on which Chaucer the poet operates, as indicated by the scathing representation of his hypothetical detractors. By setting up such knowledge as proof of intellectual and educational fitness, the poem polices the field of debate, paralleling some of the ways in which the *Confessio* polices debate. Dividing "appropriate" from "inappropriate" participants and privileging the former's point of view, the poem legitimates Chaucer's position. Readers sharing his demographics were more likely to be deemed suitable participants, since, as chapter 1 indicates, Englishmen from the ruling classes in the 1380s and 1390s possessed educations in Greco-Roman and medieval European texts more often than Englishwomen from the ruling classes. Therefore, in such contestations, male readers' interpretations were positioned to dominate. Similarly, most members of the lowest socioeconomic groups in Chaucer's audiences likely had not read *Troilus and Criseyde*'s antecedents and therefore were pronounced ill-equipped to pass judgment on the poet's construals of gender.

Percival explains that polemics about women and about *Le Roman de la Rose* were largely excuses to display scholarly competence and wit; therefore, Chaucer, demonstrating his conversance with the matter of women, is claiming a certain scholarly cachet.[23] Hence, Chaucer's choice of gender as the locus for investigating social responsibility in art places the *Legend* within an arena of cultural production where women are typically spoken for, about, and on behalf of. The *Legend* encapsulates these gendered relations. Chaucer stages an elaborate drama in which his fictional representative and two other characters debate about women, about positive representations of women, and about how well Chaucer's previous poetry fits such paradigms, ultimately concocting an elaborate excuse for his generation of more poetry—under the pretense of supporting women's interests. Operating within an exclusive praxis, the poem promotes the illusion of inclusivity, of speaking with and to women and of including large numbers of women in the conversation. With Alceste determining the narrator's assignment, the *Legend* fosters the perception that powerful female patrons commonly dictated art, a perception reinforced by linkages between Alceste and Queen Anne.[24] Since Cupid and, as Hansen argues, the narrator are highly feminized,[25] the poem generates the impression that powerful female patrons, with minimal input from castrated male partners, routinely determined the conditions of commissions, while hapless male poets meekly obeyed. The *Legend* further promotes the pretense of overwhelming female participation through female protagonists, through tales purporting to celebrate women, and through Cupid's advocation for women. An unfathomable number of female characters form the audience witnessing the exchange among Chaucer, Cupid, and Alceste and presumably auditing the legends, creating the illusion that women dominate not only poetic production but reception as well. This hyperbolic female presence camouflages affluent men's disproportionate cultural authority and disavows pronounced gendered inequities surrounding knowledge production in late fourteenth-century England. A maneuver Dympna Callaghan outlines regarding recent appropriations of identities of people of color by privileged white authors is helpful to recall here. Callaghan explains that when privileged whites appropriate the identities of people of color to compensate for the exclusion of racial "minorities" from the means of literary production, these appropriations, even when well intended, can become the very means for continuing this exclusion. Such writing attempts to control and define the culture of racial others.[26] The hyperpresence of female characters, the speaking for women, and the promotion of their (alleged) interests in the *Legend* signal an appropriation of women's identities, ostensibly compensating for their marginalization in authoritative culture while facilitating it. Masquerading as an articulation of women's stances on literature, on progressive understandings of gender, and on female desire, the *Legend* articulates and answers the question posed by the Wife of Bath and later by Freud: "What do women want?" Appearing to promote women's interests, the Wife of Bath presents ethnographic knowledge that seems to answer the question thoroughly. The *Legend* enacts a similar feat and thereby likewise attempts to obviate the need for female participation in the generation of knowledge, ultimately defining and controlling female contributions. Sawhney discusses a common mechanism in representation, where the subjectivity of the other is often erased to countenance its construction as an object, an *effect* of knowledge for the subject.[27] Similarly, the *Legend* erases female subjectivities to facilitate their constructions as effects of knowledge for affluent men. The poem thereby reinscribes women in a subject position that reinforces the centrality of men in the generation of knowledge.

The *Legend* privileges the texts of two patriarchs of Roman poetry, Ovid and Virgil, and of medieval French and Italian men, while representing women as the principal participants in poetic production. A fourteenth-century poet could have demonstrated women's cultural work by employing texts composed by women, such as Marie de France, some of whose writings Chaucer knew, as the question "Who peyntede the leon?" (3.692) attests.[28] A late medieval poet could have considered female contributions by drawing on anonymous tales that were communally authored and that therefore lent themselves to women's involvement, including Arthurian romances, troubadour poetry, or beast fables, rather than focusing on achievements of "great men." After all, Chaucer found communally generated tales of sufficient interest to employ in the *Canterbury Tales*, as the yarns of the Miller, Nun's Priest, Reeve, and Wife of Bath attest.

The *Legend*'s tales incarnate those envisioned by the Wife of Bath: women's stories of men's wickedness. The overwhelming presence of women in the *Legend* as producers and consumers of texts argues that when women are the primary agents determining poetic assignments, when men advocate for women's (alleged) interests, when a poet is subject to such patrons, and when the audience is predominantly female, the result is pejorative tales of men. More importantly, when poetry is subject to such considerations as its comprehension of gender, the result is deficient art. Characters in the legends are stripped of their conventional complexity, while tales are reduced to anemic narratives by the standards of Chaucer's usual creations, such as *Troilus and Criseyde*, which features sophisticated characters acting in a complicated drama.

While implying that women for good reason do not produce authoritative culture, the *Legend* denies that men disproportionately generate "legitimate" knowledge, disavowing this gendered disparity not only by dramatically overrepresenting women as poetic producers and consumers but also by feminizing male characters (even, as Hansen argues, the legends' antagonists).[29] Since the Prologue's two token males are emasculated, everyone in the Prologue is either female or occupies a feminized position, with no character inhabiting a position of masculine authority or displaying hegemonic masculinity, creating a certain homogeneity surrounding gender. This leveling of gendered differences among characters in a Prologue so intently interested in art, gender, and social responsibility creates a specious conundrum: can gender inequity exist in the field of cultural production if men are feminized? The instability of gender in the Prologue camouflages inequitable cultural authority.

Male privilege is further eclipsed through Alceste's defense that the narrator "was boden maken thilke tweye / Of som persone, and durste yt nat withseye; / Or him repenteth outreley of this" (F 366–68; see also G 346–47). Some powerful but now absent ruler or patron commanded the accused to write *Troilus and Criseyde* and the *Romaunt*, perhaps under duress. Cupid and Alceste enact this logic when they, rulers and patrons, mandate a poem with a specific agenda, implying that powerful people detail a poet's compositions, seemingly exonerating Chaucer for all misogyny. Moreover, the uniqueness of the duo's commission downplays patterns in work produced through patronage, as if each patron's request is so unique and unpredictable, reflecting the patron's individual temperament and eccentricities, that the resulting artifact is unconnected to a larger literary tradition, denying the presence of gendered patterns within a corpus by one or multiple poets. The insistence on idiosyncrasy also diverts attention from formal education, where works by specific authors—usually male and either Roman or influenced by Latin texts—formed the canon in late fourteenth-century England, beginning at the grammar-school level.[30] Furthermore, although the poem implies that one cannot generalize about the political economy of patronage in ways relevant to a text's gender politics, one can: literary patrons in late medieval England were disproportionately (although not exclusively, of course) ruling-class, Christian Englishmen, a demographic that heavily shaped understandings of gender in late medieval English literature. Regarding the lord of love and his lady exemplifying patrons, it is unlikely that patrons and rulers controlled a commission so heavy-handedly, unwilling to leave much to the poet's judgment, even deriding his intellect. No doubt Chaucer had to please patrons, as David Carlson argues at length.[31] But pleasing patrons does not mean that a text is insulated from the larger literary tradition or that the poet lacks creative control to such an extent that he bears no accountability for the politics of his productions. Hence, Chaucer employs false premises that he obviously did not believe, including the claim that patrons decree content, to arrive at a conclusion that he supports: poets should not be held accountable for the ideological content of their work. Therein lies a demonstration of Chaucer's artistry.

Amorous Affairs

Like the Prologue, the *Legend*'s tales frustrate recognition of gendered patterns in literature. The ensemble of tales argue that women as a group are not disadvantaged, and if women are not disadvantaged, then, the *Legend* implies, there is no need to consider the stakes of a text's rendition of gender. By disarticulating gender as a site of analysis, the poem further implies that efforts to hold a poet politically accountable for his formulations surrounding gender or to consider the potential effects of texts on readers' consciousness and behaviors makes little sense. In the tales, the poem offers a homogeneous rendition of class to buttress its homogeneity surrounding gender, an alignment that disavows that gendered paradigms exist in literature and that women, fictional or otherwise, inhabit gendered terrain. Alceste, former queen of Thrace (F 432; G 422), emerges from the ruling classes. Likewise, some of the legendary ladies (Cleopatra, Dido, Hypsipyle, and Phyllis) rule kingdoms, while several heroines (Medea, Procne, Philomela, Ariadne, Phaedra, and Hypermnestra) are kings' daughters. Although not royalty, the two remaining protagonists (Lucrece and Thisbe) are from the ruling classes. No legends center on the rank and file of women who constituted the majority of the female population in Greco-Roman and medieval English society. The tales demonstrate what Marx and Engels dub "the drama of princes," where ruling classes monopolize center stage in conventional renditions of the past.[32] The *Legend* enacts the drama of princesses, since all female characters who are individuated or who have speaking parts are ruling class, while less affluent women are invisible. Those rare figures from subordinate classes who materialize, necessary as plot devices, are male: for example, the jailer who frees Theseus (2141), the craftsmen who erect Cleopatra's shrine (672), and the servant who delivers Philomela's tapestry (2366–72). By contrast, in the *Canterbury Tales*, female characters with prominent roles emerge from a much wider socioeconomic range, including Alison in the *Miller's Tale*, Griselda in the *Clerk's Tale*, Melanie in the *Reeve's Tale*, and the widows in the *Prioress's Tale* and *Nun's Priest's Tale*. The *Legend*'s erasure of female characters from subordinate classes creates the impression that women in Chaucer's England were unhampered by the gendered disenfranchisements that frequently plagued medieval Englishwomen from the populace: for example, physically demanding labor, poorly paid occupations, political disenfranchisement, low literacy rates, and poverty. The power the *Legend*'s protagonists possess through entitlements conferred via wealth obscure many gendered disenfranchisements structuring the lives of most late medieval Englishwomen. Enjoying vast financial resources and leisure, the *Legend*'s heroines do not appear inherently disadvantaged.

Moreover, most heroines in the *Legend* are not constrained by fathers, husbands, elder brothers, or other male authorities. Rulers Cleopatra, Dido, Hypsipyle, and Phyllis answer to no patriarchs. Medea, Ariadne, Phaedra, and Thisbe, whose agency is initially circumscribed by their fathers, easily circumvent paternal dictates (Hypermnestra is the exception). Excluding Lucrece, no heroines seem to have living mothers, and no characters are hampered by matriarchs.[33] Moreover, the legends feature several women able to refuse a fairly commonplace practice in late medieval England and its literature, where daughters of the wealthy were exchanged in marriage to facilitate political, economic, and social alliances among men. By medieval conventions, the heroines' autonomy is unusual: even affluent female characters in other Chaucerian poems face much greater restraints, including Constance in the *Man of Law's Tale*, Emily in the *Knight's Tale*, and Criseyde in *Troilus and Criseyde*. Most protagonists in the *Legend* (excluding Hypermnestra, Philomela, and Lucrece) freely make choices, and when they act on their desires, they help generate scenarios that facilitate their downfalls. Exercising considerable latitude, when queens take lovers, they make poor decisions, restrict their own agency, and self-destruct. When daughters (Medea, Thisbe, Ariadne, Phaedra, and Hypermnestra) disobey paternal dictates, the daughters' demises affirm that father knows best. Most tales imply that women need male oversight to prevent them from making catastrophic decisions and that female agency *should* be circumscribed. With structural impediments to their desires seemingly nonexistent, these women face only localized troubles caused by individual male characters whose behaviors range from unfortunate (Pyramus's tardiness) to heinous (Tereus's deeds). These narratives provide sparser evidence than usual of systemic social injustice toward women, only reminders that some men behave badly—as do some women, evidenced by Phaedra's sisterly love. As Delany remarks, the legends remind readers that "neither sex has a monopoly on malfeasance."[34]

The *Legend* further obscures structural gender inequities by stripping heroines of their respective historical, geographical, social, and political contexts. The *Legend* jettisons such context associated with the protagonists, occasionally offering some for their male lovers instead. Hansen argues that the narrator demonstrates an interest in the masculine world of politics and war and "overtly indulges his own predilection for men and their affairs while omitting details that would conflict with the monotonous and debased images of the good women he portrays."[35] Focusing on Antony's career, the *Legend of Cleopatra*, Hansen notes, is two-thirds over before the narrator turns to Cleopatra, whose only acts are running away "for drede" (664), constructing a shrine in which to bury her lover, and committing suicide.[36] Similarly, the *Legend of Dido* is largely unconcerned with the politics in which Dido is immersed, preferring to discuss Aeneas's situation. Although briefer than Chaucer's *Legend of Dido*, Ovid's *Heroides* 7 provides significantly more political context surrounding Dido's reign: Dido was driven from Tyre by her brother, who killed her husband and wishes to kill her, and neighboring kingdoms envy Carthage so that, as a stranger and a woman, Dido is continually threatened with war.[37] Ovid's Dido provides several reasons for suicide: shame and her lost reputation and virtue, all mentioned multiple times; her pregnancy; and one thousand former suitors, enraged because she prefers a foreigner. Political constraints are largely alleviated in Chaucer's rendition: the murderous brother vanishes; one thousand wrathful suitors shrink to one despondent man (1245–49); and menacing kingdoms metamorphose into Dido's nobles (1317–18). Combined with the decreased emphasis on shame (1305, 1361), Chaucer is largely uninterested in the gendered obstacles confronting Dido. Furthermore, Ovid conveys that, with numerous enemies, the queen's death will significantly affect her subjects and regional geography, whereas the death of Chaucer's Dido holds no apparent repercussions. This obfuscation of the politics in which queens are embroiled is striking in the *Legend of Phyllis* and *Legend of Hypsipyle* as well. The deaths of the four queens do not impact their realms but are merely personal tragedies. The greatly diminished contexts in which the leading ladies act eclipse the ways in which each heroine's narrative is overdetermined by gendered conventions, constraints that more obviously infuse Ovid's narratives.

The *Legend*'s subject matter further thwarts recognition of structural disadvantages faced by women, fictional or historical. Love stories conventionally focus myopically on couples and on stages of their relationships. The obsession with amorous affairs, Cupid, and fidelity obscures the public sphere in favor of the private, where characters appear to enjoy near equity. The heroines seem to be equal actors with comparable volition as their lovers at the onset of romance, with the queens and princesses possessing greater power and wealth than their suitors. The legends center on being cheated in affairs of the heart, not in the public sphere where gender disparities are more easily quantifiable (for example, regarding incomes, political power, authority in the church, inheritance practices, educational opportunities, and legal rights). Although the domain of *cupiditas* is structured by gendered inequities, most legends skirt questions of privilege in this realm by portraying the heroines as unlucky individuals jilted in love, largely due to their own credulity.[38] Failing—that is, with any sincerity or nuance—to represent abandonment as gendered and instead portraying betrayal as the result of a few men behaving badly, antagonists' behaviors are extricated from gendered social praxes so that deception in love appears as part of the human condition. Accordingly, the narrator explains that *Troilus and Criseyde* was intended to convey philosophical messages about love and Truth, implying that gender is irrelevant to such universal messages and that casting a woman as the betrayer in *Troilus and Criseyde* is inconsequential. Similarly, the legends argue that there are no structural inequities in human relations, that betrayal is ultimately genderless, and that any woman can succeed and thrive, unless a Jason or Tereus is holding her down.

Male-female relations in the *Legend* also escape systemic analyses of gender as a mode of oppression through the privileging of affect, the poem's primum mobile. In keeping with his modus operandi, Cupid interacts angrily with the narrator. Similarly, most heroines are excessively emotive, as the rapidity of their devotion and devastation bespeaks. Some protagonists slaughter themselves needlessly when overwrought, including Dido, whose diluted motivations for suicide make her appear irrational. Wallowing in affect, the legends avoid loci of more easily articulable power relations and inhabit territory difficult to quantify and analyze. Such insulation from worldly concerns is characteristic of much Chaucerian poetry, as Delany, Strohm, Carlson, and others have argued.[39] As Carlson explains, what *Troilus and Criseyde* and Chaucer's complaint poems (*Anelida and Arcite*, *Complaint of Mars*, and *Book of the Duchess*) share are characters with nothing to do, except lament unhappiness in love or pine for imagined joys of romantic satisfaction, these pursuits being full-time occupations. All wrangling in the poems, about what love is, how lovers should behave, and so forth, obliterates political economy, labor, and social relations. In domesticating such literature in late fourteenth-century England, Carlson continues, Chaucer responds to contemporary, local conditions, especially to troubling conditions in the public sphere, that made amatory complaint a particularly useful and appealing literary type.[40]

Uninterested in history, cultural specificity, and social relations, the *Legend* obscures power relations and material existence. Erasing context renders analyses of gendered disparities more difficult to articulate and less comprehensible. As this discussion has demonstrated, there are several intersecting ways in which the *Legend* denies women's disenfranchisement in cultural production and in their daily lives. If women are not disadvantaged in art, knowledge production, or life, then questions about the accountability of a poet and the literary tradition regarding inequitable ideologies of gender in literature are misguided. More pointedly, neither an author nor the textual tradition bears responsibility for problematic gender politics in poetry because the question is moot. The *Legend* promotes a vision of literature and life unconcerned with gender, positioning itself above such trifles, ultimately offering an individualist understanding of human relations.[41] At the beginnings of what is now the English literary canon, Chaucer was laying the foundations of an English literary tradition, helping to determine what topics were worthy of serious consideration. Apparently, gender politics surrounding literary praxes were not worthy of sincere, sustained investigation, though this topic would, as in Latin antecedents, remain suitable for satire and intellectual displays. Most *Legend* readers likely knew that canonical texts were structured by male privilege and may have luxuriated in the amusing denial of such privilege. But these readers had rarely heard this denial executed so cleverly. More than six hundred years ago, the *Legend* raised—and settled—issues surrounding male cultural privilege and a poet's responsibility, doing so with such artistry that Chaucer helped validate these issues as worthy topics to be deliberated perennially throughout the history of English letters.

Intentions and Targets

Although the *Legend* does not seriously grapple with the gender politics of Chaucer's creations or of the larger literary heritage, the poem nonetheless rehearses pressing questions about gender and poetry and, by extension, art and accountability. When assessing the narrator's responsibility for harm in writing *Troilus and Criseyde* and the *Romaunt*, the *Legend* insists that intentions are paramount to adjudicating culpability. The *Legend*'s discussions of intentions have recently interested some Chaucerians. Percival situates Alceste's arguments about intentions alongside medieval understandings of translation. Jamie C. Fumo compares the *Canterbury Tales*' "Retraction" to the *Legend*'s Prologue regarding translation, authorial intent, authorship, and Christianity. Simon Meecham-Jones discusses the *Legend*'s understanding of intentions in relation to ethics and virtue, noting the insurmountable gap between Christian and classical ethics.[42] Neither Percival nor Fumo discuss gender, while Meecham-Jones briefly considers gender vis-à-vis ethics but not in terms of power relations. Simpson discusses intentions, ethics, and gender. Interested in a "voluntarist hermeneutics," Simpson argues that

Cupid offers a spectacular example of the *Legend*'s emphasis on the individual will of a reader and that Chaucer intentionally attempts to provoke us to recognize that our own interpretative practices have ethical implications, an understanding of readership and ethics Simpson ties to the writings of Stanley Fish, E. D. Hirsch, Augustine, and Jerome.[43] Simpson's study is helpful for my analysis because he demonstrates the privileging of intention in the *Legend*. While Simpson is interested in Chaucer's intentions and in the wills of readers, I am interested instead in how a language of intention in the poem operates politically in relation to gender and power. The poem's formulations surrounding intention frustrate understandings of structural privilege and gender inequity.

Granted a brief chance to speak, the narrator proclaims his intentions honorable:

> Ne a trewe lover oght me not to blame
> Thogh that I speke a fals lovere som shame.
> They oghte rather with me for to holde
> For that I of Creseyde wroot or tolde,
> Or of the Rose; what so myn auctour mente,
> Algate, God woot, yt was myn entente
> To forthren trouthe in love and yt cheryce,
> And to ben war fro falsnesse and fro vice
> By swich ensample; this was my menynge.
>
> (F 466–74; see also G 456–64)

The faux Chaucer maintains that because his intentions were admirable, true lovers ought not blame him; they should be beholden to him. Alceste believes the narrator bears no responsibility possibly because, as Percival notes, he is too stupid to comprehend his actions, but especially because he (stupid or not) neither writes with malice nor generates original material.[44] Alceste's excuses, including her emphasis on patrons, foreground intention as the key criterion for assessing culpability.

The poem endorses Alceste's and the narrator's positions on intentions via Cupid, whose modus operandi contrasts starkly with that of his nemesis. As demonstrated earlier, Cupid's motivations are often problematic, G-Cupid being particularly suspect, his ad hominem invectives suggesting the unjust behavior of which his partner accuses him (F 373–413; G 353–400). Alceste advises Cupid to "weyen every thing by equytee" (F 398; see also G 384), a comment the *Middle English Dictionary* employs to demonstrate the first definition of "equite": "Impartiality or fairness in dealing with others; justice" and "what is just, fair, or right."[45] Alceste admonishes Cupid for failing to handle the accused impartially, fairly, and justly. Myopic and self-interested, Cupid is an unsuitable advocate for morality, rectitude, or divine law, characteristics the *Middle English Dictionary* also employs to define "equite." Given Cupid's vituperation and Alceste's reproof, when the demideity criticizes ideologies of gender in the narrator's poetry, readers are encouraged to understand Cupid, especially G-Cupid, to be uninterested in equity but in pursuit of some other agenda. The god of love is less committed to advocating for women than in engaging in vendettas and indulging personal animosities. Cupid's problematic intentions, especially in G, are the primary means to discredit his complaint. The *Legend* thereby elevates intentions as crucial to assessing a speaker's accountability.

The *Legend* implicitly defines unfair treatment or discrimination as an intentional, malicious act by one person against another or against a group. The fictional author demonstrates this comprehension of discrimination, as his self-defense indicates, through its insistence that his intentions were honorable and his criticisms aimed at false lovers. Cupid shares his understanding: F-Cupid accuses the narrator of deliberately attacking him and his devotees, of intentionally disparaging a specific group; G-Cupid accuses his opponent of ad hominem attacks and of deliberately maligning him. The poem endorses Cupid and the narrator's suppositions that unfair treatment or discrimination requires malicious intent and specific targets. This endorsement is evident both in Cupid's maltreatment of the defendant and in the legends, where most antagonists possess ignoble designs deliberately enacted on particular women.

What are the implications for the authoritative literary tradition, given that the poem elevates intention as the primary factor in determining culpability for harm? How could a compilation of disparate authors writing at different times in various locales for sundry purposes be collectively guilty of promoting unfair treatment or discrimination? The literary canon is a decentralized conglomeration, with no obvious sites to locate accountability; its greatness is understood to lie in its constellation of differences. To accuse the canon is to demonstrate, like Cupid, the Philistinism of not appreciating poetry. The absence of collusion in a literary tradition—which possesses no agency of its own, which has blurred parameters, and which often endorses contradictory ideologies of gender—contrasts sharply with the heavy-handed decrees of Cupid and his consort. By privileging intentions, the poem diverts attention from the more urgent issue: the question is not one of locating the origins of a mandate (such as dictatorial patrons) or finding the sources of material (such as foundational poets with unjust views of women) but of uncovering who is entitled to participate in the writing of literature, in producing and reproducing the tradition. The crucial determination is between who participates in knowledge production and who is largely, or entirely, excluded from generating authoritative culture.[46]

The poem thwarts understandings of discrimination that interrogate structural inequities, focusing instead on the maltreatment of individuals. Foregrounding intention and the specificity of targets, the legends camouflage institutions and structures that disadvantage women. Featuring wealthy, powerful heroines, the poem denies group disenfranchisement, insisting that the primary determinants of a woman's lot are a combination of the intentions and behaviors of individual men in her life and her own choices, again ultimately promoting an individualist ideology. Moreover, the Prologue sets up women as a group (trusted less because of Criseyde) against an individuated Chaucer, who endures personalized attacks from a clearly biased ruler-patron-judge. Structural inequities recede from view while an individual treated unfairly looms large to occupy center stage and is rendered more compellingly. The poem thus subverts a discourse of group marginalization, a discourse articulated through Cupid, and undermines the view that some groups are advantaged over others. By extension, the nexus of issues surrounding gender inequities and cultural production—inequities toward which the Prologue, especially G, occasionally gestures (for example, by positioning Chaucer as a clerk within a scholarly tradition)—are discounted.

The political nature of F-Cupid's critiques is personalized in G. Carrie Tirado Bramen explains that, as if recrafting the 1960s and 1970s feminist slogan "the personal is political," structural and political difficulties are sometimes reformulated into "the political is personal," a dangerous individualist approach, where politics are deceptively individualized and where personal behaviors, attitudes, and lifestyles stand in for a political analysis of society. Sincere interrogations of society are thwarted, while the individualized analysis operates as a mode of evasion, avoiding examinations of structural relations, institutional power, and social praxes subtending oppression. Individual anecdotes and accounts of individual experience lend themselves to personalizing the political.[47] In personalizing the political, complete with Chaucer's fantastical autobiographical encounter, the *Legend* forecloses productive understandings of what a complaint about the gender politics of Chaucer's poetry might mean. The figure of Cupid suggests that those who critique the gender politics of Chaucer's poetry—or of poetry in general—do so from malicious personal intent, not for progressive purposes. Anyone raising concerns about the potential effects of a literary text demonstrates poor judgment or personal biases against an author. In effect, the poem places under suspicion readers who claim that poetry is political discourse.

Given the narrow parameters within which the *Legend* acknowledges biases, it seems impossible for poets to discriminate against women as a category; only an individual poet could write pejoratively about a specific woman or specific women. An author crafting a poem with problematic formulations surrounding gender cannot legitimately be accused of participating in sexism, since no malicious intent or individualized attacks are involved. The *Legend* absolves poetry as a site of gender inequity because a poem is only a poem, whose literary conventions are produced not by an individual agent but collectively by an ensemble of authors. In other words, "indiscriminate discrimination," a term discussed by Ellen Messer-Davidow, has no place in poetry.[48] Unfair treatment entails concrete acts against specific individuals and cannot be indiscriminate. Disavowing the structural marginalization of groups, the poem insists on knowledge's neutrality. But as Michel Foucault, Eve Kosofsky Sedgwick, Edward Said, and countless other contemporary cultural theorists have demonstrated, political interests are, as Terry Eagleton succinctly remarks, "*constitutive* of . . . knowledge, not merely prejudices which imperil it."[49] Cupid and those who demand that poets consider the gendered implications of their creations are condemned by the *Legend* as special interest groups with agendas that destroy art. By contrast, Chaucer's representative appears alone, not accompanied by any entourage whose interests he promotes. The fictive Chaucer is unaligned with specific political interests and does not appear to speak from any particular position, producing protohumanist art above such mundane considerations as gender and inequitable distributions of wealth and power. Concurrently, Chaucer the poet positions himself outside the text, removed from power struggles. This stance is recognizable as the beginnings of canonical English literature as it is currently celebrated. Not surprisingly, Chaucer often currently escapes culpability for the politics of his poetry, gendered or otherwise, by the attribution of irony. Although impressive scholarship, Hansen's "Irony and the Antifeminist Narrator in Chaucer's *Legend of Good Women*" exemplifies the common strategy, a legacy of New Criticism, of critiquing the politics of the *Legend* and then exonerating the poet through the defense that he is "being ironic."[50] Like the *Canterbury Tales*, with the layering and slipperiness of the narrator, Chaucer the poet's position in the *Legend* is never locatable but always seemingly sufficiently distanced from articulated stances.

The *Legend* ultimately clears Chaucer of accusations that he defamed women, though this was never really the issue. Within the world of the *Legend*, Cupid's concern about texts shaping readers' consciousness makes little sense, and his complaint is ultimately rendered uncompelling. In fact, the poem disarticulates Cupid's stance as largely incomprehensible, a rhetorical maneuver that acts as the primary means through which Chaucer is acquitted. The defendant is also exonerated through Cupid's inability to be a compelling witness, exculpating the fictive Chaucer through a logic resembling that of defamation trials in Renaissance England. As Lisa Jardine explains, defamation cases involving ordinary citizens were common in sixteenth-century English ecclesiastical courts, which enjoyed jurisdiction over violations of acceptable practices in domestic, marital, and sexual matters. In defamation cases, a complainant publicly accused of a social misdemeanor sought restitution from a defendant for slander. The plaintiff offered a deposition that functioned as his own character witness and that strove to expose the slanderer as unreliable and therefore the defamation as unfounded. If unable to undermine the credibility of the slanderer, the plaintiff stood in danger of being charged, while the repetition of the defamation in court granted the accusations a public audience and wider circulation.[51] The *Legend*'s Prologue resembles such proceedings in that the dialogue among Cupid, Alceste, and Chaucer's persona is staged as a trial, where Cupid's accusations against the narrator are granted audience and found faulty, largely because the accuser is unreliable. Chaucer is exculpated, while Cupid is deemed guilty of defamation. This strategy of exoneration demonstrates the political-is-personal maneuver in that Chaucer's name—and the poetic tradition for which he stands—is cleared not because the poem proved that his writings do not disadvantage women but because the accuser is unreliable and his criticisms less than coherent.

Conclusion

In the *Legend* Chaucer takes a crucial nexus of issues surrounding art and social responsibility and fashions a scenario staging these complaints as an amusing performance, starring semideities and wildly reinvented literary ladies. The Prologue and legends raise multiple possible sites for accountability for the gender politics of Chaucer's poetry and of the literary tradition but offer no productive places to locate responsibility. The selection of a confrontational trial as the forum for investigation maintains that holding a poet accountable is extremely aggressive, even persecutory, and thoroughly inappropriate. Failing to implicate individual authors, the textual tradition, or social praxes for gender inequities in the field of cultural production, and comically reducing responsibility for the *Legend*'s gender politics to two ridiculous patrons, the poem implies that no one ultimately bears culpability for inscriptions of gender in Chaucer's poetry or in hegemonic classical and medieval literature. This theater attempts to thwart a reader's ability to imagine a serious articulation of accountability at any locus. The poem maintains that it is irrational to interrogate earnestly the issue of art and social responsibility. Chaucer's disparaging portrayal of the articulator of this complaint makes Cupid's position one few would want to admit to holding: anyone genuinely concerned about art and social responsibility is, it appears, an idiot. I take up this abject position to reveal the *Legend*'s contempt toward those who wish to hold cultural producers accountable for their work. While the poem's lure is to be on the side of clever, witty artistry, I prefer Cupid's complaint. Obscuring inequitable access to the means of cultural production, and to the profound implications thereof, the poem deems gender a futile category through which to examine literature, insisting on a gender evasive discourse. At the nascence of an erudite English literary tradition, the *Legend* attempted to degender poetry in the service of male privilege.

The *Legend*'s process of degendering is synecdochical for the poem's stance on the propriety of analyzing poetry politically: the poem's dismissal of gender as unworthy of serious consideration condemns ideological analysis as a lens through which to examine texts. Ultimately, the *Legend* claims that social responsibility is a superfluous, unfruitful area of inquiry when contemplating literature, rendering the question of texts shaping consciousness and behavior moot. The poem works to circumscribe the field of debate regarding appropriate responses to poetry and acceptable categories of analysis for understanding and adjudicating texts. To deploy terms used by Antonio Gramsci and Stuart Hall,[52] the *Legend* disarticulates explicitly political approaches to literature, rendering them uncompelling and incoherent.

The *Legend* signals the emergence of an English literary practice that guaranteed privilege at the cultural level without having to answer for it. Crafting poetry that later became a cornerstone of the English literary canon, the man now conventionally celebrated as the father of English letters helped create the perception, which ultimately gained hegemony, that literature existed in a realm divorced from the social, thereby making literature more effective ideologically. Opposing John Gower and William Langland, Chaucer was one of the first English poets, certainly the first author of such monumental consequence in English letters, to declare equity and social justice outside the domain of poetics.

5

CHAUCER ON THE EFFECTS OF POETRY

In the *Legend of Good Women*, the narrator begins the *Legend of Philomela* with an outrageous claim:

> And, as to me, so grisely was his [Tereus's] dede
> That, whan that I his foule storye rede,
> Myne eyen wexe foule and sore also.
> Yit last the venym of so longe ago,
> That it enfecteth hym that wol beholde
> The storye of Tereus, of which I tolde.

(2238–43)

The jarring assertion that Tereus's "foule storye" makes the narrator's eyes "wexe foule and sore" raises the conundrum of how one determines what can legitimately be deemed textual influence. In foregrounding this dilemma, the narrator's claim gestures dramatically toward the problem of how to assess the specific effects of a text, a problem involving a complicated nexus of issues in which the *Legend* is keenly interested.

Chapter 4 reveals that a central concern of the *Legend* is art and social responsibility, an investigation instigated narratively by Cupid's complaint about construals of gender in Chaucer's earlier writings, since cultural artifacts shape readers' consciousness and affect lives. In part, chapter 4 shows that, at the founding of the English literary tradition, the *Legend* attempted to help construct the parameters of debate regarding acceptable responses to poetry and to establish which conversations about literature were possible; the chapter also demonstrates that the *Legend* simultaneously worked to disarticulate understandings that cultural artifacts shape consciousness and hence affect lives—while proceeding as if poetry can do exactly that.

Keeping these ideological maneuvers in mind, chapter 5 argues that the *Legend* offers a second pronounced set of strategies, very different than those outlined in the previous chapter, for dealing with concerns about the effects of Chaucer's poetry. Chapter 5 scrutinizes the *Legend*'s extensive theoretical interrogation surrounding the effects of a text. Through such mechanisms as the repeated staging of attempts by authors and narrators to elicit a defined response from readers, the poem investigates methodological complications involved in a claim that a text produces a specific result. The *Legend* investigates at length difficulties surrounding how to comprehend and gauge the influence of a piece of literature, and the poem explores the mediation of various factors in the production of the meaning of a cultural artifact or social praxis. Most importantly, this chapter analyzes the political implications of the *Legend*'s assessments of the difficulties surrounding the adjudication of the effects of a text.

Adjudicating Effects

Both Prologues initially appear to support Cupid's insistence that texts have effects. The opening lines declare that one cannot be certain of the existence of heaven and hell, since no living man has seen them, knowing them only through reading and hearing; but because men should not restrict their beliefs to that which they have witnessed, they should place faith in respected texts (F 1–28; G 1–28). Heaven and hell offer striking examples of Cupid's point that texts shape consciousness and behavior, since the Bible had tremendous impact on subjectivities and lives in late medieval England. Even while forwarding this powerful example, the poem simultaneously undermines it through the nexus of issues surrounding authority, evidence, experience, and knowledge raised in its formulation. Several Chaucerians, including Sheila Delany, Florence Percival, and Peter L. Allen, argue that the beginning of the *Legend* discusses the uncertainty of written knowledge and difficulties surrounding ways of knowing.[1] Delany, for example, maintains that the poem "opens with an epistemology inquiry: how do we know, and what are the sources of knowledge?" reflecting preoccupations by the medieval intelligentsia about the nature of evidence.[2] One could argue that the opening lines offer an epistemological dilemma that sets the stage for skepticism about Cupid's claim, questioning how one can definitively know and interrogating the nature of evidence. Since it is impossible to prove the existence of a place as foundational to medieval English social praxes as heaven and hell, how could one prove something as seemingly elusive as a text's impact on readers? Furthermore, there are even more fundamental questions surrounding literal meaning. The opening lines illustrate particularly well the difficulties surrounding deciphering a text's meaning at a basic denotative level. Because, as these opening lines demonstrate, one cannot decisively determine a text's meaning, an interpretation on which all readers can agree, how can one predict a phenomenon as seemingly speculative as a text's effects?

The opening passage's criticism of both experience and authority as reliable sources of knowledge, a topic frequently discussed by *Legend* scholars,[3] further erodes Cupid's stance regarding effects. Peter L. Allen remarks that the opening lines warn readers that "as interpreters we are on our own."[4] Articulating such sentiment, in the G-Prologue, the narrator issues the following announcement: "The naked text in English to declare / Of many a story, or elles of many a geste, / As autours seyn; leveth hem if yow leste" (G 86–88). The line "Leveth hem if yow leste" highlights readers' roles in the production of meaning and promotes an individualist understanding of reception, indicating that it is up to the reader—as if consciously, through agency and volition—how to construe a text, rather than offering a model of reception that privileges historical and cultural context or subject position, subject position being a category to which Cupid's comments point. A humanist, individualist understanding of reception anticipates and counters Cupid's stance through the logic that, since various readers interpret texts differently, reception is personal rather than being inflected by gender, culture, or historical context. When perceived as idiosyncratic, it is difficult to make compelling claims about reception.

The opening simultaneously offers a contradictory line of reasoning to discredit Cupid's claim. Linking "olde appreved stories" from the Bible with stories from other authoritative texts from the past (F 17–24; see also G 17–24), the opening argues that one must listen to the great tradition, which provides a way of knowing beyond the immediacy of the present. Readers who cut themselves off from this grand legacy ignore a rich, complex means of understanding the world. The apparent jettisoning of a rubric as structuring of medieval society as heaven and hell argues that readers must take up a relationship with texts from the past and give countenance to knowledge beyond personal experience; when they do not, the foundations of their knowledge—and of Knowledge itself—is in jeopardy. The legends, which fulfill the explicitly politicized demands of Alceste and

Cupid, speciously demonstrate the ludicrousness of rewriting texts to accommodate the interests of the current moment. Recrafting a great intellectual heritage from the interests of such a narrow viewpoint severely limits this impressive legacy, with the subsequent legends serving as a warning about explicitly connecting texts to contemporary politics. Such demands, symbolized by the poem's apparent dismissal of heaven and hell, bespeak an inappropriate desire to reinvent the world. When one disregards cultural experts, and when people without extensive formal educations seize control over cultural meaning, the result is a thorough denigration of Culture: the result is Philistinism, exemplified by Cupid, Alceste, and the legends. Hence, while the opening lines appear to liquidate authority through a radical challenge to knowledge, these lines and the larger poem merely camouflage authority. The lines immediately following the opening passage exemplify this strategy: the narrator announces that, with little provocation, he happily abandons his books to frolic in May, while, as explained in the previous chapter, subtending such apparent anti-intellectual sentiment is a complex web of erudite literary allusions, functioning as a wink to the well-educated. Revered texts from the past are affirmed as important means through which to understand the world.

The heroines' letters in the *Legend* further discredit Cupid's stance that writing produces effects on readers' consciousness and behavior. Several of the *Heroides'* protagonists appear in the *Legend*: Dido, Medea, Hypermnestra, Ariadne, Hypsipyle, and Phyllis. Although in the *Heroides* all heroines craft elaborate epistles, some of which are answered, in the *Legend* these meager four letters, which are startlingly brief, accomplish much less narratively. By dramatically narrowing the letters, Chaucer creates what appear to be four empirical test cases for the question "Do texts produce effects?" The heroines' letters generate no effects plotwise, with the exception of Philomela's tapestry. Because the flaccid missives appear after the action has played out, the letters operate largely as chronicles of events after the fact. These letters imply that Chaucer's tales likewise function in a curatorial role, as chronicles of past tales and lives, rather than generating effects and spurring action. Letters are a crafty choice for investigating effects on audience members, because letters are usually one form of writing with a direct impact on readers and hence, more than most types of writing, would be expected to attest that writing affects readers' understanding and behavior.

Hypsipyle generates the one letter that seems to shape outcomes. With her tale beginning immediately after Dido's futile letter, Hypsipyle's note is inefficacious in that it begs her lover to pity her (1567). Her letter appears to produce profound consequences otherwise, wishing that Jason's new lover would be betrayed and kill his two future children (1571–75). This vindictive missive ushers in Medea's legend, creating the impression that Hypsipyle's curse orchestrated Jason's abandonment of Medea and the death of their children, seemingly sapping all agency from Jason and Medea and making the outcome of their relationship a foregone conclusion. Hypsipyle's letter, where the response is so hyperbolic as to be untenable, creates a straw-man position. To claim that writing produces effects, the case of Hypsipyle's letter argues, these effects must be thoroughly deterministic, with a clear one-to-one correspondence between written dictates and their outcomes. Furthermore, the text must somehow possess the ability to sap agency from its readers and to make the outcomes foregone conclusions. The reductio ad absurdum strategy behind Hypsipyle's letter indicates a refusal to investigate agency in more complex terms or to acknowledge explicitly that the effects of texts are mediated, subtle, and overdetermined.

The *Legend* raises the complication of transmission to further challenge Cupid's claims about effects. Chaucer's jarring truncations and reformulations of the Greco-Roman tales emphatically illustrate that a text is altered through its dissemination, a phenomenon also foregrounded through the narrator's complaints about the lengths of some of the Ovidian epistles and his dramatic refusals to reiterate them fully, including Ariadne's "compleynyng" (2218) and Phyllis's missive (2513–2517), complaints that simultaneously foreground transmission and reception. The complication of transmission is further underscored through the lack of clarity surrounding the reception of the women's letters: there are no indications that Dido's or Medea's letters travel anywhere; Hypsipyle's letter is the only document sent to a specific target, namely, Jason (1564); and Phyllis's letter "was forth sent anon" (2555), without a specified recipient. Dido's and Medea's stationary writings and the ambiguity surrounding the recipient of Phyllis's missive emphasize that there is not simply an addresser, addressee, and a message to consider when adjudicating a text's effects. There is also the difficulty of tracking the dissemination of a text. How does one know when a text is dispersed and arrives at a destination? Chaucer's letters argue that it is impossible to gauge effects in part because dissemination is varied and unpredictable, if it happens at all. Writing means nothing without the act of transmission and without a reader. Although undeniable, these points represent some of the many arguments the poem musters to shift responsibility for a text's meaning away from the author.

The problem of transmission is also foregrounded through the narrator's explicit directive to his readers regarding Dido's letter. After reciting eleven lines penned by Dido (1355–65), the narrator writes, "But who wol al this letter have in mynde, / Rede Ovyde, and in hym he shal it fynde" (1366–67). This directive not only highlights the dramatic disparities between Chaucer's and Ovid's renditions of Dido's letter but also encourages an unlikely scenario: that upon completion of the *Legend of Dido*, audience members consult Ovid's version. It is doubtful that this intervention inspires most readers to turn, upon completion of the tale, to this source. When readers fail to do so, the *Legend* appears to demonstrate in two intersecting ways, within the narrative frame of Dido's tale and within Chaucer's audience, that it is highly possible for a text to possess no effect on audience members, even when an effect is specific and targeted and when the desired outcome is explicitly prescribed. It is difficult *not* to dismiss claims that literature affects consciousness and lives, when one is empiricist and when one conceptualizes literature in a direct cause-and-effect relation, and the poem often does exactly that, disregarding considerations of mediation, accretion, and overdetermination. This logic reduces the much more complex understanding of effects to which Cupid points into isolated, insular cases and offers these test cases to prove that texts do not generate effects. As a footnote, embedded in the narrator's directive is a further acknowledgement of reader's agency, for his directive is formulated as "who would al this letter have in mynde" (1366), meaning that the prescription is designed for readers who desire to do so, implying that readers' volition trumps, even neutralizes, any impact or address a text might have.

Just as there are no responses to the letters, Cupid, Alceste, and the sprawling host of women speak neither after individual tales nor after the compilation. Cupid and Alceste fail to indicate how well the narrator executed his assignment. The frame simply dissolves, with Cupid, Alceste, and their entourage disappearing after the Prologue, allowing for no registration of effects on these fictive readers. Hence, the issue of effects on readers disappears at the diegetic level. Such silence is deafening when compared to the *Canterbury Tales*, where pilgrims routinely comment on each other's stories and where tales provoke a range of affects. In some ways, the *Legend* does foreground audience responses: the narrator complains at length about the tedium of the Ovidian epistles, and the premise for the legends is

Cupid's disgruntlement about Chaucer's earlier compositions. Likewise, Alceste explains that the narrator's poems have made "lewed folk" (F 415; G 403) delight to serve love, implying that while unlearned audience members turn to love, more enlightened readers perceive greater things in these texts. This divide indicates that reception and effects follow patterns, based on such traits as readers' educational levels and gender, a logic that reinforces Cupid's complaint. This predictability connected to subject position is slightly disrupted by a male character's condemnation, and a female character's endorsement, of constructions of gender in Chaucer's writings. This predictability is more significantly disrupted by differences between Cupid's responses in F- versus G-Prologue to Chaucer's writings, as demonstrated in the previous chapter. The shifting of Cupid's complaint argues that reception is unpredictable and unstable, *even within the same individual*. Disparities between Alceste's and Cupid's reception and, more importantly, inconsistencies in Cupid's responses pose this conundrum: if there are multiple unstable and mutable receptions for the same text, how can one determine a text's effects?

Editorializing Remarks

The narrator's editorializing remarks throughout the *Legend* participate in the poem's interrogation of poetry's effects. The most striking of these remarks is the narrator's complaint about Tereus, beginning the *Legend of Philomela*:

> Whi sufferest thow that Tereus was bore,
> That is in love so fals and so forswore,
> That fro this world up to the firste hevene
> Corrumpeth whan that folk his name nevene?
> And, as to me, so grisely was his dede
> That, whan that I his foule storye rede,
> Myne eyen wexe foule and sore also.
> Yit last the venym of so longe ago,
> That it enfecteth hym that wol beholde
> The storye of Tereus, of which I tolde.
>
> (2234–43)

The narrator's complaint about his eyes being sullied by the account of Tereus's sordid deeds proposes a one-to-one correspondence between a text and its effects. The repetition of "foule" and the emphasis on eyes, the body part exposed to the words on the page, posit a functionalist response, as if a one-to-one correspondence between the text and the result is necessary to prove a text's impact, implying that claims that texts affect readers employ such puerile deductions. Such reductive determinism echoes Hypsipyle's curses in her letter to Jason. Moreover, this passage asserts that the mere mention of Tereus's name corrupts earth up to the first heaven, that his name produces a monolithic, totalizing response in everyone. The passage posits two binaristic effects on readers of Tereus's tale: a precise, localized impact and a deterministic, globalized effect. Both options are easily dismissible understandings of reception, in part, because they explicitly erase readers' agency, and Delany rightfully scorns the passage's denial of readers' free will.[5] More importantly, both are either so reductive or so hyperbolic that they disarticulate productive ways to discuss the effects of texts in nuanced, complex terms and work against the possibility of imagining reasonable means of conceptualizing and conversing about effects. These formulations bespeak a refusal to consider seriously the issues Cupid raises, namely, how literary texts perform ideological work and shape readers' consciousness.

The comment about venom disarticulates, through another means, complicated ways in which to consider textual influence. The "venym of so longe ago . . . enfecteth hym that wol beholde" implies that relaying a tale of a noxious man infects male readers with the same toxins, like the poisons infecting the narrator's eyes.[6] Reading about a man's malice toward women teaches male audience members to behave in similar ways, offering a model to emulate. Through the terms "foule," "venym," and especially "enfecteth," such bad behavior is portrayed as transmitting contagion, so that coming in contact with the tale of Tereus besmirches a reader. Lisa J. Kiser argues that Cupid advocates for a form of censorship rooted in the assumption that only stories about "'good' people" serve as vehicles for moral aims, while stories about "'wicked' people can do nothing but promote immoral goals"; rather than viewing these texts as vehicles for philosophical truth, Cupid sees them as exempla.[7] This logic recalls the Man of Law's apparent fear that relaying fictional tales of incest, such as "thilke wikke ensample" (2.78) of Gower's "Tale of Canace and Machaire" or "Apollonius of Tyre," might somehow encourage readers to engage in "swiche unkynde abhomynacions" (2.88). Regarding his comprehension of literature, the Man of Law, as the second chapter explains, possesses cultural lessons only half-learned. Failing to take into account overdetermination and mediation, the Man of Law's comment and the logic of the passage about contagion imply that texts have profound effects and that certain readers need to be protected from exposure, since texts will directly influence readers' actions. This is a theory of infection through vision, literal and metaphorical, through imagining the drama, like a culturally transmitted disease, creating syphilitic vision and arousing perversity. Such a formulation derides readers who express concern about the influence of texts, condemning them as misguided and ill-informed about culture.

Following such hyperbolic statements about the contagion surrounding Tereus, the narrator issues a strikingly different proclamation about the rapist: "For I am wery of hym for to tell" (2258). Within a brief span of time, the tale of Tereus ceases to cause the narrator distress, suddenly inducing ennui instead. This dramatic shift of effects on the narrator echoes disparities between Cupid's responses in F- versus G-Prologue. When one has two starkly contrasting reactions from the same reader to the same tale, the narrator's abrupt shift in affect argues, even an individual reader's responses are unpredictable and fickle, implying that one cannot predict reception by a large readership.

The narrator's further editorializing at the end of the tale continues the fragmentation of possible ways to articulate a text's effects on readers:

> Ye may be war of men, if that yow liste.
> For al be it that he wol nat, for shame,
> Don as Tereus, to lese his name,
> Ne serve yow as a morderour or a knave,
> Ful lytel while shal ye trewe hym have—
> That wol I seyn, al were he now my brother—
> But it so be that he may have non other.
>
> (2387–93)

It is striking that the warning to "be war of men" concludes the *Legend of Philomela* because this tale is the poem's most outrageous account of a man's maltreatment of a woman. This vicious treatment of Philomela undermines potential readerly claims that Chaucer's writings harm women. Next to the horrors Tereus inflicts on Philomela, and the suffering all the heroines endure, how can female readers of Chaucer's writings claim to have been harmed by his poetry? Alceste explicitly articulates this logic when she admonishes her partner for criticizing the fictional Chaucer, explaining that Cupid should be less condemnatory, "syth no cause of deth lyeth in this caas" (F 409; see also G 395). The narrator's remarks concluding Philomela's legend work in another way as well. While behaviors of other male characters are within the realm of realistic possibilities (including abandoning women for other lovers or for self-interested advantage), Tereus viciously destroys his sister-in-law. Tereus's rape, mutilation, and incarceration of Philomela constitute behavior too exceptional for audience members to encounter in everyday life. Hence, a warning at *this* juncture to beware of men counters the belief that literature intersects with readers' lives, positing too great a disjunction. The hyperbolic and overgeneralized nature of the narrator's warning foregrounds the gap between the text and audience members' experiences, a disparity further underscored by the narrator's explanation that a male lover is not likely to serve "ye" as Tereus did (presumably, as an incestuous rapist, abductor, and mutilator) or as a murderer or knave. These local comments about Tereus reinforce the larger, emphatic insistence on disparities between literature and life, a disjunction writ large in the poem's most pronounced gendered pattern: men seduce and abandon, while women are unflinchingly faithful. This gendered binary, like the warning to "be war of men," constructs a fallacious argument, conveying that those who express concern about the politics of textual content assess content in broad, crass ways. The poem then mocks such didactic messages, as the inanity of this caution to beware of men attests.

How does one appropriately discuss the impact of a text on readers? In the *Legend* Chaucer is disingenuously incapable of conceptualizing such effects, apart from Cupid's glimmers of insight. The poem otherwise refuses to consider explicitly in any compelling way a tale's subtle, nuanced participation in the shaping of an ideological terrain. The poem avoids articulating sophisticated understandings of literature's construction of readers' perceptions of themselves, others, and the world, reducing this understanding to something explicitly didactic—and obviously failing. All the while, the poem's constructions of straw-men arguments work to reshape readers' understandings regarding how objections to the potential political effects of a text should be understood.

The warning to beware of men immediately follows the jarring omission of Procne and Philomela's vengeance, a slaughter that testifies that the sisters are capable of great cruelty, as is Medea, the *Legend*'s other murderous mother, whose saga is likewise truncated. Only by ignoring a fuller account of Procne and Philomela's deeds could one derive the lesson to beware of men—but not to be wary of at least some women. Blindness to the fuller rendition could result from a lack of knowledge about Chaucer's antecedents or from perverse willfulness. The text highlights the latter through the specific terms of its warning. "Ye may be war of men, if that yow liste," which echoes the narrator's earlier advice to find Ovid's rendition of Dido's letter, "who would al this letter have in mynde" (1366). "If that yow liste" similarly indicates that readers do as they please, despite what any narrator recommends. By implication, uninformed readers reap morals they are predisposed to draw, especially readers undereducated in the Greco-Roman tradition. Such audience members derive reductive, skewed interpretations of tales, despite what tales actually convey. Female readers are specifically implicated through the gendered address of the statement that although a man "ne serve yow" like Tereus, "ful lytel while shal ye trewe hym have." Catering to a female audience and its agenda, the stated premise for the legends, the narrator dramatically truncates Philomela's tale. This abridgement implies that (female) readers isolate select moments from a tale and then celebrate these insulated fragments, ignoring the larger narrative. Cupid, Alceste, and their exclusively female entourage seek key elements that reaffirm their sense of the world, showing no interest in information countering what they wish to see.

The *Legend of Phyllis* extensively indites imagined female readings. In the *Heroides* Demophoon replies to Phyllis's letter, explaining compellingly that he longs to return but that pressing dynastic issues detain him. Chaucer's *Legend of Phyllis*, however, neglects to mention Demophoon's letter and reasons for delay. On the heels of "ye may be war of men, if that yow liste" (2387), the *Legend of Phyllis* begins as follows:

> By preve as wel as by autorite,
> That wiked fruit cometh of a wiked tre,
> That may ye fynde, if that it like yow.
> But for this ende I speke this as now,
> To tellen yow of false Demophon.
> In love a falser herde I nevere non,
> But if it were his fader Theseus.
> "God, for his grace, fro swich oon kepe us!"
> Thus may these women preyen that it here.
> Now to the effect turne I of my matere.

(2394–403)

The stated moral of the tale, "that wiked fruit cometh of a wiked tre," circumscribes fuller comprehension of Phyllis and Demophoon's affair. Through the declarations "for this ende I speke this as now" and "now to the effect turne I of my matere," the narrator announces that he deliberately manipulates his material to demonstrate this moral. However, the comment "that may ye fynde, if that it like yow"—recalling "ye may be war of men, if that yow liste" (2387)—maintains that if female readers are predisposed to see a certain moral in the tale, they will: anyone who wishes to view Demophoon as despicable will see him as such. The apparent contradiction between the narrator's agency and that of readers is negotiated through the comment "'God, for his grace, fro swich oon kepe us!' / Thus may these women preyen that it here." Most obviously, these lines convey that women who hear this tale will pray to be shielded from such men. "Women preyen that it here," though, can easily be read as "women pray to hear such a tale," a yarn about a heartless bastard. Demophoon is unfaithful in the *Legend* not because he necessarily was unfaithful in his previous literary incarnations but because certain readers demand that he be false. Moreover, readers clamor for stories of villainy signified in simple ways, villainy that is obvious and apparent, as the trite maxims accompanying this legend attest: "wiked fruit cometh of a wiked tre" (2395); "as doth the fox Renard, the foxes son" (2448); and "for fals in love was he, ryght as his syre" (2492). The latter two maxims imply that such (imagined) readers clamor for stories of a villainy that is an obvious, self-evident, didactic demonstration of identity. Hence, the narrator's heavy-handed *moralitates* are represented as being induced by readers. In shaping his "matere" to "the effect," the narrator caters to the dictates of Cupid, Alceste, their female entourage, and, most importantly, to the (alleged) demands of Chaucer's female readership. This portrayal of female reception posits women's reception, and more generally those who lack rigorous training in Greco-Roman literature, as uninformed, even foolish.

The passage's opening lines, "By preve as wel as by autorite, / That wiked fruit cometh of a wiked tre, / That may ye fynde, if that it like yow," claim that, during consumption, authority and experience are molded into whatever readers want to make of them, that the text's meaning resides with the hermeneutical activities of a readership. Through more contorted logic, the larger passage also insists on the primacy of reception. The multivalent comment that women who hear the tale will pray "God, for his grace, fro swich oon kepe us!" (2401) operates in conjunction with the narrator's two announcements that his tale is designed to elicit a certain effect ("for this ende I speke" and "now to the effect turne I of my matere") to make obvious the impossibility of a text generating a monolithic outcome. The inability to elicit a specific response from all female readers—unless they are already heavily predisposed to draw such conclusions about men— argues that even when a storyteller is deliberately didactic in an attempt to solicit a particular response, he will not succeed unless a reader is already inclined to draw the same conclusion. These formulations deflect responsibility for a text's meaning away from the author, text, and literary tradition onto audiences, as if willful readers, especially the uninformed and those with agendas, bear responsibility for fraught gender politics in a text because they chose to perceive a text perversely.

The narrator's explicit directives regarding what he hopes to achieve through his redaction of the *Legend of Phyllis* foregrounds another argument that undermines Cupid's stance on effects. Rarely does a literary text possess an agenda as explicit and narrow as the one the narrator outlines for the *Legend of Phyllis* or the one dictated by Alceste and Cupid. If heavy-handed directives cannot induce a stated effect, the logic of the narrator's editorializing remarks and Alceste and Cupid's mandate runs, then how might other literary texts that do not offer such heavy-handed directives generate specific outcomes? By foregrounding such a specious conundrum, the *Legend* demonstrates its unwillingness to acknowledge explicitly a textual address that is not overt but present nonetheless, with multiple and often contradictory ideologies speaking through a text. This conundrum also attests to the *Legend*'s resistance to acknowledging political overdetermination in the field of cultural production. The passage, like the larger poem, explicitly recognizes reductive responses that are specific and localized (for example, women will or will not exclaim "God, for his grace, fro swich oon kepe us!" upon hearing the *Legend of Phyllis*) rather than the ideological accumulation of years of exposure to tales from a privileged, Greco-Roman tradition, disproportionately produced by authors from similar demographics: white, predominantly affluent European men. In short, the narrator's directives, like Alceste and Cupid's mandate, work to thwart more complex ways of thinking about textual address and its potential implications.

Phyllis's letter continues the indictment of female audience members, while forwarding the poem's arguments that a text's message cannot be easily controlled and that effects are difficult to determine. In her epistle to Demophoon, Phyllis pens these remarks:

"Now certes, yif ye wol have in memorye,
It oughte be to yow but lyte glorye
To han a sely mayde thus betrayed!
To God," quod she, "preye I, and ofte have prayed,
That it mot be the grettest prys of alle
And most honour that evere the shal befalle!
And whan thyne olde auncestres peynted be,
In which men may here worthynesse se,
Thanne preye I God thow peynted be also
That folk may rede forby as they go,
'Lo! this is he that with his flaterye
Bytraised hath and don hire vilenye
That was his trewe love in thought and dede!'
Bot sothly, of oo poynt yit may they rede,
That ye ben lyk youre fader as in this,
For he begiled Adriane, ywis,
With swich an art and with swich subtilte
As thow thyselven hast begyled me.
As in that poynt, althogh it be nat fayr,
Thow folwest hym, certayn, and art his ayr."

(2530–49)

Phyllis is among those female readers who anticipate men's maltreatment
of their lovers. Just as the *Legend* truncates the tales of Medea and of Procne
and Philomela to cater to female readers, Phyllis readily cries "foul" before
waiting for her entire love story to unfold, preempting the possibility of a
more favorable outcome, one where, as in the *Heroides*, Demophoon is not
false, only delayed because of weighty political affairs in his kingdom. With
the lengthiest epistle in the *Legend*, Phyllis waits only for as much of the
narrative as she is inclined to hear. This passage explicitly connects Phyllis's
preemptive response to her reading habits. When musing about future literary representations of Demophoon, Theseus, and their ancestors, Phyllis's
accusation "ye ben lyk youre fader as in this" (2544) reveals that her opinions about her lover have been shaped by tales about his father. Whether
reading accounts of Theseus or merely hearing gossip, Phyllis interprets
Demophoon's actions through those of his sire. Rooted in her assumptions
that wicked fruit falls from a wicked tree and that Reynard's son acts like
Reynard, Phyllis possesses a monolithic understanding of the situation and

closes down other potential readings of events. A typical female reader looking for treachery in men, Phyllis quickly finds villainy in her lover. Ignoring the larger context, including pressing dynastic affairs, Phyllis isolates the action she expected, identifies with Ariadne, and prematurely ends her tale. When a female reader expects a given outcome, she will see that outcome. Moreover, deriving a lesson from Theseus and Ariadne's affair, Phyllis applied an apparent meaning of this tale to her own circumstances, producing an impoverished perspective on her own situation, an example that argues against applying a lesson from a tale to one's personal life and, more generally, against the practical application of literature to life.

The impoverishment of Phyllis's skills in textual analysis is further evident in her plan to float as a corpse in the Athenian harbor. Desiring such a theatrical display of grief, which suggests that Phyllis craves drama, she makes a grand, spectacular complaint through her letter and through her scheme to have her unsepulchred body indite Demophoon, before a large audience, for the grievous harm done to her. However, it is not self-evident that Demophoon is entirely to blame for Phyllis's grief. Furthermore, Phyllis cannot predict the reception of her corpse. Upon death, she cannot insure that her revenge fantasy would occur: that her body would remain unburied by its caretakers or that her corpse would be cast onto the water and navigate successfully into Athenian waters and into Demophoon's view. Nor can the queen be certain that the significations she intends her lifeless corpse to convey would be interpreted by Demophoon and by other viewers in ways she expects. Her plans and the larger quotation reveal that a central concern of Phyllis's missive and of her larger tale is reception. Her prayers about the future portrayal of Demophoon betray Phyllis's understanding, or perhaps hope, that the love story between the pair, buttressed by the fame of Demophoon's ancestors, is significant enough to be perceived as worth recording. Phyllis's repetition of her prayer ("'To God,' quod she, 'preye I, and ofte have prayed,'" 2533) acknowledges that her comprehension of Demophoon's actions do not reflect a universal reception. Through the uncertainties surrounding the fate and signification of the corpse and surrounding future portrayals of the love story, Phyllis's epistle inadvertently argues that reception is unpredictable. Chaucer's revisions to the tale underscore the instability of reception, for example, omitting references to Demophoon's epistle and dynastic disasters and greatly decreasing Phyllis's self-recriminations for her eagerness in accepting Demophoon as a lover. Phyllis's myopic interpretation of Demophoon's absence, the contingencies in Phyllis's plans for her corpse, the uncertainties surrounding later redactions, and Chaucer's dramatic rewriting of Ovid's tale argue that reception is unpredictable. Since reception cannot be predicted, logic the poem frequently musters, how can one then attach any accountability to a poet for the reception of his work?

At the end of the *Legend of Phyllis*, the narrator issues his oft-quoted warning:

> Be war, ye wemen, of youre subtyl fo,
> Syn yit this day men may ensaumple se;
> And trusteth, as in love, no man but me.

(2559–61)

The first two lines of this passage are ambiguous and may be read in multiple ways.[8] One could gloss these lines as a warning to women to beware of the subtle foe that defeated Phyllis: female tendencies to read reductively. Phyllis single-mindedly interprets Demophoon's behavior, prematurely acts on her reductive construal, and harms herself gravely as a result, suggesting that women's worst enemies may be themselves. The tale insinuates that women project, overreact, and launch injudicious complaints, behavior echoing Cupid's. "Yit this day men may ensaumple se" could be understood as saying that the *Legend of Phyllis* provides men with an example of women's inability to read appropriately.

"Trusteth, as in love, no man but me" toys with the issue of effects in relation to the burden of representation. Obviously, the narrator's admonition, the preceding tale, and the larger compilation will not persuade every female reader to mistrust all men except the narrator. The unlikelihood of convincing all female readers, through Phyllis's saga or the larger compilation, of the falsity of men can be read as a comment on the likelihood of Criseyde persuading men of the falsity of women. "Trusteth, as in love, no man but me" implies that one unfaithful character, or even several unfaithful characters, will not induce an entire group to dismiss the opposite sex: one cannot legitimately make globalizing statements about a group based on one character or person, because no single figure can sustain such a burden of representation. Through this turn in logic, Cupid's complaint about a gendered system of representation appears flattened into an erroneous lament that Criseyde somehow stands in for all women. As explained in the previous chapter, Cupid's concerns, however, indite something much larger than a single poem or isolated narrative; Cupid points to the power of hegemonic construals of gender in a Greco-Roman–based literary tradition, overdetermined understandings of gender in a dominant system of cultural representation. Moreover, the proclamation "trusteth, as in love, no man but me" places the discussion about effects in the realm of heavy determinism—not in the realm of nuanced, mediated, overdetermined effects, where it is more appropriate and productive to stage this discussion—and implies that Cupid and, more importantly, others who express concern about the potential effects of cultural artifacts do the same.

Collectively, the narrator's editorializing remarks raise a nexus of issues surrounding the problem of how to adjudicate the effects of a literary text. This web of issues offers several reasons why it is difficult to prove—or to even convincingly conjecture about—a text's influence on readers' consciousness and behaviors. In the *Legend* specious arguments appear alongside more legitimate rationales for shifting responsibility for the consequences of a text away from an author and his cultural productions, while the poem's staging of explicit directives to readers, ignoring such important factors as ideological overdetermination, reduces effects to absurd models that work to foreclose sophisticated understandings of effects. The *Legend*'s heavy-handed and ineffectual directives point out the impossibility of aligning a narrator's and/or author's intentions with actual outcomes and beg the question whether an author can be held responsible for the impact of his texts, even when he explicitly states specific intentions that contravene possible consequences of his writings. These interjections disingenuously demonstrate that readers interpret documents as they see fit, irrespective of pronounced narratorial and/or authorial interventions. Betsy McCormick emphasizes the *Legend*'s insistence on readers' interpretations. Employing modern game theory, McCormick argues that the poem participates in an elaborate, well-established literary game where the reader, drawing upon his ethical memory, "is left to determine the ethical wheat from the chaff for him (or her) self." McCormick writes, "readers of the *Legend* are forced into a pro-active stance by Chaucer's multi-layered editorial displacement; they/we must accept responsibility for their own hermeneutical authority."[9] I would not disagree that the *Legend* promotes this proposition, but this stance ultimately thrusts responsibility for textual meaning disproportionately onto readers. The *Legend* repeatedly enacts the point that a text cannot command a monolithic response and that the effects of one poem cannot be determined by a narrator and/or author because an individual reader's volition and interpretative apparatus are the primary sites of the production of meaning. Apart from the centrality of the readers' alleged determination of meaning, the narrator's comments foreground other complications that the *Legend* construes as eliminating authors' and texts' culpability for content. The poem insists that there is too much uncertainty surrounding consumption: one cannot know who consumes a given text, if a text reaches its intended target, or if a text reaches any audience at all. The tales point out disparities between tales and readers' lived experiences, most dramatically through the example of Tereus, insisting that one cannot apply literature to life. The cumulative result of these comments is the stance that if one cannot prove a text's effects, how can one criticize a poet or hold him or his writings culpable for such effects? By extension, how can one justly question the political propriety of a cultural artifact?

Uncontrolled Reception

This discussion of effects occurs in a poem that participates heavily, as several Chaucerians have demonstrated, including Percival and McCormick, in a long-standing scholarly debate among male intellectuals about women.[10] By staging a complaint about his earlier poetry's impact on women and by aligning this complaint with women and femininity, as discussed in the previous chapter, Chaucer not only speaks *about* women in the *Legend* but speaks *for* them, a common conflation, as Linda Martín Alcoff points out.[11] Alcoff argues that to evaluate attempts to speak for others, we must analyze the probable or actual effects of the words on the discursive and material context, acknowledging that, although when meaning is plural and deferred we can never know the totality of effects, we *can* know some effects our speech generates. I can find out, for example, Alcoff notes, whether the people I spoke for are angry as a result. In one conventional view, Alcoff explains, the author is credited with creating ideas and with being their authoritative interpreter. However, because the meaning of any discursive event is shifting, plural, and inconsistent, as it ranges over diverse spaces and transforms in recipients' minds, the speaker or author inevitably loses some control over the meaning of his/her utterance. While this loss of control may be taken by some speakers to mean that no speaker should be held accountable for his/her discursive action, "a *partial* loss of control does not entail a *complete* loss of accountability": we do not need fully conscious acts or containable, fixed meanings to maintain that speakers can alter their discursive practices and be held accountable for at least some of the effects. It is a false dilemma to pose the choice as being between complete causal power or no accountability. As an erasure and a reinscription of sexual, national, and other kinds of hierarchies, Alcoff continues, speaking for others often emerges from a desire for mastery, privileging oneself as the person who more correctly understands the truth about another's situation, while the impetus to always be the speaker reflects a desire for mastery and domination. Claims to speak only for oneself, which Alcoff dubs "the retreat position," attempt to avoid the problematic of speaking for another by retreating into an individualist realm, based on an illusion that one can separate from others to such an extent as to avoid affecting them. This may be the intention of a person's speech, but there is no neutral place to stand in which a person's words do not participate in the creation and reproduction of discourses through which other selves are constituted. The retreat response may be motivated by a desire for mastery, an attempt to establish a privileged discursive position wherein one cannot be undermined or challenged. Speaking must carry with it accountability and responsibility, entailing a serious commitment to remain open to criticism and to attempt actively, attentively, and sensitively to understand the criticism.[12]

Through his ambassador, Chaucer represents himself in the *Legend* as unswervingly patient, willing to listen quietly to all criticisms, regardless how inappropriate or facile. His persona's defense of *Troilus and Criseyde* and the *Romaunt of the Rose* sounds unassuming:

> What so myn auctour mente,
> Algate, God woot, yt was myn entente
> To forthren trouthe in love and yt cheryce,
> And to ben war fro falsnesse and fro vice
> By swich ensample.

(F 470–74)

By emphasizing something as seemingly personal as intentions, Chaucer's fictive spokesman declares that he speaks only for himself. The narrator claims a place immune from criticism because few would condemn such noble intentions as promoting truth in love and decrying falsity. These sentiments sound so lofty, or at least so innocuous, that they are difficult to indite.

Simultaneously, this statement of intentions acknowledges the instability of signification, foregrounding disparities between Chaucer's texts and their sources and between authorial intent and readerly interpretation. As this chapter has illustrated, the *Legend* continuously demonstrates that a rich plurality of textual interpretations exists at any given moment, and the poem explicitly plays with the narrator's and author's lack of control over reception and hence over their speech acts. Chaucer understands well that the speaker is not the master of the situation, that the poet loses some portion of control over the meaning and truth of his utterance. Although an author's lack of complete mastery does not absolve him of accountability, the *Legend* enacts this logical leap through its continual insistence on the unpredictability of reception and its assertion that a text's meanings reside primarily with readers. This loss of control is represented by Chaucer to mean that he cannot be held accountable for his discursive actions. The *Legend*, yet again, but this time through a different logic than outlined in the previous chapter, maintains that any attempt to hold a poet accountable is thoroughly inappropriate, if not absurd.

Diane Elam's discussion of speaking for others, where she rather takes up Alcoff's argument, further illuminates Chaucer's stance. Elam maintains that Alcoff's analysis brings us a long way toward understanding difficulties behind speaking for oneself but that what Alcoff "has not understood is that such analysis is both necessary *and endless*." Although, Elam explains, we may long to determine the precise effects of speech, the possibility of all utterances, including "speaking for," depends on the inexhaustibility of contexts. Any given utterance is situated in an infinitely expanding context, which includes an infinite number of senders and receivers. Elam deploys Derrida to argue that while intention does not disappear, "it will no longer be able to govern the entire scene and the entire system of utterances." Derrida's point is that "being taken out of context" and being "misused" are structural hazards of language use, and it would be naive to think otherwise.[13] Elam's logic elucidates Chaucer's. Through the incomprehensibly large host of women witnessing the dialogue among Cupid, Alceste, and the fictive poet, Chaucer conveys that there are an infinite number of receivers for any message and hence limitless possibilities for the reception of any given speech act. Chaucer also demonstrates the potential for his utterances to be taken out of context and misconstrued, as Cupid's objections attest. Furthermore, the disparities between F-Cupid's and G-Cupid's responses to Chaucer's work demonstrate the instability of reception, not only across a vast audience but within the same individual. Ultimately, an author cannot be held responsible for his work, the poem argues, because the possibilities for construals of a text's meaning are endless.

Preoccupied with the multiplicity of interpretation, the *Legend* is unconcerned, in a sincere manner, with what any consequences of a text might be. The richness of potential interpretations, the *Legend* insists, makes anticipating outcomes impossible. The poem's staging of a debate about women does not express sincere concern about the potential impact of poetry on readers' consciousness or on their subsequent lived experiences of gender. Chaucer deems the effects of his poetry a question worth considering, but a question that is ultimately moot, except as an abstract philosophical musing through which to display a poet's brilliant artistry. Positioning himself as the inheritor of a grand paternal poetic tradition, Chaucer claims to be the scion who best knows how to transmit this legacy. Even while insisting on the multiplicity of interpretation, in a contradictory move Chaucer positions himself as *the* authoritative interpreter of his earlier poetry and the owner and originator of the *Legend*, generating its ideas and being its foremost translator. Those (imagined or actual) readers who question constructions of gender in his poetry are deemed incapable of truly comprehending his art. Imagined criticisms of his poetry, such as those mouthed by Cupid and Alceste, are condemned as naive and inappropriate.

In the *Legend* Chaucer speaks for women to demonstrate his poetic prowess and linguistic brilliance, ultimately enacting a strategy for rhetorical command. This strategy works in tandem with a way in which Chaucer seeks mastery: the language of the *Legend* is so slippery and, like the *Canterbury Tales*, so thickly stratified with levels of narration, that it is difficult to determine either the poet's stance or the politics of his text. It is unclear who has responsibility for the point of narration or the utterance, constructed as a type of play, where Chaucer, eluding being pinned down, involves the reader in a game of decipherment. This elusiveness places Chaucer in a privileged discursive position: because the reader cannot catch Chaucer, Chaucer and his writings thereby remain above criticism. He finds a privileged discursive position wherein he cannot be undermined or challenged and thus becomes master of the situation. Chaucer's speaking for women is tied to a maneuver for political control, privileging himself as the one who more correctly understands the truth about poetry's relation to women, deriding the possibility that poetry that could harm women. The

Legend works to carve out this position of mastery and lack of accountability for an author in the new English literature.

Conclusion

The *Legend* insists that poetry is above such mundane considerations as genuine concern about its political effects. Proclaiming that effects are indeterminate, that a text's consequences are too speculative to contemplate seriously, the *Legend* offers a disingenuous—albeit clever and entertaining—dismissal of the stakes of poetry. Chaucer's dream-vision works to camouflage poetry's participation in the ideological battleground that is culture. Rather than locating any accountability for the potential consequences of a cultural artifact in the producer's hands or in the artifact itself, the *Legend* insists that, *if*, in the unlikely event there is any culpability, it lies with a reader for his/her construal of a text. The *Legend* promotes an ideology of individualism that holds a reader disproportionately responsible for how literature, and cultural production more generally, helps to produce the ways in which people understand their own identities, the identities of others, and the world around them. The *Legend* declares such considerations irrelevant to poetic endeavors, although a topic worth contemplating at great length from an allegedly disinterested point of view.

Ultimately, the *Legend* works to render the recognition that poetry is inherently political incomprehensible. This poem disarticulates connections between literature and power relations, partitioning literature from political discourse. Moreover, Chaucer carves out a hallowed place for the poet, setting up a privileged discursive position wherein he and other English poets are above responsibility for their creations. The poet, according to Chaucer, has autonomy beyond the social. The *Legend* signals the emergence in English letters of an art practice that has the ability to guarantee privilege at the cultural level without having to answer for it. Chaucer is one of the first English poets, certainly the first of such monumental consequence, to declare poetry divorced from the social realm, heralding the historical emergence of a type of author that has been familiar to readers of English literature over the past six hundred years. This is not to claim that English authors prior to Chaucer always conceptualized their poetry in explicitly political terms or as socially useful; however, it is to claim that Chaucer, a foundational figure in the English literary canon, actively argued against the utility of poetry and did so sustainedly in the *Legend*. At the beginnings of the English literary tradition, Chaucer worked to foreclose the possibility of ideology being a legitimate category through which to analyze this new body of knowledge, pronouncing poetry primarily entertainment, proclaiming that it is more important for the artist to be witty and clever than to be politically progressive, and disingenuously disencumbering literature in a way that makes it more effective in terms of social control. Promoting this notion of artistry, Chaucer helped found a modern sense of the author and authorship, a cultural worker with no little or no accountability to social justice. Chaucer helped found a bourgeois notion of the poet.

CONCLUSION

The poetry of Chaucer and Gower defined what the new English literature would become. In many ways their respective writings promoted similar understandings of the emergent literature and of the nature of its participation in the field of cultural production, while in other ways their texts diverged greatly regarding possibilities for this nascent cultural praxis. Both the *Confessio* and the *Legend* forward poetry as a means of categorizing and controlling readers and nonreaders alike. The *Confessio* offers a full-blown articulation of conversance with the Greco-Roman literary tradition as an indicator of intellectual, moral, and spiritual superiority over the populace. In a much less systematic, less nuanced manner than the *Confessio*, the *Legend* also ascribes familiarity with this tradition to superior intellectual capacities and vision, as the example of Cupid attests. Poorly versed in the Greco-Roman heritage, Cupid resembles the Man of Law, possessing cultural lessons half-learned. Readers with limited knowledge of this cultural heritage may rise above the multitude, but they should assume only meager roles in the production of knowledge, and the example of Cupid illustrates some of the reasons why. Gower's and Chaucer's poetry conveyed to Englishmen and women from the upper strata of nonruling urban classes a treasure trove not previously available in such an accessible medium, transmuting into plain English cultural riches heretofore stored largely only in other tongues.[1] While doing so, these texts pronounced readers inadequately prepared, if they were not already fully familiar with the great intellectual tradition, which both the *Confessio* and the *Legend* dispense. Hence, these texts worked to limit the possibilities of this new knowledge and to circumscribe readers' potential uses of these highly literate texts.

Chaucer's and Gower's writings offer some convergent and some disparate stances regarding this new vernacular poetry in relation to what would now be considered identity politics. The writings of both poets feature the discursive position of a neutral, even sacred, enlightened place from which the author speaks, a realm beyond socioeconomic position and beyond gender, where affluent, privileged cultural producers are not registered as such and where male cultural producers are not marked as men. Class and gender are rendered invisible at the sites of poetic production and articulation, the poet appearing disinterested, removed from contemporary power struggles. Although Gower's writings locate the author above categories of identity, his poetry does not otherwise generally deny that positionalities exist. Maintaining that the social order is decreed by God and nature alike, Gower's poetry recognizes that people speak from various socioeconomic situations. Even in his own case, despite his construction of the sagacious author removed from society, Gower intermittently concedes that he speaks from within a certain class as, for example, in book 1 of the *Vox*, when he depicts himself cowering in the forest while the rebellious lower orders rule the land. In his extended account of the rebellion, Gower admits the possibility that subaltern groups might speak, even if only in animal grunts rendered incomprehensible in his writings. Gower also concedes that other groups' experiences and perspectives on the world possess the potential to become ubiquitous, a stance reflected in his tremendous anxiety surrounding the uprising.

In the *Legend* Chaucer adopts a much stronger anti-identity stance. The glaring absurdity of the *Legend*'s identity-based assertions (for example, all women are faithless, all men are deceptive, and a poet who disparages love and women must be impotent) creates straw-men versions of late medieval identity politics. Commonalities surrounding gender and class are understood in only the crassest terms. Rendered ridiculous, it is easy to dismiss identity-based claims within the universe of the poem, and readers are encouraged to dismiss such claims more generally. While Chaucer speaks from nowhere in particular, women who complain speak from marked positions, constituting special interests, and the *Legend* dramatizes what happens when special interests are given audience: the imperilment of art, tradition, and, apparently, civilization itself. People who argue from identity, the *Legend* maintains, are not legitimate intellectuals, since they muster no intellectual arguments. As the martyrdom of Cupid's saints attests, claims rooted in identity are ultimately cries of victimization, mere claims of suffering; how can one intellectually engage with such protestations? The *Legend* delegitimates gender as a suitable rubric to consider in relation to textual production, constructing for poetry a place of gender indifference at the site of articulation, and, according to the poem, this is true not only for the literary author but for speakers more broadly. At the beginnings of English literature, Chaucerian poetry instructed readers how to recognize and understand identity-based claims and encouraged them to discount such concerns as inartful, ignorant, and ultimately dismissible.

The *Canterbury Tales* follows a slightly different logical trajectory vis-à-vis identity politics but ultimately promotes a similar stance. Each pilgrim stands for a social type and narrates a story that corresponds to that identity, according to "al the condicioun / Of ech of hem . . . and of what degree" (1.38–40). Each pilgrim possesses fairly predictable characteristics, such as the drunk, churlish Miller and the loquacious, duplicitous Wife of Bath. Regarding their readerly receptions, the pilgrims respond in ways that are predictable, if not essentialist: for example, the Friar advises the Wife of Bath to leave preaching to authorities (3.1270–77), and the Host, who owns a Southwark tavern, understands Malkin's rape as "hir wantownesse" (2.30–31). Each pilgrim bears a burden of representation. The identities of these Canterbury-bound characters are mapped out and portrayed as familiar figures, though not for readers to identify with, but to classify and pronounce knowable. Chaucer mimics sundry social positions and speaks for them all, simultaneously inhabiting each and none of them. Chaucer claims to know these positions so well that he can occupy them and speak their limited truths; he can, for instance, thoroughly investigate and answer the question "What do women want?" The compelling nature of the poet's mimicry is evident in the character of the Wife of Bath, who has often been understood as protofeminist or as an authentic spokesperson for women's interests. By creating the illusion of successfully inhabiting many subjectivities, Chaucer conveys that wives, pardoners, millers, lawyers, and others perceive the world through limited points of view, while the poet possesses a comprehensive perspective that rises above that of average people, that understands the (class-based and gendered) interests of others who speak, but that is itself disinterested. The *Canterbury Tales* celebrates late medieval Englishmen and women since, although they cannot all represent themselves, they are part of what makes England great and hence must be spoken for and about. Chaucer weaves an elaborate tapestry of identities, erasing differences through an illusory inclusiveness, creating the fiction that people speak for themselves, while he merely records voices, from a perch above the sociopolitical fray. In speaking so cleverly for the people, Chaucer's *Canterbury Tales* asserts the unmarked but seminal position of wealthy white Christian men in the production of knowledge in late medieval England.

Chaucer places potential objections to his poetry (and to poetry resembling his) from members of other groups in the mouths of characters prone to complaint, exemplified by Cupid's concerns on behalf of women or the Wife of Bath's heavily recited remarks about clerks in their oratories (2.692–96). Hence, hypothetical objections to his poetry appear as instances of a culture of complaint, voiced by unthinking malcontents. Chaucer pronounces these voices meaningless, emptying them out and reinscribing them as he sees fit, turning potential objections to his work into the artistry that is the greatness of his poems. Chaucer's refusal to endorse identity as a legitimate ground from which to produce knowledge about the world promotes an ideology of individualism, making his work more compelling to humanists than the poetry of Gower, which insists on the naturalness and inevitability of socioeconomic place.[2] As Lee Patterson argues, "For it is as the great champion of the individual that Chaucer has displaced his rivals (like Gower and, especially, Langland—both of whom haunt the *Canterbury Tales* as rejected possibilities) in order to established [*sic*] himself as the Father of English Poetry."[3]

Not only does Chaucer delegitimate sociohistorical identity as a locus from which to generate knowledge but in the *Legend* Chaucer represents identity-based claims as an impediment to Art. Florence Percival explains that, in representing himself as a poet writing under compulsion, in the *Legend* Chaucer aligns himself with (medieval understandings of) Ovid's motivations. Hence, the narrator's lamentations about persecution distinguish him as the inheritor of Ovid, a strategy that, as Yoshiko Kobayashi argues, Gower's persona adopts in book 1 of the *Vox*.[4] The *Legend*'s narrator assumes a marginalized status, an emphatically hollow posture, just as the poem renders all claims about disenfranchisement hollow. The emptying out of claims of marginalization thwarts the ability to hold sincere conversations about disadvantage and privilege in relation to poetry. The narrator's stance as victim in the *Legend* mocks the idea that Chaucer's poetry—or that any poetry—might harm groups of readers. After all, Chaucer as narrator is not besmirched by any heavy-handed indictment, nor, as Lisa J. Kiser points out, are the male antagonists in the tales sullied,[5] which begs the specious question "How can anyone be injured by poetry?" According to the *Legend*, the most legitimate claim of damage is the poet's: the poet is the one potentially harmed by the suggestion that literature has pejorative effects, because the demand for a poet to be held accountable is a demand for artistic constraint, attenuating his means of self-expression. Asking Chaucer to consider the political implications of his art is to censor the poet, to reign in his vision, whereby the poet becomes the aggrieved party, a logic replicated particularly well in John M. Fyler's comment that the legends "do not answer a male bias with a female one, but replace a pose of benevolent detachment with a predetermined moral message. . . . The *Legend* shows what happens when art becomes propaganda. More important, and truer to Chaucer's cast of thought, the *Legend* and *Troilus* together reveal . . . the difference between an ironic narrowing of the poet's vision and the poet with his powers fully extended."[6] To ask that a poet be held accountable is to tether his creative genius.

Implying that the poet is oppressed by demands for responsible representations of women, Chaucer employs what Robyn Wiegman calls a "discourse of injury and . . . minoritization," where a member of a privileged group assumes marginal status and claims to be oppressed, camouflaging the real relations of power.[7] From this victimized stance, all analytical concerns raised by readers from nondominant groups are damaging to the author, not crucial contributions to his self-examination and thoughtful articulation. When Cupid says that the narrator's poetry makes men trust women less, Chaucer supplants the issue of social responsibility through a discourse of personal injury—I as an individual am injured—and an ideology of individualism. The *Legend*'s implicit injury-based logic regarding the author thwarts conversations about the social responsibility poet and poetry should bear to specific groups. Demands for political accountability are portrayed as reactionary complaints impinging on free speech, while those who articulate them are represented as being closed to the human experience and naive to the edificatory project and the humor and pleasures of humanist poetry. Chaucer offers an art that guarantees the poet's right to liberal self-expression, without repercussions or accountability. Chaucer engages in cultural pastimes as a game, demonstrating casualness, mannered elegance, and statutory assurance, characteristics that, as Bourdieu and Passeron explain, indicate a mastery of culture and signal membership in the elite.[8]

By contrast, Gower, it seems, takes culture too seriously, in addition to which his poetry intermittently reveals the vulgar mark of toil and effort.

Consequently, according to now long hegemonic understandings of English letters, Gower fails as a model of a cultural producer worthy of emulation. As part of his seriousness, Gower, as his oeuvre attests, operates on the premise that culture is a battleground, a view shared by many late medieval English poets, the most celebrated being Langland.[9] Many late medieval English texts that fail to explicitly discuss political economy nonetheless acknowledge that texts shape readers' consciousness and spur readers to action, texts that include, to name only a few, compilations of saints' lives, *Everyman*, *Mankind*, the Croxton *Play of the Sacrament*, and the late medieval English cycle plays. Gower proceeds as if poetry is a means of social reformation and a vehicle for social engineering. Chaucer, by contrast, consistently evades explicit discussions of contemporary events, as several medievalists have noted.[10] Situating Chaucer's distance from such events within the larger canon of English writers, Sheila Delany argues that authors, with few exceptions, write in ways removed from political struggles, insulated from topicality through their class privilege. In this context "Chaucer's notorious silence about the 1381 revolt and other important national and international events of his time appears not especially unusual: indeed, it appears prototypical."[11] Chaucer's writings frustrated the possibilities for poetry that Gower pursued. Chaucer's writings helped thwart the likelihood of politics being a primary category through which to conceptualize the new body of knowledge and attempted to make derisive any demand that poetry be political or any recognition that poetry is political by nature. Chaucer pronounced great literature to be above ideological struggle, and poetry and poetics inappropriate forums for orchestrating social change. Consequently, Chaucerian poetry has become more effective at intervening in the production of the sociopolitical terrain by appearing not to do so.

Chaucer's mocking title for his colleague has enjoyed tremendous longevity, and, as Diane Watt points out, the moniker "moral Gower" "has proved sufficient to dissuade many from exploring his poetry."[12] The dullness associated with Gower's poetry through the appellation "moral Gower" is part of a larger nihilism associated with Gower's art. Gower has been conventionally aligned with morbidity. After pronouncing himself "John Gower," Gower's personification, Amans, learns of his hoary locks and visage defaced by Eld (8.2321–2439); signifying sterility, Amans squanders his time unsuccessfully pursuing a lady until Venus pronounces him aged and impotent. This proximity to death is not isolated to Amans, for most of Gower's writings are deeply concerned with death, the afterlife, and the salvation of souls. Gower's oeuvre is associated with decline, because he wrote two of his three major works in what were languishing languages in late fourteenth-century England, Latin and Anglo-Norman. Gower the man is frequently aligned with feebleness and superannuation. In the Dedicatory Epistle to the *Vox* in MS 98 (S) All Souls College, Oxford, the manuscript used as the basis for G. C. Macaulay's critical text—and, as Jeremy Dimmick points out, in the Dedicatory Epistle in *Vox* manuscripts generally—Gower declares himself old and blind.[13] Gower's biography is often figured through images of the frailty of old age because, excluding the Septvauns scandal, little is known of his youth and midlife, although he spent his later years, from the 1370s until his death, living at a property owned by St. Mary Overie Priory.[14] Likewise, medievalists know of no marriage of Gower as a young man nor of any offspring, only of a marriage in 1398 to Agnes Groundolf, a younger woman whom the poet is conventionally believed to have wed to gain a nurse, not due to a romantic predilection for younger women.[15] Gower has been immortalized by a heavily photographed, spectacular sepulcher (in the current Southwark Cathedral), while Chaucer's tomb (in Westminster Abbey) does not generally figure in representations of Chaucer as a synecdoche for the poet.

While the effigy on Gower's tomb is the most frequently reproduced likeness of Gower, one of the most heavily reproduced likenesses of Chaucer is the depiction of him as a pilgrim astride a horse.[16] Chaucer, in his twenties, married Philippa, and he may have had as many as four children: a son, Thomas Chaucer; a son, Lewis; and perhaps two daughters, Elizabeth and Agnes.[17] Chaucer is believed to have had extramarital relations with Cecilia Chaumpaigne, possibly without her consent, a union from which "Lyte Lowys" may have issued.[18] Extensive records exist from various stages of Chaucer's life, leaving to the world more than a portrait of an aged man. Abandoning dead and dying tongues, Chaucer composed in the emergent vernacular literary language. Chaucer's poetry is viewed as endlessly productive of new meanings, as the sheer volume of Chaucer scholarship over the past century attests, while Gower scholarship has been slim by comparison.

Regarding futurity, the *Legend* can be read, in part, as a statement about the type of art Gower's poetry represents. The *Legend* argues that socially accountable art is by definition sterile, a stance evident not only in the characters' flatness and in the starkness of the narratives but also in the protagonists' barrenness as a group, since very few of them (including Thisbe, Ariadne, Hypermnestra, Lucrece, Dido, Philomela, and Phyllis) give birth and since the specter of murderous mothers haunts some of the tales (such as the legends of Medea and of Philomela and Procne). Similarly, several protagonists (Dido, Cleopatra, Phyllis, Lucrece, and Thisbe) slaughter themselves, while others are left in positions that offer no apparent future (such as Ariadne, Medea, Procne, Philomela, and Hypermnestra). This annihilating force in these legends figures political poetry as antilife and antihumanist. Lee Edelman has described how political discourse is often misread as morality and how heterosexual coupling and reproduction are the conventionally deployed as markers of potential, artistry, and futurity.[19] The perverted, thwarted heterosexual couplings in the *Legend* act as testimonies to the perils of writing socially accountable art. Chaucer would have us believe that political English poetry was stillborn in the late fourteenth century.

Hence, Chaucer's writings helped to thwart one of the most politically progressive possibilities of Gower's poetry and of similar literature in late medieval England. In many other ways, however, the poetry of these two foundational authors worked in tandem to produce the terms for the new English legacy. Chaucer and Gower were instrumental in transmuting heavily fortified cultural riches into an accessible tongue, rendering these treasures available for widespread enjoyment and for innovative uses by the English populace, who possessed different ways of perceiving and being in the world than the ruling classes. At the same time, the poetry of Chaucer and Gower helped to construct another fortress around these cultural riches, one to prevent them from being despoiled by the socially unfit and underprepared.

In short, English literature from its nascence did not offer a democratization of culture but represented a new means of constructing authority and imposing social control as a form of education. Lacking an appropriate pedigree to become the legitimate inheritors of this cultural tradition, readers from the nonruling classes were still refused entry into the inner sanctum of culture. As Thomas Walsingham remarked in his account of the English Rising of 1381,

> Rustici quidem fuistis et estis; in bondagio permanebitis, non ut hactenus, sed incomparabiliter viliori. Nam ad hoc dum vivimus, et regno, Deo dante, præfuerimus, sensu, viribus, et catallis nostris, elaborabimus vos suppeditare, taliter ut exemplum sit posteris vestræ

servitutis offensum, et habeant præsentes et futuri vobis similes sem-
per coram oculis, et tanquam pro speculo vestram miseriam, et vobis
maledicendi materiam, et timorem vobis similia perpetrandi.

[Peasants/rustics you were, and peasants/rustics you shall remain. You
will remain in bondage, not as before, but incomparably worse. For
as long as we live and, by the grace of God, rule this kingdom, we
shall work with our minds, powers, and property to keep you in such
subjection that your servitude may be a lesson to posterity, and so
that now and in the future, men like you will always have before their
eyes, as if in a mirror, your miseries and reasons for cursing you and
for fearing to commit similar crimes.][20]

Chaucer served as a justice of the peace on the peace commission in Kent
from 1385 to 1389, at a time when these commissions were the primary
instrument for enforcing the 1349 Ordinance of Laborers.[21] As a long-term
strategy, however, the dissemination of English literature represented a
much more effective means than peace commissions for thwarting a reprise
of the English Rising of 1381.

NOTES

INTRODUCTION

1. These prerequisites are evident in the *Vox*'s language and dense textual allusions, reflected in Stockton's copious endnotes in Gower, *Major Latin Works*, 340–470.

2. Fisher, *John Gower*, 108–9.

3. Compare the *Visio Anglie* to the *Confessio*'s Prologue (499–584 and Latin verses at Prol.iv). All quotations from the *Confessio* are from Gower, *English Works*. Discussions of the *Confessio* and insurrection include Ferster, "O Political Gower"; Ferster, *Fictions of Advice*; and Peck, "Social Conscience."

4. I deliberately borrow "crisis of authority" from Gramsci, *Prison Notebooks*.

5. Although Butterfield, *Familiar Enemy*, xxvi, conceptualizes both English and French as England's vernaculars, by "vernacular" I specifically mean English, the first language of the overwhelming majority of English men and women in late medieval England.

6. Justice, *Writing and Rebellion*.

7. Middleton, "Chaucer's 'New Men,'" 15; Strohm, *Social Chaucer*, esp. 1–23, 47–83; Strohm, "Social and Literary Scene," 9–12; Strohm, "Fifteenth-Century Audience," esp. 6–7.

8. Examples include Penn, "Literacy and Literary Production," 121–24; and Watt, *Amoral Gower*, 9–10.

9. Middleton, "Idea of Public Poetry"; Middleton, "Audience and Public."

10. Examples include Breen, *English Reading Public*; and Benson, *Public "Piers Plowman,"* esp. chap. 4. Cf. Sponsler, "London's Public Culture."

11. Kerby-Fulton and Justice, "Langlandian Reading Circles."

12. Examples include Copeland, *Rhetoric, Hermeneutics, and Translation*; and Minnis, *Translations of Authority*.

13. See especially Gramsci, "Modern Prince"; and Hall, *Hard Road to Renewal*, esp. chap. 10.

14. Williams, *Marxism and Literature*, 115–17.

15. Justice, *Writing and Rebellion*.

16. Strohm, "Revelle!"

17. On the fragmentary nature of subaltern consciousness, see, for example, Gramsci, *Prison Notebooks*, 158–59, 196–200.

18. Although numerous, the best-known examples include Salisbury, "Remembering Origins"; and Peck, "Book of Daniel."

19. Aers, "Reflections on Gower"; Aers, "Third Estate," 345–47.

20. This removal is encapsulated by the image of Gower as an archer reproduced (from London, British Library, MS Cotton Tiberius A.iv., fol. 9) in the frontispiece to Gower's *Complete Works*, vol. 4, on the front cover of Yeager's *Re-visioning Gower*, and in Yeager's positioning of Gower as Arion in *John Gower's Poetic*.

21. Alongside Aers's two articles on Gower, Carlson's scholarship stands as a notable exception, particularly "Gower's Beast Allegories" and discussions of Gower in *Chaucer's Jobs*.

22. Bowers, *Chaucer and Langland*, 3.

23. See especially Bowers, "Antagonistic Tradition."

24. Conventional areas of discussion include their personal relationship, explicit references to each other by name, comparisons of their writings as mutual sources and analogues for each other's poetry, and textual allusions and parallels between their writings. One of Yeager's several edited collections, *Chaucer and Gower*, pairs the poets.

25. Mitchell, *Ethics and Exemplary Narrative*; Mitchell, "Gower's *Confessio Amantis*." See also Aers, "Reflections on Gower."

26. Watt, *Amoral Gower*, xi; E. Allen, "Chaucer Answers Gower," 649–50, 50n9; Fisher, *John Gower*, 207.

27. Urban, *Fragments*, esp. 224. Urban's book, like mine, is interested in Chaucer's and Gower's constructions of the past in relation to the historical and discursive context in which the poets wrote, although Urban adds a third term to his study: the postmodern reader. Focusing on different texts than I do, Urban produces a series of close readings that, although interesting, do not produce a clear overarching argument.

28. Patterson, "No Man," esp. 146–55; Delany, *Naked Text*, 9–10; Strohm, *Social Chaucer*, 164–66; Strohm, "Social and Literary Scene," 14.

29. Gower's most respected biographer, John H. Fisher, believes that Gower composed the *Confessio* from 1381 to 1390 (*John Gower*, 108–9). G. C. Macaulay dates the completion of the Ricardian *Confessio* at 1390 and the completion of the Lancastrian version at 1392 or 1393 (Gower, *English Works*, xxii–xxiii). Regarding key premises in attempts to assign chronologies to the *Legend*'s two Prologues, see Delany, *Naked Text*, 34–43.

30. Coleman, "King Richardes Sake."

31. See A. Edwards's, Askins's, and Robertson's reviews of *Chaucer's Jobs*. See also Mead, "Subject of Bureaucracy," 50–51.

32. Carlson, *Chaucer's Jobs*, esp. 33–74.

33. Bourdieu, *Distinction*.

34. Bourdieu and Passeron, *Inheritors*, esp. 1–27, 67–76.

CHAPTER I

1. Cavanaugh, "Study of Books," 12, 158, 196–97, 649, 670, 781.

2. Middleton, "Chaucer's 'New Men'"; Middleton, "Idea of Public Poetry"; Middleton, "Audience and Public."

3. Strohm, *Social Chaucer*, 1–23, 50–51; Strohm, "Fifteenth-Century Audience"; Strohm, "Social and Literary Scene," 3, 6, 10–13; Strohm, "Chaucer's Audience," 29; Strohm, "Chaucer's Audience(s)," 141–44. For a critique of Strohm's category of "middle strata," see Patterson, review of *Social Chaucer*.

4. Examples include Watt, *Amoral Gower*, 9; Penn, "Literacy and Literary Production," 121, 124; Phillips, "Register," 107; Echard, "Designs for Reading," 72; and Coleman, "Lay Readers," 235. Parkes's influential "Literacy of the Laity," 561–65, and Meale's "Patrons, Buyers, and Owners," 216–17, helped foster medieval English scholars' frequent conflation between the protobourgeoisie and middle classes. Watts, "Pressure of the Public," critiques tendencies by medieval English literary scholars to employ the amorphous categories of "middle strata" and "middle class."

5. Kerby-Fulton and Justice, "Langlandian Reading Circles."

6. On Chaucer as a civil servant, see Carlson, *Chaucer's Jobs*; Mead, "Subject of Bureaucracy"; and Robertson, *Laborer's Two Bodies*, 51–58.

7. Kerby-Fulton and Justice, "Langlandian Reading Circles," 66.

8. Doyle and Parkes, "Production of Copies." On Hoccleve's clerical work, see Mooney, "Some New Light."

9. Kerby-Fulton and Justice, "Langlandian Reading Circles," 64–67. See also Horobin, "Manuscripts and Scribes," 68–71.

10. Kerby-Fulton and Justice, "Langlandian Reading Circles," esp. 63–64, 75–76. On Usk's father and occupations, see Strohm, *Hochon's Arrow*, 146–48.

11. Kerby-Fulton and Justice, "Langlandian Reading Circles," 76.

12. See especially Horobin, "Manuscripts and Scribes"; Horobin, "Professionalization of Writing"; and Mooney, "Locating Scribal Activity."

13. These categories are rooted in the work of Hilton, especially "Popular Movements" and "Status and Class," and Dyer, "Late Medieval Society."

14. Dyer, *Standards of Living*, 19–21. Storey, "Gentleman-Bureaucrats," explains that "esquire" was also a title for certain royal domestic servants (as the king's esquires) and that some men adopted the title "gentleman" because of their administrative occupations.

15. Given-Wilson, "Problem of Labour," 97.

16. Dyer, "Were There Any Capitalists?" 19; Dyer, *Standards of Living*, 23; Hilton, *Class Conflict*, 156.

17. Dyer, *Standards of Living*, 20–25; Hilton, *Class Conflict*, 154–56; Hilton, "Status and Class," 11–13; Thrupp, *Merchant Class*, 6, 84; Swanson, *Medieval Artisans*, 1–5. See also Bolton, *Medieval English Economy*, 259–67.

18. Barron, *Later Middle Ages*, 207–8, 230–33; Barron, "Richard II and London," 134–35; Thrupp, *Merchant Class*, 84. See also Unwin, *Gilds and Companies*, 74–81.

19. Thrupp, *Merchant Class*, 6; Unwin, *Gilds and Companies*, 77, 88.

20. Thrupp, *Merchant Class*, 27–32. This does not mean there were no divisions within the London mercantile elite. See Barron, "Richard II and London," 135–36; Strohm, *Hochon's Arrow*, chaps. 1 and 7; and Nightingale, *Medieval Mercantile Community*, chaps. 10–12.

21. Thrupp, *Merchant Class*, 204–5, 225, 258, 260–63. See also Hilton, *Class Conflict*, 154. Regarding lawyers' relation to gentlemen, see Storey, "Gentleman-Bureaucrats," 95–97.

22. Kermode, "Three Northern English Towns," 7; Kermode, *Medieval Merchants*, 4–6, 38–52. See also Swanson, *Medieval Artisans*, chaps. 9–11, esp. 109, 113, 120–24, 149–50, 170; Dobson, "Risings in York," 119–20, 125–26, 130–31; and Hilton, *Class Conflict*, 161.

23. Thrupp, *Merchant Class*, 28–29; Barron, "Education and Training," 144, 150; Barron, "Widow's World."

24. Examples include Watt, *Amoral Gower*, 1; Fisher et al., "John Gower," 2196; and Fisher, *John Gower*, 41. Penn mistakes the mercantile class as middle class, places Chaucer in the middle class, and claims that the middle class comprised a sector of Chaucer's readership ("Literacy and Literary Production," 121).

25. Crow and Olson, *Chaucer Life-Records*, 1–12; Pearsall, *Life of Geoffrey Chaucer*, 11–16.

26. Patterson, *Subject of History*, 253.

27. Crow and Olson, *Chaucer Life-Records*, 151, 269–70, 298–99, 302–39, 525–34; Pearsall, *Life of Geoffrey Chaucer*, 96–97.

28. Robertson, *Laborer's Two Bodies*, 51–58; Carlson, *Chaucer's Jobs*, 15–20.

29. Fisher, *John Gower*, 41. See also Watt, *Amoral Gower*, 1; and Fisher et al., "John Gower," 2196.

30. Nicolas, "John Gower, the Poet"; Fisher, *John Gower*, 37–54; Hines, Cohen, and Roffey, "*Iohannes Gower*," 24.

31. Fisher, *John Gower*, 55–59.

32. Ibid., 47–69.

33. Arundel, *Register*, 1, fols. 256r–257r. A transcription of Gower's will appears in Nicholas, "John Gower, the Poet," 103–4n1. The translation of the clause about the rental income is

from W. Taylor, *St. Mary Overy*, 79–80, where Gower's will appears in modern English. Regarding Gower's landholdings, see Fisher, *John Gower*, 47–67.

34. Carlin, *Medieval Southwark*, 172–74, 184–85.

35. Barron, *Later Middle Ages*, 130–31, 207–8, 218–23.

36. Hilton, "Popular Movements"; Hilton, "Status and Class"; Dyer, "Late Medieval Society." See also Swanson, *Medieval Artisans*, introduction.

37. Swanson, *Medieval Artisans*, 113, 120–24; Hilton, *Class Conflict*, 161. See also Kermode, *Medieval Merchants*, 38–48.

38. Swanson, *Medieval Artisans*, 5–6, 113; Hilton, *Class Conflict*, 156.

39. On women traders and artisans, see, for example, Hilton, "Women Traders"; Goldberg, "Women and Work"; Kowaleski, "Women's Work"; McIntosh, "Women's Participation"; and Mate, *Medieval English Society*, 46–56.

40. Hilton, "Status and Class," 11. See also Swanson, *Medieval Artisans*, 6.

41. Hilton, *Class Conflict*, 156; Hilton, "Status and Class," 11–12; Dyer, "Were There Any Capitalists?" 7–8; Swanson, "Industrial Investment." Cf. Rosser, "Workers' Associations."

42. Barron, "Richard II and London," 135.

43. Prescott, "Peasants' Revolt," 132–33.

44. Barron, "Richard II and London," 149.

45. On the 1377 oaths and the Northampton-Brembre struggle, see Barron, "Richard II and London," 145–50; Strohm, *Hochon's Arrow*, chaps. 1 and 7; and Nightingale, *Medieval Mercantile Community*, chaps. 10–12. On Chancery returns, see Barron, "Parish Fraternities"; and Barron, *Later Middle Ages*, 206–9. Regarding Ralph Holland's cause, see Barron, "Ralph Holland."

46. Dobson, "Risings in York," 124–30.

47. Swanson, *Medieval Artisans*, 122–23.

48. Butcher, "English Urban Society," 104–10.

49. William Smith of Leicester becomes one such example of exceptionalism. See S. Justice, *Writing and Rebellion*, 30–31.

50. The lack of conscious cohesion among artisans as a group is one of the central premises of Swanson's *Medieval Artisans*.

51. Ibid., esp. 172–73, 122–24, 139; Rosser, "Workers' Associations"; Rosser, "Negotiation of Work." See also Giles, "Framing Labour."

52. Orme, *Education and Society*, 34–35; Orme, *English Schools*, 210–15; Barron, "Education and Training," 147–49. See also Barron, "Expansion of Education."

53. Moran, *Growth of English Schooling*, 160–62; Moran, "Literacy and Education," 14–23.

54. On curricula in late medieval English grammar schools, see Orme, *English Schools*, 68–70; and Orme, "Study of Grammar."

55. Orme, *English Schools*, 60, 167; Orme, *Education and Society*, 53.

56. Orme, *English Schools*, 87, 178–96, 214, 224; Orme, *Education and Society*, 25.

57. On tuition, see Orme, *English Schools*, 118; on wages, see Kowaleski, *Medieval Towns*, 371.

58. Orme, *English Schools*, 118–19.

59. Moran, *Growth of English Schooling*, 164, see also 94; Moran, "Literacy and Education," 17.

60. Moran, "Literacy and Education," 14. See also Orme, *English Schools*, 69–70, and Orme, *Education and Society*, 192–93.

61. Orme, *Education and Society*, 192–93; Orme, *English Schools*, 69–70.

62. Zieman, *Singing the New Song*, chap. 1.

63. Orme, *English Schools*, 64, 175; Zieman *Singing the New Song*, 6, 23; Orme, *Education and Society*, 192–95.

64. Orme, *Education and Society*, 191–92.

65. Barron, "Expansion of Education," 224; Hines, Cohen, and Roffey, "*Iohannes Gower*," 32–34.

66. Orme, *English Schools*, 65–67, 196, 232, 243–51; Orme, *Education and Society*, 45–46; Moran, *Growth of English Schooling*, 82–84, 114–15.

67. Christianson, *Directory of London Stationers*, 88–89.

68. S. Justice, *Writing and Rebellion*, 30–31.

69. Barron, "Education and Training," 147–48; Barron, "Expansion of Education," 225. See also Moran, *Growth of English Schooling*, 70.

70. Orme, *English Schools*, 66–67.

71. Quoted in Dobson, "Later Middle Ages," 67. See also Orme, *English Schools*, 66.

72. Orme, *English Schools*, 66–68.

73. Adamson, *Illiterate Anglo-Saxon*, 41. On unlicensed schools teaching grammar in London, see Barron, "Expansion of Education," 231–32.

74. Ives, "Common Lawyers," 198.

75. Moran, *Education and Learning*, 25.

76. Orme, "Schoolmasters," 220–22, 226.

77. Swanson, *Medieval Artisans*, 165–68.

78. Orme, *Education and Society*, 203–4. See also Moran, *Growth of English Schooling*, 115.

79. On reaching the age of ordination, on marrying before taking up major orders, and on pursuing other occupations, consult Cullum, "To Be a Man," esp. 141–44.

80. Kerby-Fulton and Justice, "Langlandian Reading Circles," 64. See also Cullum, "To Be a Man," 142–46.

81. Orme, *Education and Society*, 1–2; Salzman, *English Industries*, 340–41; Orme, *English Schools*, 48; Thrupp, *Merchant Class*, 159–60; Barron, "Education and Training," 139–47. On apprenticeship to crafts, see Lipson, *Economic History of England*, 279–96.

82. Orme, *English Schools*, 48; Moran, *Growth of English Schooling*, 67–68.

83. Moran, *Growth of English Schooling*, 171. See also Barron, "Education and Training," 146.

84. Moran, *Growth of English Schooling*, 67–68.

85. Sharpe, *Calendar of Wills*, 576.

86. Orme, *English Schools*, 48.

87. Barron, "Education and Training," 146.

88. Orme, *English Schools*, 45–46; Barron, "Expansion of Education," 220–21; Barron, "Education and Training," 150.

89. Barron, "Education and Training," 150–53; Barron, "Expansion of Education," 244–45.

90. Quoted in Chambers and Daunt, *Book of London English*, 139.

91. Fisher, "Language Policy," 1172.

92. Thrupp, *Merchant Class*, 6, 35. See also Unwin, *Gilds and Companies*, 77.

93. Dobson, *Peasants' Revolt*, 226–28.

94. Gabel, "Term *Clericus*," esp. 76–77, 81. See also Zieman, *Singing the New Song*, 53–62.

95. Gabel, *Benefit of Clergy*, 81.

96. Kaeuper, "Two Early Lists," 365. Zieman, *Singing the New Song*, 49–62, offers a rich explanation of the term *litteratus*.

97. Kaeuper, "Two Early Lists."

98. Thrupp, *Merchant Class*, 156–58. Cf. Moran, *Growth of English Schooling*, 20, 172.

99. Cavanaugh, "Study of Books," 12, 781. Regarding the contents of the "Clensyngsyne," see Hanna, *London Literature*, 14–15.

100. Cavanaugh, "Study of Books," 670, 196–97. See also Hanna, *London Literature*, 12. On *The Mirror*, see 7–8.

101. Moran, *Education and Learning*, 35.

102. Swanson, *Medieval Artisans*, 164.

103. Cavanaugh, "Study of Books," 649.

104. Ibid., 12, 158; Allison, *County of York*, 57–62.

105. Furnivall, *Fifty Earliest English Wills*, 100–103; Cavanaugh, "Study of Books," 288.

106. See, for example, Cavanaugh, "Study of Books," 2–3, 8–17; and Moran, "Literacy and Education," 9.

107. On the inventories of these guilds, see Smith, *English Gilds*, 6–13. On these three parish fraternities, see Barron, "Parish Fraternities," 30–31.

108. Sponsler, "London's Public Culture," 20–21; Lancashire, *London Civic Theatre*, 123–24. Regarding the tapestry, see Floyd, "Steyned Halle."

109. Parkes, "Literacy of the Laity."

110. Edwards and Pearsall, "Major English Poetic Texts," 257; Horobin, "Professionalization of Writing," 57. See also Doyle and Parkes, "Production of Copies," 198.

111. Christianson, "Evidence for the Study," 89.

112. Doyle and Parkes, "Production of Copies," 198; Christianson, "Community of Book Artisans," 207, 212; Christianson, "London's Book-Trade," 128. See also Mooney, "Locating Scribal Activity."

113. Edwards and Pearsall, "Major English Poetic Texts," 258.

114. Bell, "Price of Books," 313. Cf. Doyle, "English Provincial Book Trade," 19–20.

115. Friedman, "Books, Owners, and Makers," 112.

116. Mooney, "Locating Scribal Activity." See also Horobin, "Professionalization of Writing."

117. Parkes, "Literacy of the Laity," 564.

118. Cavanaugh, "Study of Books," 13.

119. Thrupp, *Merchant Class*, 162.

120. Barron, "Expansion of Education," 240–41.

121. Cavanaugh, "Study of Books," 12–13, 15–16.

122. Christianson, "Manuscript-Book Trade," 155.

123. Bell, "Price of Books," 330–31.

124. Christianson, "Manuscript-Book Trade," 155.

125. Cavanaugh, "Study of Books," 12, 210; Hanna, *London Literature*, 12–13; Thrupp, *Merchant Class*, 162.

126. Orme, *Education and Society*, 73.

127. Pollard, "English Market," 10; Harris, "Patrons, Buyers, and Owners," 172–83; Christianson, "Manuscript-Book Trade," 148–50; Christianson, "London's Book-Trade," 133.

128. Bell, "Price of Books," 331.

129. On booklets and pamphlets in the second half of the fifteenth century, see Boffey and Thompson, "Anthologies and Miscellanies." See also Meale, "Patrons, Buyers, and Owners," 217, 234–35, 235–36n96; and Christianson, "Manuscript-Book Trade," 156.

130. Knoop and Jones, *Mediaeval Mason*, 85–100.

131. Thrupp, *Merchant Class*, 113.

132. Rosser, "Workers' Associations," 299. Kowaleski explains that *unskilled* workers in late fourteenth-century London made 4d. to 5d. per day (*Medieval Towns*, 371).

133. See Dyer, *Standards of Living*, 188–210; and Swanson, *Medieval Artisans*, 150–71.

134. Barr, "Minster Library," 494–96.

135. Orme, "Schools and School-Books," 454.

136. Barr, "Minster Library," 494. See also Friedman, "Books, Owners, and Makers," 118.

137. Moran, *Education and Learning*, 30; Moran, *Growth of English Schooling*, 210; Kisby, "London Parish Churches," 306–13.

138. Gee, "Parochial Libraries," 219.

139. Barron, "Education and Training," 152.

140. Barron, *Medieval Guildhall*, 33–34.

141. Rye, *Students' Guide*, 11.

142. Regarding these bequests, see Arundel, *Register*, 1, fols. 256–57r. On the relation among the institutions, see Hines, Cohen, and Roffey, "*Iohannes Gower*," 30–31.

143. In empiricist terms, little is known of the ownership of early *Confessio* manuscripts. Of the cases discussed in Harris's "Ownership and Readership," the Cambridge, Gonville, and Caius MS 176/97 is the earliest extant manuscript—whose provenance is known—that contains excerpts from the *Confessio* and that was owned by members of the upper strata of nonruling urban classes. London's Barber-Surgeons, a lesser guild, owned this manuscript, into which portions of the *Confessio* were added circa 1475 (30). See also Voigts and McVaugh, *Latin Technical Phlebotomy*, 32.

144. Moran, *Growth of English Schooling*, 211.

145. Examples of women book artisans include bookbinders Alice Drax and Dionisia le Bokebyndere; apprentice limner Joan Boefe (Christianson, "Community of Book Artisans," 213; Christianson, "Manuscript-Book Trade," 151; Christianson, *Directory of London Stationers*, 69, 99); illuminators Joan Lymner, Alice Le Lumenur, Agnes la Luminor, and Matilda Lumynour (Michael, "English Illuminators," 83, 86, 88, 94); and scrivener Petronilla (Veale, "Matilda Penne, Skinner," 49).

146. Christianson, "Community of Book Artisans," 210–11.

147. Some of the numerous examples involve the following men listed in Christianson's *Directory of London Stationers*: Robert Blakemore, 69; John Carswell, 84; Roger Cole, 90–91; John Corby, 94–95; John Donce, 99; Roger Dunce, 99–100; Nicholas Holford, 117–18; Thomas Housewyfe, 121; Thomas Kellow, 125; Thomas Lesyngham, 127–28; John Roulande, 154; and Richard Waltham, 170–71.

148. Christianson, "Manuscript-Book Trade," 151–53.

149. Aston, *Lollards and Reformers*, 199–206.

150. S. Justice, *Writing and Rebellion*, 33.

151. Coleman, *Public Reading*; Coleman, "Aurality." See also Clanchy, *Written Record*, 268–78.

152. Coleman, *Public Reading*, esp. xii–xiii, 185–88; Coleman, "Lay Readers," esp. 217–19; Minnis, *Magister Amoris*, 299–300. See also Emmerson, "Reading Gower," 171–78.

153. Coleman, "Lay Readers," 235.

154. Coleman, "Aurality," 71.

155. Strohm, "Social and Literary Scene," 13.

156. Echard, "Pre-Texts," 270, 283n1.

157. Sargent, "Numbers," 206; Pearsall, "Manuscripts and Illustrations," 80.

158. Doyle "English Books," 171.

159. Kerby-Fulton and Justice, "Langlandian Reading Circles," 74.

160. Althusser, "Ideological State Apparatuses."

CHAPTER 2

1. Dyer, "Work Ethics," 36–37.

2. Friedman, "Books, Owners, and Makers," 112.

3. Meale, "Patrons, Buyers, and Owners," 218.

4. Middleton, "Chaucer's 'New Men,'" 16–17, 30.

5. The Man of Law refers to two tales (those of Apollonius and Canace) and narrates a third from the *Confessio*; he and Gower share striped garments and apparent occupations; his

description as a "purchasour" (1.318) recalls the *Mirour de l'Omme*'s discussion of lawyers' wealth and possibly Gower's suspect land acquisition in the Septvauns scandal; the Man of Law praises merchants and is intensely interested in mercantilism, while Gower is understood to have invested in the wool trade; and, like the *Confessio* but unlike the *Canterbury Tales*, the *Man of Law's Tale* contains an unusually large number of glosses, attributed to the author. On Gower's striped garments, associations with law, mercantilism, and Septvauns affair, see Fisher, *John Gower*, 51–58; see also Giancarlo, "Property, Purchase, and Parliament." Regarding the Man of Law's mercantilism, see Dinshaw, "Law of Man"; and Ladd, "Mercantile (Mis)reader." On glosses in the *Man of Law's Tale*, see Caie, "Thrifty Tale."

6. All quotations of Chaucer's poetry are from *The Riverside Chaucer*.

7. E. Allen, "Chaucer Answers Gower," 647.

8. On the Man of Law's errors, see Eberle, *Riverside Chaucer*, 854–56; and Caie, "Thrifty Tale."

9. See Eberle, *Riverside Chaucer*, 856; and Caie, "Thrifty Tale," 57.

10. Bourdieu, *Distinction*.

11. Bourdieu and Passeron, *Inheritors*, esp. 1–27, 67–76.

12. Williams, *Marxism and Literature*, 115–17.

13. I deliberately borrow Gramsci's language, whose *Prison Notebooks* influence my discussion of ideological address.

14. Copeland, *Rhetoric, Hermeneutics, and Translation*, 179; Minnis, "*De Vulgari Auctoritate*," 54; Minnis, "Authors in Love," 162–63, 165, 172–73; Echard, "With Carmen's Help," 10–13; Echard, "Glossing Gower," 238.

15. Breen has recently published a study, *Imagining an English Reading Public*, which utilizes Bourdieu's concept of *habitus*, arguing that the habitus of Latin grammar and clerical culture inflected late medieval English grammar and select English-language writings. Breen's study and mine differ greatly, however, in that Breen is interested primarily in a habitus aligned with Christianity and because Breen discusses neither cultural capital nor Gower.

16. Many Gowerians, such as Schmitz in "Classics," have discussed Ovid's influence.

17. Simpson, *Sciences and the Self*.

18. Weatherbee, "Latin Structure"; Weatherbee, "Classical and Boethian Tradition."

19. Fanger, "Metaphysics of Gender"; Olsson, "Reading, Transgression, and Judgment."

20. Porter, "Gower's Ethical Microcosm"; Schmitz, "Classics"; Mitchell, *Ethics and Exemplary Narrative*, 22–35.

21. Schlauch, "*Man of Law's Tale*"; Correale, "Gower's Source Manuscript."

22. On the penitential tradition, see Kinneavy, "Penitentials." On *Handlyng Synne*, see McNally, "Exemplum."

23. On the influence of Jean de Meun, Guillaume de Lorris, Guillaume de Machaut, and Jean Froissart on the figure of Amans, see Butterfield, "French Tradition," 172–80. Regarding the *Confessio*'s debt to *Le Roman de la Rose*, see Dean, "Gather Ye Rosebuds." On Dante's influence, see Olsson, "Aspects of *Gentilesse*," 226, 238–42, 244.

24. For an annotated bibliography of source studies, see Yeager, *John Gower Materials*, 54–72.

25. The text reads "Sortes." In Gower, *Confessio Amantis*, 2000, 1:347–48, note for line 2718, Peck conjectures that "Sortes" refers to Socrates.

26. All quotations from the Ricardian version are indicated by asterisks after line numbers.

27. These statistics are from Echard, "Last Words," 100.

28. On allusions in the conversion scene to the *Legend*, see Coleman, "King Richardes Sake," esp. 108–14.

29. The Ricardian reads, "A bok for king Richardes sake" (Prol.24*).

30. See Pearsall, "Gower Tradition," regarding Gower scholars' reinscription of the moniker "moral Gower." For critiques of this epithet, see Watt, *Amoral Gower*; and Aers, "Reflections on Gower."

31. Kinneavy, "Penitentials" and McNally, "*Exemplum*," demonstrate the *Confessio*'s resemblance to penitential guides.

32. For discussions of Gower's claims men must turn to God, see Peck, *Kingship and Common Profit*, 3–4, 14.

33. Bourdieu, *Distinction*, 7.

34. Bourdieu, *State Nobility*, 108.

35. Bourdieu, *Language and Symbolic Power*, 117–21; Bourdieu, *State Nobility*, 102–3, 108.

36. In "Fear of Flying" Davis also understands Amans to be engaged in a rite of passage, but she understands the rite of passage dramatically differently. Using Victor and Edith Turner's scholarship, Davis focuses on Amans's masculinity and sexuality.

37. Meecham-Jones, "Prologue," 22.

38. Pearsall, "Gower's Latin," 14.

39. Meecham-Jones, "Prologue," 27–28.

40. White, *Nature, Sex, and Goodness*, 206.

41. Bourdieu and Passeron, *Inheritors*, 20–21, 28, 69–76; Bourdieu, *Distinction*, 3, 68, 72, 88, 330.

42. Kurath, Kuhn, and Lewis, *Middle English Dictionary*, pt. G, 283–88.

43. This is one reason why Amans is not the Augustinian sinner who, through contemplative labor, prepares his soul to receive grace. Also, my interpretation of Amans's transformation is incompatible with Augustine's understanding of grace, because, like other fathers of the church, Augustine believed in the universality of the offer of grace. By contrast, I argue that the *Confessio* offers grace only to a select few.

44. Pearsall, "Gower's Latin," 20.

45. Enlightenment is a male privilege in the *Confessio*. While associated with a woman, Amans is the furthest from reason. Only upon renouncing her can he achieve enlightenment.

46. Bourdieu, *Language and Symbolic Power*, 122.

47. Bourdieu and Passeron, *Inheritors*, 22.

48. Bourdieu, *Distinction*, 447, explains that secondary schools, by slightly initiating its pupils into legitimate culture and its values, introduce a break with the popular worldview.

49. Bourdieu, *Language and Symbolic Power*, 122; Bourdieu, *State Nobility*, 103–4.

50. Peck, *Kingship and Common Profit*.

51. Gower, *Confessio Amantis*, 2000, 279.

52. Aers, "Third Estate," 345.

53. Echard, "With Carmen's Help," 11–13.

54. Pearsall, "Gower's Latin," 13.

55. Echard, "With Carmen's Help," 16–17.

56. Pearsall, "Gower's Latin," 14.

57. Echard, "With Carmen's Help," 17–20; see also 21–25. The apparent disparity between the number of *Confessio* manuscripts with Latin (i.e., forty-three versus forty-four) is Echard's.

58. Almost all Gower scholars believe Gower wrote the glosses. Examples include Butterfield, "French Tradition," 81; Echard, "With Carmen's Help," 4, 13; and Yeager, "Text as 'Other,'" 262.

59. Minnis, *Medieval Theory of Authorship*, xii.

60. Butterfield, "French Tradition," 94.

61. Cf. Minnis, *Medieval Theory of Authorship*, 190; Pearsall, "Gower's Latin," 14, 81; Echard, "With Carmen's Help," 5, 9, 29, 39; and Weatherbee, "Latin Structure," 7, 9.

62. Meecham-Jones, "Prologue," 19.

63. See Bourdieu and Passeron, *Inheritors*, 63 and 70, regarding how working-class students adopt the essentialism of the upper classes and experience disadvantage as their predestined failure.

64. Bourdieu, *Distinction*, 399, 409–14, 443–44, 453.

65. Loomba, "Post-Colonial English Studies," 19.

66. Bourdieu remarks that the petit bourgeois typically possess an avid but anxious way of clutching at legitimate culture; legitimate culture is not made for them and is often made against them, and they are not made for it (*Distinction*, 327).

CHAPTER 3

1. On disparities between Gower's rendition of Nebuchadnezzar's dream and the biblical account, see Watt, *Amoral Gower*, 107–9; and Dean, *World Grown Old*, 257.

2. For translations of the colophons, see Fisher, *John Gower*, 88–91.

3. Echard, "Designs for Reading," 65n23; Griffiths, "*Confessio Amantis*," 177; Emmerson, "Reading Gower."

4. Peck, *Kingship and Common Profit*, 3–4; Dean, "Time Past and Present," 407.

5. Regarding the ages man motif in Nebuchadnezzar's dream, see Nitzsche, *Genius Figure*, 126–27; Dean, "Time Past and Present," 401–2, 407; and Watt, *Amoral Gower*, 108.

6. Fisher, *John Gower*, 185–87.

7. Examples include McKisack, *Fourteenth Century*, 422; Postan, *Medieval Economy and Society*, 154; and Dobson, *Peasants' Revolt*.

8. Peck discusses the apocalyptic tone ("Book of Daniel," 159–60, 173–75).

9. Fisher, *John Gower*, 186–87.

10. See Hall, *Hard Road to Renewal*, 129–49, for a discussion of how Thatcherism helped generate a sense of national crisis and thereby encouraged the populace to call for repressive rule.

11. Froissart, *Chroniques de J. Froissart*, 129–31; Knighton, *Knighton's Chronicle*, 240–41; Walsingham, *Historia Anglicana*, 13–22.

12. Dobson, *Peasants' Revolt*, 303–4.

13. The concept of a "change of course" is indebted to Chomsky, *Culture of Terrorism*.

14. Benjamin, "Philosophy of History," 260.

15. As Macaulay points out, Emperor Leo died the year before Charlemagne was born (Gower, *English Works*, 1:464, note for line 745).

16. As additional proof of this synecdochical relation, one could consider Watt's point that Nebuchadnezzar's statue can be read in terms of the king's two bodies (*Amoral Gower*, 110).

17. In *The German Ideology*, Karl Marx and Frederick Engels write, "civil society is the true source and theatre of all history, and how absurd is the conception of history held hitherto, which neglects the real relationships and confines itself to high-sounding dramas of princes and states" (57).

18. In book 3, chapter 10, of *The Republic*, Plato disassociates caste and family from metal.

19. Gower, *Confessio Amantis*, 1980 and 2000.

20. Dyer, "Work Ethics," 30.

21. Walsingham, *Historia Anglicana*, 321.

22. See Gramsci, "Modern Prince"; Hall, "Popular-Democratic"; and Hall, "Gramsci and Us."

23. Similarly, no distinctions are made between the *types* of rule enjoyed by the emperors or kings of Persia, Babylon, Greece, Rome, and England. This lack of distinction reflects a larger pattern in the *Confessio*. Several Gower scholars argue that the *Confessio*, was written, in

part, as a handbook for princes. Examples include Ferster, "O Political Gower"; Ferster, *Fictions of Advice*, chap. 7; Porter, "Gower's Ethical Microcosm," 135–62; Coffman, "Mentor for Royalty"; Peck, *Kingship and Common Profit*, 139–59; and Fisher, *John Gower*, 180–85. For the *Confessio* to be a guide for Gower's monarchs, historical differences among various rulers within the text must be leveled to such a degree that the text could perceived to have been helpful to a late fourteenth-century English king.

24. Lukács, *History and Class Consciousness*, 48.

25. Watt, *Amoral Gower*, 108.

26. See especially the introduction and prologue of Peck's *Kingship and Common Profit*. On "common profit" as a rhetorical and political strategy in late medieval England, see Robertson, *Laborer's Two Bodies*, 78–118.

27. Fisher, *John Gower*, 183.

28. In *The World Grown Old*, Dean cites this line and remarks, "Gower is not specific about the nature of this diversity; it seems to be related linguistically but not conceptually to division" (258). Unfortunately, Dean does not explain his logic.

29. See Gower, *English Works*, 1:464, note for line 745.

30. Examples of claims about either type of division include Prol.889, 893, 896, 928, 966, 967, 971, 976, 980, 992, 996, 998, 1077.

31. Hilton, "Status and Class," 9.

32. Knight, "Voice of Labor," 107.

33. See Watt, *Amoral Gower*, regarding some of the complexities of gender and sexuality in the *Confessio*.

34. Coleman, "King Richardes Sake."

35. E. Allen, "Chaucer Answers Gower," 650n9.

36. A central premise of Carlson's *Chaucer's Jobs* is that much of Chaucer's poetry is myopically interested in love and insufficiency invested in social issues.

37. Dinshaw, *Chaucer's Sexual Poetics*, chap 2.

38. Kurath, Kuhn, and Lewis, *Middle English Dictionary*.

39. Examples include Kiser, *Telling Classical Tales*, 129–31; and Fyler, *Chaucer and Ovid*, 115.

CHAPTER 4

1. Hagedorn, *Abandoned Women*, 159.

2. Best-known examples include Hansen, "Antifeminist Narrator"; Kiser, *Telling Classical Tales*; P. Allen, "Reading Chaucer's Good Women"; Dinshaw, "English to Declare"; Delany, "Reading and Writing"; Delany, "Women, Nature, and Language"; Delany, *Naked Text*; and Simpson, "Ethics and Interpretation."

3. Kiser, *Telling Classical Tales*, 71–94, esp. 71, 78; Delany, *Naked Text*, 102.

4. Hansen, "Antifeminist Narrator," esp. 12–13, 28–29.

5. Percival, *Chaucer's Legendary Good Women*, 299–323; McCormick, "Remembering the Game"; McDonald, "Chaucer's *Legend*"; McDonald, "Games Medieval Women Play."

6. Dinshaw, *Chaucer's Sexual Poetics*, esp. 67–68, 87.

7. R. Edwards points out that two versions of the F-Prologue—British Library Additional MS 9832, London, and Trinity College R.3.19, Cambridge—omit lines 332–33, replacing them with "[Thou] makest wise folk from me withdrawe, / That ben as trewe as ever was any steel" ("Ricardian Dreamwork," 66).

8. Simpson, "Ethics and Interpretation," 77–81.

9. Bloch, "Medieval Misogyny."

10. Several Chaucerians have noted this shift, including R. Edwards, "Ricardian Dreamwork," 70–73.

11. Simpson claims that Cupid provokes female suffering ("Ethics and Interpretation," 91).

12. Regarding key premises in attempts to assign chronologies, see Delany, *Naked Text*, 34–43.

13. Percival, *Chaucer's Legendary Good Women*, 130.

14. On this homage, see Hagedorn, *Abandoned Women*, 172–73.

15. Ovid is mentioned in lines 1367, 1465, 1678, 2220, while Guido delle Colonne is mentioned in line 1464.

16. For studies of the well-documented sources of Froissart, Machaut, and Deschamps for the *Legend*, see Palmer, "Chaucer's *Legend*"; Coleman, "Philippa of Lancaster"; and Meecham-Jones, "Myn Erthly God"; for Livy and Vincent de Beauvais, see Phillips, "Register," 114; for Boccaccio, see D. Wallace, *Chaucerian Polity*, 337–78.

17. Percival, *Chaucer's Legendary Good Women*, 13.

18. Phillips identifies "Valerye" as Valerius Maximus's *Facta et dicta memorabilia* ("Register," 114).

19. McCormick, "Remembering the Game," 112–15; Percival, *Chaucer's Legendary Good Women*, 13, 17, 146.

20. Noting the repetition of a single narrative, Dinshaw compares the tales to saints' lives (*Chaucer's Sexual Poetics*, 86).

21. Sawhney, "Joke and the Hoax," 214.

22. M. Wallace, "Negative/Positive Images." McCormick's understanding of *La Querelle des Femmes* provides an example, since, she argues, although a writer could adopt a "profeminist" stance, an "antifeminist" stance, or both, the terms of the debate were stable, and even a "profeminist" text had to address the "antifeminist" counterarguments, rather than basing itself on a separate foundation ("Remembering the Game," 114).

23. Percival, *Chaucer's Legendary Good Women*, 4, 10, 108.

24. On connections between Alceste and Queen Anne, see A. Taylor, "Anne of Bohemia."

25. On the narrator's feminization, see Hansen, *Fictions of Gender*, 8–10; and Simpson, "Ethics and Interpretation," 87–88.

26. Callaghan, "Vicar and Virago," 197.

27. Sawhney, "Joke and the Hoax," 210.

28. Delany, *Medieval Literary Politics*, 113–14.

29. Hansen, *Fictions of Gender*, 3–10.

30. On the curricula in late medieval grammar schools, see Orme, *English Schools*, 68–74, 102–6; and Orme, *Education and Society*, 65–69.

31. Chaucer's work of pleasing patrons is a foundational concern of Carlson, *Chaucer's Jobs*.

32. In *The German Ideology*, Marx and Engels write, "civil society is the true source and theatre of all history, and how absurd is the conception of history held hitherto, which neglects the real relationships and confines itself to high-sounding dramas of princes and states" (57).

33. Antagonists also lack mothers. Absent mothers are not uncommon in early British literature; witness Shakespearean plays.

34. Delany, *Naked Text*, 202.

35. Hansen, *Fictions of Gender*, 1; Hansen, "Antifeminist Narrator," 26.

36. Hansen, "Antifeminist Narrator," 17.

37. Baswell maintains that Chaucer used Ovid and Virgil equally as sources for the "Legend of Dido," borrowing Virgil's tone and Ovid's plot (*Virgil in Medieval England*, 256–57).

38. Lucrece and Hypermnestra are exceptions. On the heroines' credulity, see Hansen, "Antifeminist Narrator," 24–27.

39. Delany, *Naked Text*, 9–10; Strohm, *Social Chaucer*, 164–66; Carlson, *Chaucer's Jobs*.

40. Carlson, *Chaucer's Jobs*, 35–36, 44; see also 54.

41. In *Chaucer and the Subject of History*, Patterson observes, "it is as the great champion of the individual that Chaucer has displaced his rivals (like Gower and, especially, Langland—both of whom haunt the *Canterbury Tales* as rejected possibilities) in order to established [*sic*] himself as the Father of English poetry" (246). On Chaucer's promotion of individualism, see Patterson, "No Man," 125, 149–55.

42. Percival, *Chaucer's Legendary Good Women*, 130–48; Fumo, "God of Love," esp. 159; Meecham-Jones, "Intention, Integrity, and 'Renoun.'"

43. Simpson, "Ethics and Interpretation."

44. Percival, *Chaucer's Legendary Good Women*, 130–40.

45. Kurath, Kuhn, and Lewis, *Middle English Dictionary*, 3:210.

46. This logic is influenced by Messer-Davidow, "Constructing Sex Discrimination."

47. Bramen, "Minority Hiring," 114–16.

48. Messer-Davidow, "Constructing Sex Discrimination," 60–61.

49. Eagleton, *Literary Theory*, 12.

50. For a particularly striking example, see Hansen, "Antifeminist Narrator," 28. See also Kiser, *Telling Classical Tales*, 79–80.

51. Jardine, "Why Should He?" esp. 133–44.

52. Gramsci, *Prison Notebooks*; Hall, *Hard Road to Renewal*.

CHAPTER 5

1. Delany, *Naked Text*, 43–59, 123; Percival, *Chaucer's Legendary Good Women*, 62–69; P. Allen, "Reading Chaucer's Good Women," 421–22.

2. Delany, *Naked Text*, 43; see also 43–59.

3. Examples include P. Allen, "Reading Chaucer's Good Women," esp. 421–22; Percival, *Chaucer's Legendary Good Women*, 62–63; Delany, *Naked Text*, 44–45; R. Edwards, "Ricardian Dreamwork," 69–70; and McCormick, "Remembering the Game," 122.

4. P. Allen, "Reading Chaucer's Good Women," 422.

5. Delany, *Naked Text*, 216.

6. Cf. Shoaf, *Chaucer's Body*, 1–3.

7. Kiser, *Telling Classical Tales*, 77. Cf. Percival, *Chaucer's Legendary Good Women*, 133–34.

8. See Delany, *Naked Text*, 224, for some possible readings.

9. McCormick, "Remembering the Game," 110, 129–30.

10. Percival, esp. "Legend as Courtly Game"; Percival, introduction to *Chaucer's Legendary Good Women*; McCormick, "Remembering the Game."

11. Alcoff, "Speaking for Others," 100–101.

12. Ibid., 105–16.

13. Elam, "Speak for Yourself," 233.

CONCLUSION

1. Olsson remarks that one of Gower's claims to be among important fourteenth-century English poets lies in the vast knowledge his three encyclopedic poems "made available to his public" (*Structures of Conversion*, 1).

2. On Chaucer's promotion of individualism, see Patterson, *Subject of History*, 3–13, 32, 246, 283, 337–38, 422–25; and Patterson, "No Man," 125, 150–51.

3. Patterson, *Subject of History*, 246.

4. Percival, *Chaucer's Legendary Good Women*, 141–42; Kobayashi, "Voice of an Exile."

5. Kiser, *Telling Classical Tales*, 131.

6. Fyler, *Chaucer and Ovid*, 115.

7. Wiegman, "What Ails Feminist Criticism?" 377.

8. On such casualness, see Bourdieu and Passeron, *Inheritors*, 19–21; see also Bourdieu, *Distinction*, 33.

9. For a discussion of Chaucer's anxiety of influence regarding Langland, his more politicized predecessor, see Bowers, *Chaucer and Langland*.

10. Examples include Strohm, *Social Chaucer*, 164–66; Strohm, "Social and Literary Scene," 14; Patterson, "No Man," 146–55; and Phillips, "Register," 101.

11. Delany, *Naked Text*, 9–10.

12. Watt, *Amoral Gower*, xi.

13. Gower, *Complete Works*; Dimmick, "Gower's Effortful *Otium*."

14. Regarding the Septvauns affair, see Fisher, *John Gower*, 51–54; and Giancarlo, "Property, Purchase, and Parliament." Regarding Gower's living arrangements at the priory, see R. Allen, "John Gower and Southwark," 111–14.

15. Fisher, *John Gower*, 65; Hines, Cohen, and Roffey, "*Iohannes Gower*," 26–27; Peck, *Confessio*, 1:62.

16. The image appears in the Ellesmere manuscript of the *Canterbury Tales* (Henry E. Huntington Library, MS EL 26. C. 9 fol. 153v, San Marino, California). Examples of front covers of books featuring this image include Carlson, *Chaucer's Jobs*; Shoaf, *Chaucer's Body*; Howard, *Canterbury Tales*; and Rowland, *Companion to Chaucer Studies*.

17. Pearsall, *Life of Geoffrey Chaucer*, 278.

18. Chaucer, *Treatise on the Astrolabe*, line 1. For a range of positions on the Chaumpaigne case, cf. Delany, *Medieval Literary Politics*, 128; Pearsall, *Life of Geoffrey Chaucer*, 135–38; and Cannon, "Chaucer and Rape," 266.

19. Edelman, *No Future*.

20. Walsingham, *Historia Anglicana*, 18; translation mine.

21. Robertson, *Laborer's Two Bodies*, 51–58.

Adamson, John William. *The Illiterate Anglo-Saxon and Other Essays on Education, Medieval and Modern.* Cambridge: Cambridge University Press, 1946.

Aers, David. "Reflections on Gower as '*Sapiens* in Ethics and Politics.'" In *Faith, Ethics, and Church: Writing in England, 1360–1409*, 102–18. Cambridge, U.K.: Brewer, 2000. Reprinted in Yeager, *Re-visioning Gower*, 185–201.

———. "Representations of the 'Third Estate': Social Conflict and Its Milieu Around 1381." *Southern Review* 16, no. 3 (1983): 335–49.

Alcoff, Linda Martín. "The Problem of Speaking for Others." In Roof and Wiegman, *Who Can Speak?*, 97–119.

⚡ Allen, Elizabeth. "Chaucer Answers Gower: Constance and the Trouble with Reading." *ELH* 64, no. 3 (1997): 627–55.

Allen, Peter L. "Reading Chaucer's Good Women." *Chaucer Review* 21, no. 4 (1987): 419–34.

Allen, Rosamund S. "John Gower and Southwark: The Paradox of the Social Self." In *London and Europe in the Later Middle Ages*, edited by Julia Boffey and Pamela M. King, 111–47. London: Centre for Medieval and Renaissance Studies, Queen Mary and Westfield College, University of London, 1995.

Allison, Keith John, ed. *A History of the County of York, East Riding.* Vol. 6, *The Borough and Liberties of Beverley.* London: Oxford University Press, 1989.

Althusser, Louis. "Ideology and Ideological State Apparatuses (Notes Towards an Investigation)." In *Lenin and Philosophy and Other Essays*, translated by Ben Brewster, 127–86. New York: Monthly Review Press, 1971.

Arundel, Thomas. *Register of Thomas Arundel*, 1. London: Lambeth Palace Library.

Askins, William. Review of *Chaucer's Jobs*, by David Carlson. *Speculum* 83, no. 1 (2008): 182–84.

Aston, Margaret. *Lollards and Reformers: Images and Literacy in Late Medieval Religion.* London: Hambledon Press, 1984.

Barr, C. B. L. "The Minster Library." In *A History of York Minster*, edited by G. E. Aylmer and Reginald Cant, 487–538. Oxford: Clarendon Press, 1977.

Barron, Caroline M. "The Education and Training of Girls in Fifteenth-Century London." In *Courts, Counties, and the Capital in the Later Middle Ages*, edited by Diana E. S. Dunn, 139–53. New York: St. Martin's Press, 1996.

———. "The Expansion of Education in Fifteenth-Century London." In *The Cloister and the World: Essays in Medieval History in Honour of Barbara Harvey*, edited by John Blair and Brian Golding, 219–45. Oxford: Clarendon Press, 1996.

———. *London in the Later Middle Ages: Government and People, 1200–1500.* Oxford: Oxford University Press, 2004.

———. *The Medieval Guildhall of London.* London: Corporation of London, 1974.

———. "The Parish Fraternities of Medieval London." In *The Church in Pre-Reformation Society: Essays in Honour of F. R. H. Du Boulay*, edited by Caroline M. Barron and Christopher Harper-Bill, 13–37. Woodbridge, U.K.: Boydell, 1985.

———. "Ralph Holland and the London Radicals, 1438–1444." In *The Medieval Town: A Reader in English Urban History, 1200–1540*, edited by Richard Holt and Gervase Rosser, 160–83. London: Longman, 1990.

———. "Richard II and London." In *Richard II: The Art of Kingship*, edited by Anthony Goodman and James L. Gillespie, 129–54. Oxford: Clarendon Press, 1999.

———. "The Widow's World in Later Medieval London." In *Medieval London Widows, 1300–1500*, edited by Caroline M. Barron and Anne F. Sutton, xiii–xxxiv. London: Hambledon Press, 1994.

Baswell, Christopher. *Virgil in Medieval England: Figuring the Aeneid from the Twelfth Century to Chaucer*. Cambridge: Cambridge University Press, 1995.

Bell, H. E. "The Price of Books in Medieval England." *Library*, 4th ser., 17, no. 3 (1936): 312–32.

Benjamin, Walter. "Theses on the Philosophy of History." In *Illuminations*, edited by Hannah Arendt and translated by Harry Zohn, 253–64. New York: Schocken Books, 1968.

Benson, C. David. *Public "Piers Plowman": Modern Scholarship and Late Medieval English Culture*. University Park: Pennsylvania State University Press, 2004.

Bloch, Howard R. "Medieval Misogyny." *Representations* 20 (Autumn 1987): 1–24.

Boffey, Julia, and John J. Thompson. "Anthologies and Miscellanies: Production and Choice of Texts." In Griffiths and Pearsall, *Book Production*, 279–315.

Bolton, J. L. *The Medieval English Economy, 1150–1500*. London: Dent and Sons, 1980.

Bothwell, James, P. J. P. Goldberg, and W. M. Ormrod, eds. *The Problem of Labour in Fourteenth-Century England*. York: York Medieval Press; Woodbridge, U.K.: Boydell and Brewer, 2000.

Bourdieu, Pierre. *Distinction: A Social Critique of the Judgement of Taste*. Translated by Richard Nice. Cambridge: Harvard University Press, 1984.

———. *Language and Symbolic Power*. Edited by John B. Thompson. Translated by Gino Raymond and Matthew Adamson. Cambridge: Harvard University Press, 1991.

———. *The State Nobility: Elite Schools in the Field of Power*. Translated by Lauretta C. Clough. Stanford: Stanford University Press, 1996.

Bourdieu, Pierre, and Jean-Claude Passeron. *The Inheritors: French Students and Their Relation to Culture*. Translated by Richard Nice. Chicago: University of Chicago Press, 1979.

Bowers, John M. *Chaucer and Langland: The Antagonistic Tradition*. Notre Dame: University of Notre Dame Press, 2007.

———. "Introduction: The Antagonistic Tradition." In *Chaucer and Langland*, 1–42.

Bramen, Carrie Tirado. "Minority Hiring in the Age of Downsizing." In *Power, Race, and Gender in Academe: Strangers in the Tower?*, edited by Shirley Geok-Lin Lim and María Herrera-Sobek, 112–31. New York: Modern Language Association, 2000.

Breen, Katherine. *Imagining an English Reading Public, 1150–1400*. Cambridge: Cambridge University Press, 2010.

Butcher, A. F. "English Urban Society and the Revolt of 1381." In *The English Rising of 1381*, edited by R. H. Hilton and T. H. Aston, 84–111. Cambridge: Cambridge University Press, 1984.

Butterfield, Ardis. "*Confessio Amantis* and the French Tradition." In Echard, *Companion to Gower*, 165–80.

———. *The Familiar Enemy: Chaucer, Language, and Nation in the Hundred Years War*. Oxford: Oxford University Press, 2009.

Caie, Graham D. "'This Was a Thrifty Tale for the Nones': Chaucer's Man of Law." In *Chaucer in Perspective: Middle English Essays in Honour of Norman Blake*, edited by Geoffrey Lester, 47–60. Sheffield: Sheffield Academic Press, 1999.

Callaghan, Dympna. "The Vicar and Virago: Feminism and the Problem of Identity." In Roof and Wiegman, *Who Can Speak?*, 195–207.

Cannon, Christopher. "Chaucer and Rape: Uncertainty's Certainties." In *Representing Rape in Medieval and Early Modern Literature*, edited by Elizabeth Robertson and Christine M. Rose, 255–79. New York: Palgrave Macmillan, 2001.

Carlin, Martha. *Medieval Southwark*. London: Hambledon Press, 1996.

Carlson, David R. *Chaucer's Jobs*. New York: Palgrave Macmillan, 2004.

———. "Gower's Beast Allegories in the 1381 *Visio Anglie*." *Philological Quarterly* 87, nos. 3–4 (2008): 257–75.

Cavanaugh, Susan H. "A Study of Books Privately Owned in England, 1300–1450." PhD diss., University of Pennsylvania, 1980.

Chambers, R. W., and Marjorie Daunt, eds. *A Book of London English, 1384–1425*. Oxford: Clarendon Press, 1967.

Chaucer, Geoffrey. *The Riverside Chaucer*. Edited by Larry D. Benson. 3rd ed. Boston: Houghton Mifflin, 1987.

Chomsky, Noam. *The Culture of Terrorism*. Boston: South End Press, 1988.

Christianson, C. Paul. "A Century of the Manuscript-Book Trade in Late Medieval London." *Medievalia et Humanistica*, n.s., 12 (1984): 143–65.

———. "A Community of Book Artisans in Chaucer's London." *Viator* 20 (1989): 207–18.

———. *A Directory of London Stationers and Book Artisans, 1300–1500*. New York: Bibliographical Society of America, 1990.

———. "Evidence for the Study of London's Late Medieval Manuscript-Book Trade." In Griffiths and Pearsall, *Book Production*, 87–108.

———. "The Rise of London's Book-Trade." In Hellinga and Trapp, *Cambridge History*, 128–47.

Clanchy, M. T. *From Memory to the Written Record: England, 1066–1307*. Oxford: Blackwell, 1993.

Clough, Cecil H., ed. *Profession, Vocation, and Culture in Later Medieval England: Essays Dedicated to the Memory of A. R. Myers*. Liverpool: Liverpool University Press, 1982.

Coffman, George R. "John Gower, Mentor for Royalty: Richard II." *PMLA* 69, no. 4 (1954): 953–64.

Coleman, Joyce. "Aurality." In *Middle English*, edited by Paul Strohm, 68–85. Oxford: Oxford University Press, 2007.

———. "'A Bok for King Richardes Sake': Royal Patronage, the *Confessio*, and the *Legend of Good Women*." In *On John Gower: Essays at the Millennium*, edited by R. F. Yeager, 104–23. Kalamazoo: Medieval Institute, 2007.

———. "The Flower, the Leaf, and Philippa of Lancaster." In Collette, *"Legend of Good Women,"* 33–58.

———. "Lay Readers and Hard Latin: How Gower May Have Intended the *Confessio Amantis* to Be Read." *Studies in the Age of Chaucer* 24 (2002): 209–35.

———. *Public Reading and the Reading Public in Late Medieval England and France*. Cambridge: Cambridge University Press, 1996.

Collette, Carolyn P., ed. *The "Legend of Good Women": Context and Reception*. Cambridge, U.K.: Brewer, 2006.

Copeland, Rita. *Rhetoric, Hermeneutics, and Translation in the Middle Ages: Academic Traditions and Vernacular Texts*. Cambridge: Cambridge University Press, 1991.

Correale, Robert M. "Gower's Source Manuscript of Nicholas Trevet's *Les Cronicles*." In Yeager, *John Gower*, 133–57.

Crow, Martin M., and Clair C. Olson, eds. *Chaucer Life-Records*. Oxford: Clarendon Press, 1966.

Cullum, P. H. "Learning to Be a Man, Learning to Be a Priest in Late Medieval England." In *Learning and Literacy in Medieval England and Abroad*, edited by Sarah Rees Jones, 135–53. Turnhout, Belgium: Brepols, 2003.

Davis, Isabel. "John Gower's Fear of Flying: Transitional Masculinities in the *Confessio Amantis.*" In *Rites of Passage: Cultures of Transition in the Fourteenth Century*, edited by Nicola F. McDonald and W. M. Ormrod, 131–52. York: York Medieval Press; Woodbridge, U.K.: Boydell and Brewer, 2004.

Dean, James M. "Gather Ye Rosebuds: Gower's Comic Reply to Jean de Meun." In Yeager, *John Gower*, 21–37.

———. "Time Past and Present in Chaucer's Clerk's Tale and Gower's *Confessio Amantis.*" *ELH* 44, no. 3 (1977): 401–18.

———. *The World Grown Old in Later Medieval Literature.* Cambridge: Medieval Academy of America, 1997.

Delany, Sheila. *Medieval Literary Politics: Shapes of Ideology.* Manchester: Manchester University Press, 1990.

———. *The Naked Text: Chaucer's "Legend of Good Women."* Berkeley: University of California Press, 1994.

———. "Reading and Writing." In *Naked Text*, 13–69.

———. "Women, Nature, and Language." In *Naked Text*, 115–52.

Dimmick, Jeremy. "Gower's Effortful *Otium.*" Sixteenth International Congress of the New Chaucer Society, University of Wales, Swansea, U.K., July 18–22, 2008.

Dinshaw, Carolyn. *Chaucer's Sexual Poetics.* Madison: University of Wisconsin Press, 1989.

———. "The Law of Man and Its 'Abhomynacions.'" In *Chaucer's Sexual Poetics*, 88–112.

———. "'The Naked Text in English to Declare': The *Legend of Good Women.*" In *Chaucer's Sexual Poetics*, 65–87.

Dobson, R. B. "The Later Middle Ages, 1215–1500." In *A History of York Minster*, edited by G. E. Aylmer and Reginald Cant, 44–109. Oxford: Clarendon Press, 1977.

———, ed. *The Peasants' Revolt of 1381.* 2nd ed. London: Macmillan, 1983.

———. "The Risings in York, Beverley, and Scarborough, 1380–1381." In *The English Rising of 1381*, edited by R. H. Hilton and T. H. Aston, 112–42. Cambridge: Cambridge University Press, 1984.

Doyle, A. I. "English Books In and Out of Court from Edward III to Henry VII." In *English Court Culture in the Later Middle Ages*, edited by V. J. Scattergood and J. W. Sherborne, 163–81. London: Duckworth, 1983.

———. "The English Provincial Book Trade Before Printing." In *Six Centuries of the Provincial Book Trade in Britain*, edited by Peter Isaac, 13–29. Winchester: St. Paul's Bibliographies, 1990.

Doyle, A. I., and M. B. Parkes. "The Production of Copies of the *Canterbury Tales* and the *Confessio Amantis* in the Early Fifteenth Century." In *Medieval Scribes, Manuscripts, and Libraries: Essays Presented to N. R. Ker*, edited by M. B. Parkes and Andrew G. Watson, 163–210. London: Scolar Press, 1978.

Dyer, Christopher. "Late Medieval Society." In *Standards of Living*, 10–26.

———. *Standards of Living in the Later Middle Ages: Social Change in England, c. 1200–1520.* Cambridge: Cambridge University Press, 1989.

———. "Were There Any Capitalists in Fifteenth-Century England?" In *Enterprise and Individuals in Fifteenth-Century England*, edited by Jennifer Kermode, 1–24. Stroud, U.K.: Sutton, 1991.

———. "Work Ethics in the Fourteenth Century." In Bothwell, Goldberg, and Ormrod, *Problem of Labour*, 21–41.

Eagleton, Terry. *Literary Theory: An Introduction.* 2nd ed. Minneapolis: University of Minnesota Press, 1996.

Eberle, Patricia J. Explanatory notes to the *Introduction to the Man of Law's Tale* and to the *Man of Law's Prologue.* In *The Riverside Chaucer*, 3rd ed., edited by Larry D. Benson, 854–56. Boston: Houghton Mifflin, 1987.

Echard, Siân, ed. *A Companion to Gower.* Cambridge, U.K.: Brewer, 2004.

———. "Designs for Reading: Some Manuscripts of Gower's *Confessio Amantis.*" *Trivium* 31 (1999): 59–72.

———. "Glossing Gower: In Latin, in English, and *in Absentia*: The Case of Bodleian Ashmole 35." In Yeager, *Re-visioning Gower,* 237–56.

———. "Last Words: Latin at the End of the *Confessio Amantis.*" In *Interstices: Studies in Middle English and Anglo-Latin Texts in Honour of A. G. Rigg,* edited by Richard Firth Green and Linne R. Mooney, 99–121. Toronto: University of Toronto Press, 2004.

———. "Pre-Texts: Tables of Contents and the Reading of John Gower's *Confessio Amantis.*" *Medium Ævum* 66, no. 2 (1997): 270–87.

———. "With Carmen's Help: Latin Authorities in the *Confessio Amantis.*" *Studies in Philology* 95, no. 1 (1998): 1–40.

Edelman, Lee. *No Future: Queer Theory and the Death Drive.* Durham: Duke University Press, 2004.

Edwards, A. S. G. Review of *Chaucer's Jobs,* by David Carlson. *Journal of English and Germanic Philology* 106, no. 4 (2007): 540–42.

Edwards, A. S. G., and Derek Pearsall. "The Manuscripts of the Major English Poetic Texts." In Griffiths and Pearsall, *Book Production,* 257–78.

Edwards, Robert R. "Ricardian Dreamwork: Chaucer, Cupid, and Loyal Lovers." In Collette, *"Legend of Good Women,"* 59–82.

Elam, Diane. "Speak for Yourself." In Roof and Wiegman, *Who Can Speak?,* 231–37.

Emmerson, Richard K. "Reading Gower in a Manuscript Culture: Latin and English in Illustrated Manuscripts of the *Confessio Amantis.*" *Studies in the Age of Chaucer* 21 (1999): 143–86.

Fanger, Claire. "Magic and the Metaphysics of Gender in Gower's 'Tale of Circe and Ulysses.'" In Yeager, *Re-visioning Gower,* 203–19.

Ferster, Judith. *Fictions of Advice: The Literature and Politics of Counsel in Late Medieval England.* Philadelphia: University of Pennsylvania Press, 1996.

———. "O Political Gower." *Medievalia* 16 (1993 [for 1990]): 33–53.

Fisher, John H. *John Gower: Moral Philosopher and Friend of Chaucer.* New York: New York University Press, 1964.

———. "A Language Policy for Lancastrian England." *PMLA* 107, no. 5 (1992): 1168–80.

Fisher, John H., R. Wayne Hamm, Peter G. Beidler, and Robert F. Yeager. "John Gower." In *A Manual of the Writings in Middle English, 1050–1500,* vol. 7, edited by Albert E. Hartung, 2195–210. New Haven: Connecticut Academy of Arts and Sciences, 1986.

Floyd, Jennifer. "St. George and the 'Steyned Halle': Lydgate's Verse for the London Armourers." In *Lydgate Matters: Poetry and Material Culture in the Fifteenth Century,* edited by Lisa H. Cooper and Andrea Denny-Brown, 139–64. New York: Palgrave Macmillan, 2008.

Friedman, J. B. "Books, Owners, and Makers in Fifteenth-Century Yorkshire: The Evidence from Some Wills and Extant Manuscripts." In *Latin and Vernacular: Studies in Late-Medieval Texts and Manuscripts,* edited by Alastair J. Minnis, 111–27. Cambridge, U.K.: Brewer, 1989.

Froissart, Jean. *Chroniques de J. Froissart.* Vol. 10, *1380–1382.* Edited by Gaston Raynaud. Paris: Renouard, 1897.

Fumo, Jamie C. "The God of Love and Love of God: Palinodic Exchange in the Prologue of the *Legend of Good Women* and the 'Retraction.'" In Collette, *"Legend of Good Women,"* 157–75.

Furnivall, Frederick J., ed. *The Fifty Earliest English Wills in The Court of Probate, London A.D. 1387–1439.* Early English Text Society, o.s., 78. London: Oxford University Press, 1964. First published 1882.

Fyler, John M. *Chaucer and Ovid*. New Haven: Yale University Press, 1979.

Gabel, Leona. *Benefit of Clergy in England in the Later Middle Ages*. New York: Octagon Books, 1969.

———. "The Term *Clericus*." In *Benefit of Clergy*, 62–91.

Gee, Stacey. "Parochial Libraries in Pre-Reformation England." In *Learning and Literacy in Medieval England and Abroad*, edited by Sarah Rees Jones, 199–222. Turnhout, Belgium: Brepols, 2003.

Giancarlo, Matthew. "Property, Purchase, and Parliament: The Estates of Man in John Gower's *Mirour de l'Omme* and *Cronica Tripertita*." In *Parliament and Literature in Late Medieval England*, 90–128. Cambridge: Cambridge University Press, 2007.

Giles, Kate. "Framing Labour: The Archaeology of York's Medieval Guildhalls." In Bothwell, Goldberg, and Ormrod, *Problem of Labour*, 65–83.

Given-Wilson, Chris. "The Problem of Labour in the Context of English Government, c. 1350–1450." In Bothwell, Goldberg, and Ormrod, *Problem of Labour*, 85–100.

Goldberg, P. J. P. "Women and Work." In *Life Cycle*, 82–157.

———. *Women, Work, and Life Cycle in a Medieval Economy: York and Yorkshire, c. 1300–1520*. Oxford: Clarendon Press, 1992.

Gramsci, Antonio. "The Modern Prince." In *Prison Notebooks*, 123–205.

———. *Selections from the Prison Notebooks of Antonio Gramsci*. Translated and edited by Quintin Hoare and Geoffrey Nowell Smith. New York: International, 1987.

Gower, John. *The Complete Works of John Gower*. Vol. 4, *The Latin Works*, ed. G. C. Macaulay. Oxford: Clarendon Press, 1902.

———. *Confessio Amantis*. Edited by Russell A. Peck. Toronto: University of Toronto Press, 1980.

———. *Confessio Amantis*. Vol. 1. Edited by Russell A. Peck. Kalamazoo: Medieval Institute Publications, Western Michigan University, 2000.

———. *The English Works of John Gower*. Edited by G. C. Macaulay. Vols. 1–2. Early English Text Society, e.s., 81–82. London: Oxford University Press, 1900–1901.

———. *The Major Latin Works of John Gower*. Translated by Eric W. Stockton. Seattle: University of Washington Press, 1962.

Griffiths, Jeremy. "*Confessio Amantis*: The Poem and Its Pictures." In Minnis, *Gower's "Confessio Amantis,"* 163–78.

Griffiths, Jeremy, and Derek Pearsall. *Book Production and Publishing in Britain, 1375–1475*. Cambridge: Cambridge University Press, 1989.

Hagedorn, Suzanne C. *Abandoned Women: Rewriting the Classics in Dante, Boccaccio, and Chaucer*. Ann Arbor: University of Michigan Press, 2004.

Hall, Stuart. "Gramsci and Us." In *Hard Road to Renewal*, 161–73.

———. *The Hard Road to Renewal: Thatcherism and the Crisis of the Left*. London: Verso, 1988.

———. "Popular-Democratic vs. Authoritarian Populism: Two Ways of 'Taking Democracy Seriously.'" In *Hard Road to Renewal*, 123–49.

Hanna, Ralph. *London Literature, 1300–1380*. Cambridge: Cambridge University Press, 2005.

Hansen, Elaine Tuttle. *Chaucer and the Fictions of Gender*. Berkeley: University of California Press, 1992.

———. "Irony and the Antifeminist Narrator in Chaucer's *Legend of Good Women*." *Journal of English and Germanic Philology* 82, no. 1 (1983): 11–31.

Harris, Kate. "Ownership and Readership: Studies in the Provenance of the Manuscripts of Gower's *Confessio Amantis*." PhD diss., University of York, 1993.

———. "Patrons, Buyers, and Owners: The Evidence for Ownership and the Role of Book Owners in Book Production and the Book Trade." In Griffiths and Pearsall, *Book Production*, 163–99.

Hellinga, Lotte, and J. B. Trapp, eds. *The Cambridge History of the Book in Britain*. Vol. 3, *1400–1557*. Cambridge: Cambridge University Press, 1999.

Hilton, Rodney. *Class Conflict and the Crisis of Feudalism: Essays in Medieval Social History*. London: Hambledon Press, 1985.

———. "Popular Movements in England at the End of the Fourteenth Century." In *Class Conflict*, 152–64.

———. "Status and Class in the Medieval Town." In *The Church in the Medieval Town*, edited by T. R. Slater and Gervase Rosser, 9–19. Aldershot: Ashgate, 1998.

———. "Women Traders in Medieval England." In *Class Conflict*, 205–15.

Hines, John, Nathalie Cohen, and Simon Roffey. "*Iohannes Gower, Armiger, Poeta*: Records and Memorials of His Life and Death." In Echard, *Companion to Gower*, 23–41.

Horobin, Simon. "Manuscripts and Scribes." In *Chaucer: Contemporary Approaches*, edited by Susanna Fein and David Raybin, 67–82. University Park: Pennsylvania State University Press, 2010.

———. "The Professionalization of Writing." In *The Oxford Handbook of Medieval Literature in English*, edited by Elaine Treharne and Greg Walker, 57–67. Oxford: Oxford University Press, 2010.

Howard, Donald R. *The Idea of the "Canterbury Tales."* Berkeley: University of California Press, 1976.

Ives, E. W. "The Common Lawyers." In Clough, *Profession*, 181–217.

Jardine, Lisa. "'Why Should He Call Her Whore?' Defamation and Desdemona's Case." *Addressing Frank Kermode: Essays in Criticism and Interpretation*, edited by Margaret Tudeau-Clayton and Martin Warner, 124–53. Urbana: University of Illinois Press, 1991.

Justice, Steven. *Writing and Rebellion: England in 1381*. Berkeley: University of California Press, 1994.

Kaeuper, Richard W. "Two Early Lists of Literates in England: 1334, 1373." *English Historical Review* 99, no. 391 (1984): 363–69.

Kerby-Fulton, Kathryn, and Steven Justice. "Langlandian Reading Circles and the Civil Service in London and Dublin, 1380–1427." *New Medieval Literatures* 1 (1997): 59–83.

Kermode, Jennifer I. *Medieval Merchants: York, Beverley, and Hull in the Later Middle Ages*. Cambridge: Cambridge University Press, 1988.

———. "The Merchants of Three Northern English Towns." In Clough, *Profession*, 7–48.

Kinneavy, Gerald. "Gower's *Confessio* Amantis and the Penitentials." *The Chaucer Review* 19, no. 2 (1984): 144–61.

Kisby, Fiona. "Books in London Parish Churches Before 1603: Some Preliminary Observations." In *The Church and Learning in Later Medieval Society: Essays in Honour of R. B. Dobson: Proceedings of the 1999 Harlaxton Symposium*, edited by Caroline M. Barron and Jenny Stratford, 305–26. Donington, U.K.: Tyas, 2002.

Kiser, Lisa J. *Telling Classical Tales: Chaucer and the "Legend of Good Women."* Ithaca: Cornell University Press, 1983.

Knight, Stephen. "The Voice of Labor in Fourteenth-Century English Literature." In Bothwell, Goldberg, and Ormrod, *Problem of Labour*, 101–22.

Knighton, Henry. *Knighton's Chronicle, 1337–1396*. Translated and edited by G. H. Martin. Oxford: Clarendon Press, 1995.

Knoop, Douglas, and G. P. Jones. *The Mediaeval Mason: An Economic History of English Stone Building in the Later Middle Ages and Early Modern Times*. Manchester: Manchester University Press, 1967.

Kobayashi, Yoshiko. "The Voice of an Exile: From Ovidian Lament to Prophecy in Book I of John Gower's *Vox Clamantis*." In *Through a Classical Eye: Transcultural and Transhistorical Visions in Medieval English, Italian, and Latin Literature in Honour of Winthrop*

Wetherbee, edited by Andrew Galloway and R. F. Yeager, 339–62. Toronto: University of Toronto Press, 2009.

Kowaleski, Maryanne, ed. *Medieval Towns: A Reader*. Toronto: University of Toronto Press, 2008.

———. "Women's Work in a Market Town: Exeter in the Late Fourteenth Century." In *Women and Work in Preindustrial Europe*, edited by Barbara A. Hanawalt, 145–64. Bloomington: Indiana University Press, 1986.

Kurath, Hans, Sherman M. Kuhn, and Robert E. Lewis, eds. *The Middle English Dictionary*. Ann Arbor: University of Michigan Press, 1952–2001. Reprint, Ann Arbor: University of Michigan Press, Digital Library Production Services, 2001. http.quod.lib.umich.edu/m/med.

Ladd, Roger A. "The Mercantile (Mis)reader in *The Canterbury Tales*." *Studies in Philology* 99, no. 1 (2002): 17–32.

Lancashire, Anne. *London Civic Theatre: City Drama and Pageantry from Roman Times to 1558*. Cambridge: Cambridge University Press, 2002.

Lipson, E. *An Introduction to the Economic History of England*. Vol. 1, *The Middle Ages*. 4th ed. London: Black, 1926.

Loomba, Ania. "Imperialism, Patriarchy, and Post-Colonial English Studies." In *Gender, Race, Renaissance Drama*, 10–37. Manchester: Manchester University Press, 1989.

Lukács, Georg. *History and Class Consciousness: Studies in Marxist Dialectics*. Translated by Rodney Livingstone. Cambridge: MIT Press, 1968.

Marx, Karl, and Frederick Engels. *The German Ideology*. Edited by C. J. Arthur. New York: International, 1970.

Mate, Mavis E. *Women in Medieval English Society*. Cambridge: Cambridge University Press, 1999.

McCormick, Betsy. "Remembering the Game: Debating the *Legend*'s Women." In Collette, *"Legend of Good Women,"* 105–31.

McDonald, Nicola F. "Chaucer's *Legend of Good Women*, Ladies at Court, and the Female Reader." *Chaucer Review* 35, no. 1 (2000): 22–42.

———. "Games Medieval Women Play." In Collette, *"Legend of Good Women,"* 176–97.

McIntosh, Marjorie Keniston. "Women's Participation in the Skilled Crafts." In *Working Women*, 210–38.

———. *Working Women in English Society, 1300–1620*. Cambridge: Cambridge University Press, 2005.

McKisack, May. *The Fourteenth Century: 1307–1399*. London: Oxford University Press, 1959.

McNally, Joseph. "The *Exemplum* in John Gower's *Confessio Amantis*." PhD diss., University of South Carolina, 1982.

Mead, Jenna. "Chaucer and the Subject of Bureaucracy." *Exemplaria* 19 (2007): 39–66.

Meale, Carol M. "Patrons, Buyers, and Owners: Book Production and Social Status." In Griffiths and Pearsall, *Book Production*, 201–38.

Meecham-Jones, Simon. "Intention, Integrity, and 'Renoun': The Public Virtue of Chaucer's Good Women." In Collette, *"Legend of Good Women,"* 132–56.

———. "'Myn Erthly God': Paradigm and Parody in the Prologue to the *Legend of Good Women*." In *Myth and Its Legacy in European Literature*, edited by Neil Thomas and Françoise Le Saux, 93–113. Durham: University of Durham, 1996.

———. "Prologue: The Poet as Subject: Literary Self-Consciousness in Gower's *Confessio Amantis*." In *Betraying Our Selves: Forms of Self-Representation in Early Modern English Texts*, edited by Henk Dragstra, Sheila Ottway, and Helen Wilcox, 1–30. New York: St. Martin's Press, 2000.

Messer-Davidow, Ellen. "Constructing Sex Discrimination." In *Disciplining Feminism*, 49–79.

———. *Disciplining Feminism: From Social Activism to Academic Discourse*. Durham: Duke University Press, 2002.

Michael, M. A. "English Illuminators, c. 1190–1450: A Survey from Documentary Sources." *English Manuscript Studies, 1100–1700* 4 (1993): 62–113.

Middleton, Anne. "The Audience and Public of 'Piers Plowman.' " In *Middle English Alliterative Poetry and Its Literary Background*, edited by David A. Lawton, 101–54. Cambridge, U.K.: Brewer, 1982.

———. "Chaucer's 'New Men' and the Good of Literature in the *Canterbury Tales*." In *Literature and Society: Selected Papers from the English Institute*, edited by Edward W. Said, 15–56. Baltimore: Johns Hopkins University Press, 1980.

———. "The Idea of Public Poetry in the Reign of Richard II." *Speculum* 53, no. 1 (1978): 94–114.

Minnis, Alastair J. "Authors in Love: The Exegesis of Late Medieval Love-Poets." In *The Uses of Manuscripts in Literary Studies: Essays in Memory of Judson Boyce Allen*, edited by Charlotte Cook Morse, Penelope Reed Doob, and Marjorie Curry Woods, 161–89. Kalamazoo: Medieval Institute, Western Michigan University, 1992.

———. "*De Vulgari Auctoritate*: Chaucer, Gower, and the Men of Great Authority." In *Chaucer and Gower: Difference, Mutuality, Exchange*, edited by R. F. Yeager, 36–74. English Literary Studies 51. Victoria: University of Victoria, 1991.

———, ed. *Gower's "Confessio Amantis": Responses and Reassessments*. Cambridge, U.K.: Brewer, 1983.

———. *Magister Amoris: The "Roman de la Rose" and Vernacular Hermeneutics*. Oxford: Oxford University Press, 2001.

———. *Medieval Theory of Authorship: Scholastic Literary Attitudes in the Later Middle Ages*. 2nd ed. Philadelphia: University of Pennsylvania Press, 1988.

———. *Translations of Authority in Medieval English Literature: Valuing the Vernacular*. Cambridge: Cambridge University Press, 2009.

Mitchell, J. Allan. *Ethics and Eventfulness in Middle English Literature*. New York: Palgrave Macmillan, 2009.

———. *Ethics and Exemplary Narrative in Chaucer and Gower*. Cambridge, U.K.: Brewer, 2004.

———. "Gower's *Confessio Amantis* and the Nature of Vernacular Ethics." In *Ethics and Eventfulness*, 69–86.

Mooney, Linne R. "Locating Scribal Activity in Late Medieval London." In *Design and Distribution of Late Medieval Manuscripts in London*, edited by Margaret Connolly and Linne R. Mooney, 183–204. York: York Medieval Press; Woodbridge, U.K.: Boydell, 2008.

———."Some New Light on Thomas Hoccleve." *Studies in the Age of Chaucer* 29 (2007): 293–340.

Moran, Jo Ann Hoeppner. *Education and Learning in the City of York, 1300–1560*. Borthwick Institute of Historical Research. York: University of York, Borthwick Institute of Historical Research, 1979.

———. *The Growth of English Schooling, 1340–1548: Learning, Literacy, and Laicization in Pre-Reformation York Diocese*. Princeton: Princeton University Press, 1985.

———. "Literacy and Education in Northern England, 1350–1550: A Methodological Inquiry." *Northern History* 17 (1981): 1–23.

Nicolas, Harris Nicholas. "John Gower, the Poet." In *The Retrospective Review, and Historical and Antiquarian Magazine*, edited by Henry Southern and Nicholas Harris Nicolas, 2nd ser., vol. 2, 103–117. London: Baldwin and Cradock, 1828.

Nightingale, Pamela. *A Medieval Mercantile Community: The Grocers' Company and the Politics and Trade of London, 1000–1485*. New Haven: York University Press, 1995.

Nitzsche, Jane Chance. *The Genius Figure in Antiquity and the Middle Ages*. New York: Columbia University Press, 1975.

Olsson, Kurt. "Aspects of *Gentilesse* in John Gower's *Confessio Amantis*, Books III–V." In Yeager, *John Gower*, 225–73.

———. *John Gower and the Structures of Conversion: A Reading of the "Confessio Amantis."* Cambridge, U.K.: Brewer, 1992.

———. "Reading, Transgression, and Judgment: Gower's Case of Paris and Helen." In Yeager, *Re-visioning Gower*, 67–92.

Orme, Nicholas. *Education and Society in Medieval and Renaissance England*. London: Hambledon Press, 1989.

———. *English Schools in the Middle Ages*. London: Methuen, 1973.

———. "Schoolmasters, 1307–1509." In Clough, *Profession*, 218–41.

———. "Schools and School-Books." In Hellinga and Trapp, *Cambridge History*, 449–69.

———. "The Study of Grammar." In *English Schools*, 87–115.

Palmer, R. Barton. "Chaucer's *Legend of Good Women*: The Narrator's Tale." In *New Readings of Chaucer's Poetry*, edited by Robert G. Benson and Susan J. Ridyard, 183–94. Cambridge, U.K.: Brewer, 2003.

Parkes, Malcolm. "The Literacy of the Laity." In *Literature and Western Civilization: The Mediaeval World*, edited by David Daiches and Anthony Thorlby, 555–77. London: Aldus Books, 1973.

Patterson, Lee. *Chaucer and the Subject of History*. Madison: University of Wisconsin Press, 1991.

———. " 'No Man His Reson Herde': Peasant Consciousness, Chaucer's Miller, and the Structure of the *Canterbury Tales*." In *Literary Practice and Social Change in Britain, 1380–1530*, edited by Lee Patterson, 113–55. Berkeley: University of California Press, 1990.

———. Review of *Social Chaucer*, by Paul Strohm. *Speculum* 67 (1992): 485–88.

Pearsall, Derek. "Gower's Latin in the *Confessio Amantis*." In *Latin and Vernacular: Studies in Late-Medieval Texts and Manuscripts*, edited by Alastair J. Minnis, 13–25. Cambridge, U.K.: Brewer, 1989.

———. "The Gower Tradition." In Minnis, *Gower's "Confessio Amantis,"* 179–97.

———. *The Life of Geoffrey Chaucer: A Critical Biography*. Oxford: Blackwell, 1992.

———. "The Manuscripts and Illustrations of Gower's Works." In Echard, *Companion to Gower*, 73–97.

Peck, Russell A. "John Gower and the Book of Daniel." In Yeager, *John Gower*, 159–87.

———. *Kingship and Common Profit in Gower's "Confessio Amantis."* Carbondale: Southern Illinois University Press, 1978.

———. "Social Conscience and the Poets." In *Social Unrest in the Late Middle Ages*, edited by Francis X. Newman, 113–48. Binghamton, N.Y.: Medieval and Renaissance Texts and Studies, 1986.

Penn, Stephen. "Literacy and Literary Production." In *Chaucer: An Oxford Guide*, edited by Steve Ellis, 113–29. Oxford: Oxford University Press, 2005.

Percival, Florence. *Chaucer's Legendary Good Women*. Cambridge: Cambridge University Press, 1988.

———. "The Legend as Courtly Game." In *Chaucer's Legendary Good Women*, 299–323.

Phillips, Helen. "Register, Politics, and the *Legend of Good Women*." *Chaucer Review* 37, no. 2 (2002): 101–28.

Plato. *The Republic of Plato*. Translated by Francis MacDonald Cornford. Oxford: Oxford University Press, 1941.

Pollard, Graham. "The English Market for Printed Books." *Publishing History* 4 (1978): 9–48.

Porter, Elizabeth. "Gower's Ethical Microcosm and Political Macrocosm." In Minnis, *Gower's "Confessio Amantis,"* 135–62.

Postan, M. M. *The Medieval Economy and Society: An Economic History of Britain, 1100–1500.* Berkeley: University of California Press, 1972.

Prescott, Andrew. "London in the Peasants' Revolt: A Portrait Gallery." *London Journal* 7, no. 2 (1981): 125–43.

Robertson, Kellie. *The Laborer's Two Bodies: Labor and the "Work" of the Text in Medieval Britain, 1350–1500.* New York: Palgrave Macmillan, 2006.

———. Review of *Chaucer's Jobs*, by David Carlson. *Studies in the Age of Chaucer* 28 (2006): 284–87.

Roof, Judith, and Robyn Wiegman, eds. *Who Can Speak? Authority and Critical Identity.* Urbana: University of Illinois Press, 1995.

Rosser, Gervase. "Crafts, Guilds, and the Negotiation of Work in the Medieval Town." *Past and Present* 154 (February 1997): 3–31.

———. "Workers' Associations in English Medieval Towns." In *Les métiers au Moyen Âge: Aspects économiques et sociaux*, edited by Pascale Lambrechts and Jean-Pierre Sosson, 283–305. Louvain-la-Neuve: Université Catholique de Louvain, Institut d'Études Médiévales, 1994.

Rowland, Beryl, ed. *Companion to Chaucer Studies.* Rev. ed. New York: Oxford University Press, 1979.

Rye, Reginald Arthur. *The Students' Guide to the Libraries of London.* London: University of London Press, 1927.

Salisbury, Eve. "Remembering Origins: Gower's Monstrous Body Poetic." In Yeager, *Re-visioning Gower*, 159–84.

Salzman, L. F. *English Industries of the Middle Ages.* Oxford: Clarendon Press, 1923.

Sargent, Michael G. "What Do the Numbers Mean? A Textual Critic's Observations on Some Patterns of Middle English Manuscript Transmission." In *Design and Distribution of Late Medieval Manuscripts in London*, edited by Margaret Connolly and Linne R. Mooney, 205–44. York: York Medieval Press; Woodbridge, U.K.: Boydell and Brewer, 2008.

Sawhney, Sabina. "The Joke and the Hoax: (Not) Speaking as the Other." In Roof and Wiegman, *Who Can Speak?*, 208–20.

Schlauch, Margaret. "The *Man of Law's Tale*." In *Sources and Analogues of Chaucer's "Canterbury Tales,"* edited by W. F. Bryan and Germaine Dempster, 155–206. New York: Humanities Press, 1958.

Schmitz, Götz. "Gower, Chaucer, and the Classics: Back to the Textual Evidence." In Yeager, *John Gower*, 95–111.

Sharpe, Reginald Robinson, ed. *Calendar of Wills Proved and Enrolled in the Court of Husting, London, A.D. 1258–A.D. 1688.* Vol. 1. London: Francis, 1889.

Shoaf, R. Allen. *Chaucer's Body: The Anxiety of Circulation in the "Canterbury Tales."* Gainesville: University Press of Florida, 2001.

Simpson, James. "Ethics and Interpretation: Reading Wills in Chaucer's *Legend of Good Women.*" *Studies in the Age of Chaucer* 20 (1998): 73–100.

———. *Sciences and the Self in Medieval Poetry: Alan of Lille's "Anticlaudianus" and John Gower's "Confessio Amantis."* Cambridge: Cambridge University Press, 1995.

Smith, Toulmin, ed. *English Gilds: The Original Ordinances of More Than One Hundred Early English Gilds.* Early English Text Society, o.s., no. 40. London: Trübner, 1870.

Sponsler, Clare. "Lydgate and London's Public Culture." In *Lydgate Matters: Poetry and Material Culture in the Fifteenth Century*, edited by Lisa H. Cooper and Andrea Denny-Brown, 13–33. New York: Palgrave Macmillan, 2008.

Storey, R. L. "Gentleman-Bureaucrats." In Clough, *Profession*, 90–129.

Strohm, Paul. "Chaucer's Audience." *Literature and History* 5 (Spring 1977): 26–41.

———. "Chaucer's Audience(s): Fictional, Implied, Intended, Actual." *Chaucer Review* 18, no. 2 (1983): 137–45.

———. "Chaucer's Fifteenth-Century Audience and the Narrowing of the 'Chaucer Tradition.'" *Studies in the Age of Chaucer* 4 (1982): 3–32.

———. *Hochon's Arrow: The Social Imagination of Fourteenth-Century Texts.* Princeton: Princeton University Press, 1992.

———. "'A Revelle!': Chronicle Evidence and the Rebel Voice." In *Hochon's Arrow*, 33–56.

———. "The Social and Literary Scene in England." In *The Cambridge Companion to Chaucer*, edited by Piero Boitani and Jill Mann, 2nd ed., 1–19. Cambridge: Cambridge University Press, 2003.

———. *Social Chaucer.* Cambridge: Harvard University Press, 1989.

Swanson, Heather. "Industrial Investment." In *Medieval Artisans*, 127–49.

———. *Medieval Artisans: An Urban Class in Late Medieval England.* Oxford: Basil Blackwell, 1989.

Taylor, Andrew. "Anne of Bohemia and the Making of Chaucer." *Studies in the Age of Chaucer* 19 (1997): 95–119.

Taylor, William. *Annals of St. Mary Overy: An Historical and Descriptive Account of St. Saviour's Church and Parish.* London: Nichols and Son, 1833.

Thrupp, Sylvia. *The Merchant Class of Medieval London.* Chicago: University of Chicago Press, 1948.

Unwin, George. *The Gilds and Companies of London.* 4th ed. London: Cass, 1963.

Urban, Malte. *Fragments: Past and Present in Chaucer and Gower.* Oxford: Lang, 2009.

Veale, Elspeth. "Matilda Penne, Skinner (d. 1392/3)." In *Medieval London Widows, 1300–1500*, edited by Caroline M. Barron and Anne F. Sutton, 47–54. London: Hambledon Press, 1994.

Voigts, Linda, and Michael R. McVaugh. *A Latin Technical Phlebotomy and Its Middle English Translation.* Vol. 74. Pt. 2. Transactions of the American Philosophical Society. Philadelphia: American Philosophical Society, 1984.

Wallace, David. *Chaucerian Polity: Absolutist Lineages and Associational Forms in England and Italy.* Stanford: Stanford University Press, 1997.

Wallace, Michele. "Negative/Positive Images." In *Invisibility Blues: From Pop to Theory*, 1–10. London: Verso, 1990.

Walsingham, Thomas. *Historia Anglicana.* Edited by Henry Thomas Riley. Vol. 2, *1381–1422*. London: Longman, Green, Longman, Roberts, Green, 1864.

Watt, Diane. *Amoral Gower: Language, Sex, and Politics.* Minneapolis: University of Minnesota Press, 2003.

Watts, John. "The Pressure of the Public on Later Medieval Politics." In *The Fifteenth Century*, vol. 4, *Political Culture in Late Medieval Britain*, edited by Linda Clark and Christine Carpenter. Woodbridge, U.K.: Boydell, 2004.

Weatherbee, Winthrop. "Classical and Boethian Tradition in the *Confessio Amantis*." In Echard, *Companion to Gower*, 181–96.

———. "Latin Structure and Vernacular Space: Gower, Chaucer, and the Boethian Tradition." In Yeager, *Chaucer and Gower*, 7–35.

White, Hugh. *Nature, Sex, and Goodness in a Medieval Literary Tradition.* Oxford: Oxford University Press, 2000.

Wiegman, Robyn. "What Ails Feminist Criticism? A Second Opinion." *Critical Inquiry* 25 (1999): 362–79.

Williams, Raymond. *Marxism and Literature.* Oxford: Oxford University Press, 1977.

Yeager, Robert F., ed. *Chaucer and Gower: Difference, Mutuality, Exchange.* English Literary Studies 51. Victoria: University of Victoria, 1991.

———. "English, Latin, and the Text as 'Other': The Page as Sign in the Work of John Gower." *Text: Transactions of the Society for Textual Scholarship* 3 (1987): 251–67.

————, ed. *John Gower: Recent Readings*. Kalamazoo: Medieval Institute, Western Michigan University, 1989.

————. *John Gower Materials: A Bibliography Through 1979*. New York: Garland, 1981.

————. *John Gower's Poetic: The Search for a New Arion*. Cambridge, U.K.: Brewer, 1990.

————, ed. *Re-visioning Gower*. Asheville: Pegasus Press, 1998.

Zieman, Katherine. *Singing the New Song: Literacy and Liturgy in Late Medieval England*. Philadelphia: University of Pennsylvania Press, 2008.

INDEX